To the Stoddards
from
The Lynch Family'
(p. 165)
Christmas 1998

Courage
to
Love

Courage
to
Love

A Gay Priest Stands Up
for His Beliefs

Will Leckie
and
Barry Stopfel

Doubleday

NEW YORK LONDON TORONTO
SYDNEY AUCKLAND

PUBLISHED BY DOUBLEDAY

a division of Bantam Doubleday Dell Publishing Group, Inc.

1540 Broadway, New York, New York 10036

DOUBLEDAY and the portrayal of an anchor with a dolphin are trademarks of Doubleday,
a division of Bantam Doubleday Dell Publishing Group, Inc.

Book Design by Brian Mulligan

Library of Congress Cataloging-in-Publication Data
Leckie, Will, 1953–
Courage to love : a gay priest stands up for his beliefs / Will
Leckie and Barry Stopfel. — 1st ed.
p.   cm.
Includes bibliographical references.
1. Stopfel, Barry, 1947–   .   2. Leckie, Will, 1953–   .
3. Episcopal Church—United States—Clergy—Biography.   4. Christian
gays—United States—Biography.   5. Gay clergy—United States—
Biography.   6. Gay male couples—United States.   I. Stopfel,
Barry, 1947–   .   II. Title.
BX5995.S82L23   1997
283'.092—dc21
[B]   97-3840
CIP
AC

ISBN 0-385-48672-3
Copyright © 1997 by Will Leckie and Barry Stopfel
All Rights Reserved
Printed in the United States of America
June 1997
First Edition
10   9   8   7   6   5   4   3   2   1

For

Carolyn and Marlin Stopfel,

June and Bill Leckie,

first givers of love;

the Right Reverend John S. Spong,

the Right Reverend Walter C. Righter,

gentle warriors for love;

Hannah Katherine Hancock Rubinsky,

Sarah Martin Hancock Rubinsky,

our hope for love's future.

Foreword by

The Right Reverend John Shelby Spong
Bishop of Newark

Courage to Love is a dramatic story, told well and with enormous emotional power. It captures both the agony and the ecstasy of a major moment of transition in the life of the Christian Church. It reveals the pain of fear, compromise and cowardice, as well as the nobility of courage, conviction, and integrity. It is a moving and in many ways an enchanting narrative.

More than once people have observed that history is really biography. Every moment of history turns on the particular life that stands at the epicenter of that transition. Sometimes that person volunteers for the role quite consciously and moves steadfastly into the vortex. Abraham Lincoln is a person who comes to mind in that scenario. Sometimes fate, operating out of thousands of lesser and minor decisions, designates a particular life to be the person with the right ability to stand in the right place and at the right time. Through no choice of his or her own that person will become a pivotal figure of history. Martin Luther King, Jr., was such a person. The authors of this book must also be classified in this latter category.

In every religious body the world over, new learnings and new definitions are confronting the traditional stereotypes and prejudices of the past. In that process the Church is being called to new frontiers beyond the security-building limits of yesterday. The debate over justice for gay and lesbian people is the cutting edge of this uncharted territory. By God's grace or by the fate of history, the Episcopal Church in the United States became the faith community in which the battle would first be waged publicly. Through a series of decisions made over a number of years, the Diocese of Newark became the local battlefield within the Episcopal Church, and by a series of chance maneuvers, an unlikely couple, Barry Stopfel and Will Leckie, were cast in the role of change agents. They were surprised to find themselves in the center of this storm. I suspect that to them it felt as if the pyramids of Egypt had been turned upside down and placed upon their backs with the point located between their shoulder blades. It was for them, I am certain, almost too much to bear. These two human beings are gentle people. They lack the fire of social activists—they are not aggressive, out-front, agitating personalities. But they were in the right place at the right time and they were willing to do the right thing. So it was that the history of the Church quite literally turned upon their lives.

Their antagonists tried to demonize this devoted couple, but Barry and Will simply did not respond well to demonizing. Others tried to use these two persons to get at those of us whom they perceived to be the real troublers of God's people. Barry and Will proved to be poor conduits. Some bishops even tried to impose their hostile definitions of homosexual persons upon their slender frames. Those definitions simply did not fit Barry and Will.

Most of us who populate the straight world understand very poorly the lives of our gay brothers and lesbian sisters. Straight people have no sense of what it means to be defined daily in pejorative ways, or of how it feels to live inside a culture's active hate. We do not comprehend those deep recesses within our own souls wherein lurks the fear and the threat out of which our judgment and hostility flow so easily. Nor do we fully recognize how those who have been marginalized hang upon the words of hope that fall so easily from our lips. This book will serve to raise our consciousness in all of these areas.

The episodes related in this provocative story are ones with which

I am deeply and personally familiar as the text will reveal. In some ways this book is a biography of a major part of my life also. I lived through these years with Barry and Will in a unique and sometimes stressful way. However, only when I read this manuscript did I understand how these events had really looked to them. I felt the pain of those times when they thought I should have acted differently. They had no way of understanding all the forces that I was trying to balance. I had no way of making them aware of that. It was inappropriate for me to have expected that of them anyway. Perhaps the most poignant moment in this text for me was my rereading of the letter young Tim Croneberger had sent to me when I postponed Barry's ordination to the diaconate from June to September. I had known Tim well, admired his writing, and his insightful sensitivity. I had lived with his family during his attempted suicide, and had watched his mother and father grow into the realization that their son was gay. I knew that Barry had helped to carry both Tim and especially his father through that episode into a full, joyful, and holy acceptance of this wonderfully gifted young man and son. I knew Tim was disappointed that we could not move the Episcopal Church as fast as he would have wished. I was not, however, prepared for the depth of Tim's pain nor for the intensity of his anger. To reread that letter in this book was to experience an incredible discomfort yet again. I am grateful, not for the discomfort, but for the realization that I must never pretend that I can fully understand the way another feels when that person believes that his or her life is on the line.

Barry Stopfel is in every way an outstanding priest of this Diocese. He is an eloquent and perceptive preacher. He is an educator second to none. He has exceptional pastoral and administrative skills. It is easy for me to understand why those who sat in judgment upon his selection for ordination were so enthusiastic about his potential priesthood. It is also easy for me to understand how St.

George's Church in Maplewood chose him from among ninety-six prospective clergy to be their rector. By every measure Barry would rank in the top 10 percent of the Church's clergy.

Will Leckie is, in the language of our faith community, "a clergy spouse." It was a difficult stretch for many people to embrace first the fact that this category now included male husbands of female priests. When the Church looked at that role through the eyes of a professional male we understood for the first time the expectations we have always placed on the female spouses of clergy, to be unpaid employees of the churches their husbands served. When the category of clergy spouse began to include male partners of male clergy and female partners of female clergy, brand new insights were gained. There were no role models for this designation. Will Leckie has created his own niche in the affections of the people of St. George's and attends regularly the clergy spouse events of our Diocese. But he is always true to his own identity.

St. George's Church is itself remarkable. Present still in its matrix, but out of its background, are clergy of the past who challenged the boundaries of their generation and called the people of that congregation to new visions. I think of people like the elegant Albert Judd, who served as rector from 1949 to 1975, and whose ministry demanded that this congregation relate to real issues in a real world. I also think of Craig Burlington, rector from 1975 to 1992, who first began to lead this church into a probe of sexual ethics, and who invited a gay organization to use the parish house of St. George's for their regular meeting place and for social functions. I recall Craig's assisting the first out-of-the-closet gay couples when they began to venture beyond that gay organization and into the Sunday morning worship of St. George's and finally into full membership in the Church.

Then there was Diana Clark, who became St. George's first female assistant priest, serving from 1988 to 1991, who not only enhanced the place of women in that congregation, but who also developed her pastoral relationships with gay communicants in a quite remarkable way. Finally, there was a second woman priest, Ann McRae Wrede, who served as interim rector between Craig Burlington and Barry Stopfel and who solidified the new dimensions of consciousness in that congregation. That consciousness came into full bloom when this congregation, acting through its search committee and vestry, called upon this healthy, whole, talented, but out-of-the-closet gay priest, Barry Stopfel, to be its rector and his equally gifted and whole partner, Will Leckie, to be the other member of the church's "first family."

Last, but not least, I recall the devoted laypeople of St. George's Church, whose commitment to their Lord and whose growth into their vision of what the Church is called to be made Barry's rectorship possible. Included in this congregation are respected people who, though they have been leaders in that church for years, did not develop until quite recently the capacity to be honest about who they were as sexual beings. To that mix must be added traditional conservative people who were challenged so deeply by the faith they found in St. George's that they were able to put aside the prejudices of the ages and to embrace a gay man as pastor and priest and his partner as their friend.

I suppose I must also thank our sometimes bitter critics, such as those bishops who disassociated themselves from me in 1990 when I first ordained to the priesthood a gay man who was living openly with his partner. I am also grateful to those ten bishops who in 1995 filed a presentment against my associate, the Right Reverend Walter Righter, thereby suggesting that heresy had been committed when Barry was ordained, for that action forced the Church to define itself. The rhetoric of these bishops was filled with the punitive, hostile words of rejection. Their attitudes revealed a deep sexual fear and a moralistic desire to keep the Church safe inside the patterns of the prejudiced and dying past. I even thank that member of the Bishop's Court who, after casting the single and lone vote for conviction for the one who had ordained Barry, then justified his decision with such a remarkable demonstration of homophobic words that disgust was the response, even from those who leaned toward his point of view. In God's economy everyone plays a role in the drama of salvation or in the drama of ecclesiastical change. This bishop thus made a decisive contribution to the cause he opposed.

Walter Righter, who was my associate and who remains my esteemed colleague in the Episcopal Office, emerges in these pages as the hero that he in fact was. He and I shared some critical decisions in this period of change. We were both determined to accomplish our goal. Barry must be a priest, not just for Barry's sake, but for the Church's sake. We achieved that goal and we are both grateful. Both of us paid a price for our convictions. Walter bore much of the abuse that was intended for me. But when our critics chose to make him, instead of me, the target for their wrath, they miscalculated badly the steel present in the heart of this gentle and godly man. I am pleased that this Church of ours will always remember my friend as one of its most significant bishops.

This book is destined to be widely read. The lively style in which it is written will guarantee that. People will recognize it as a powerful human drama. Its message will come not only through its pages but through the other media creations it will produce. Wherever and however this story is heard, hope will be created in the hearts of millions. Those who have been our critics will either adjust or ultimately they will fade away. The world will not stop to allow them the option of getting off. No one doubts what the verdict of history will be in the Church's relationship with the gay community. The Church that once rejected Gentiles, women, divorced people, left-handed people, mentally ill people, suicidal people, ethnic minority people, and now gay and lesbian people, always at last will see the light and become the body of Christ that the Church was created to be. The only alternative is for the Church to die. Those who stand at the side of the barriers to inclusivity and fight to the bitter end will inevitably and always be swept aside. As the years go by their feeble efforts to justify their limited understanding of the infinite embrace of the love of God will be recognized for what it is, a pitiful self-serving attempt to enhance their human power at the expense of another. They will finally be numbered among those who sought in vain to convince others that their prejudice was, in fact, the expression of the will of the holy God. It is the ultimate sin, as well as the ultimate irony, to call that which is evil, holy and that which is holy, evil.

This battle is all but over. Gay and lesbian people have always been, are now, and will forever be part of the body of Christ. The Church has finally mustered the courage to speak positively on this issue. Its doors are now open to this formerly rejected and abused minority of God's special children. We, as a Church, are beginning to move on to shine the light of God's love on the next dark corner of human fear that our journey through life will inevitably disclose.

Barry Stopfel and Will Leckie were the two lives upon which this particular phase of Church history was acted out. It was an honor for me to walk with them on a part of their journey. This Church of ours is privileged that people like Barry and Will still want to serve it and people like these two courageous men will continue to transform this community of faith until it becomes what it was intended to be—a sign of the Kingdom of God in our midst, welcoming all whom God has created and indeed welcoming all whom God would welcome.

Preface

Courage to Love is a recollection of relationships. It is also a personal reflection on a dramatic moment in the debate on human sexuality and homosexuality in the Episcopal Church, and how the wedding of the divine will and human flesh was worked out in those relationships.

Along the way, from my first day in the cloister garden of Union Theological Seminary, where I met the man without whom my life would be immeasurably diminished, to the Episcopal Cathedral in Wilmington, Delaware, as witness to the Ecclesial Court for the Trial of a Bishop, my faith in God's blessing has been expanded beyond my wildest imaginings.

One of Brian Wren's hymns from his collection, *Bring Many Names*, joyfully proclaims that God delights in our human flesh.

Good is the flesh that the Word has become;
Good is the body for knowing the world;

Good is the body from cradle to grave;
Good is the pleasure of God in our flesh.

Each of us has the capacity to reflect the holy. Both heterosexual and homosexual, our flesh is good and God delights in it. As a Christian, I believe that God is incarnate in our very flesh, all of our flesh, a faith I am reminded of regularly at the Eucharist. The wonder of incarnation is good news for all of us but particularly for those of us who are gay and lesbian and who have been taught that our desire for human sexual intimacy is an abomination to God.

Courage to Love is a recollection of my falling in love with God again, falling in love with Will, and falling in love with the Episcopal Church. And, like all loving, these relationships have seen both smooth sailing and stormy passings.

Each is interwoven so tightly that I can no longer follow a single strand. But the common demand for those who love is that we devote our lives to discerning the will of the Holy Spirit using our own particular set of life experiences, our own particular hearts and minds, and our own eyes—to see this loving and challenging Spirit working its way in us. That demand is also at the heart of faith and belief in the Episcopal Church which I serve.

Courage to Love is also a series of snapshots of me and Will, doing our best to live out the love that God has graciously given to us.

Some of the pictures are good, some are blurry, but they show us doing what we all hope to do in life—building meaningful relationships with others, productively working at our vocations, trying to be good neighbors in our communities, loving each other as honestly and passionately as we can, and, as Christians, praying for the wisdom and strength to mirror the face of a reconciling Christ to our world.

As the years have passed and I have entered the debate in the Episcopal Church about gay and lesbian Christians, I find that I always choose the integrity of love over the purity of doctrine. I keep Jesus as my model. Time and time again Jesus chose compassion over law. He chose to feed the hungry rather than abide by religious form. He chose to challenge social stereotypes rather than conform to human expectations. He chose love over apathy.

In my life's journey, I have both succeeded and failed at Jesus' command to be a person of reconciliation and forgiveness in relationship to myself, God, and others. There have been many moments when I felt hurt by people and circumstances, moments when my imperfect humanity led me to remember and blame in spite of my prayers to forgive and forget. Forgiveness is not always easy, particularly when people do not recognize the hurt they have caused. The love of enemies is grueling spiritual work, and is accomplished, I have discovered, not by my own effort, but by the grace of God through Jesus Christ, whom I call Lord.

Courage to Love is a chronicle of learning that God visits us through the lives of others, often through lives in which we least expect to encounter the Divine. My life in church communities has proven many times that when we embrace our common humanity, regardless of external distinctions, and embrace the truth that all of what God has created is good, then our common differences become bridged by our common acts of love and compassion. And is not love the greatest act of faith?

The biblical narrative consists of story upon story of ordinary people who found extraordinary faith as they discovered where God has been and learned what God was instructing them to be in the midst of their ordinary lives.

God has come to me through people who have reached across any anxiety their lack of familiarity about homosexuality may have caused them, embraced me as their priest, and welcomed Will into their hearts as my partner.

God has come to me in the loving guidance of those who played in the fields of theology and intellectual rigor with me—all those who helped me love God with all my mind, meet the quandaries in life with faith, and ask the hard questions about Christian belief.

God has come to me in all the children who have taught me countless lessons about loving God and yearning for God with my own childlikeness, such as seven-year-old Sawyer, who, with her family, attends Saint George's Church. Sawyer stapled together a special prayer book of crayon drawings on construction paper for Will and me the Sunday before we went to the hearings on the trial of Bishop Walter Righter.

Will has the right to love Barry
and Barry has his right to love Will.
And what does that have to do
with Barry being a priest?
I feel sad for you guys.
God bless Barry and God bless Will.

Courage to Love is a chronicle of ordinary courage and the ebb and flow of faith in me and Will as we found our way in the Church and our culture. Proclaiming to the world that God has also blessed us is a consistent act of ordinary courage, for the cost of loving is still very high for very many.

As a young boy I walked to the altar rail of the First Evangelical United Brethren Church in Hummelstown, Pennsylvania, and claimed Jesus Christ as my personal Lord and Savior. That moment shaped me irrevocably for a life of ministry and service; it shaped the nature of my morals, values, personal ethics, and my faith. That moment convinced me that every nook and cranny of my life, body, soul, sexual loving, and simple affection, could be dedicated to the nurturing of love and joy in others.

I have never forgotten the blessing that was given to me at that altar rail. Trust. Trust in a divine love has guided and sustained me in search of a life of dignity, service, and joy. On my journey I have discovered that there is nothing within me which is beyond the reach of God's love.

—The Reverend Barry L. Stopfel
Epiphany, 1997

Acknowledgments

Along with the dozens of remarkable men and women who appear in these pages under their own names and, in a few necessary cases, under pseudonyms, we owe an overwhelming debt of gratitude to the following:

To Tom Cantone, Lee Hancock, Mark Rubinsky, Diana and Lee Clark, Ann Evans, Sue McBride, Mary Ann Morrison, Mark Polo, Butch Stopfel, and Alice Stopfel, who exuberantly encourage us and believe in us.

To Jimmy Vines, our agent, and Mark J. H. Fretz, our editor, who steadfastly guided us with their insistent faith, uncompromising skill, and not always gentle urgings. To Karen Roche, whose support, friendship, and humor sustain us both; Don Winslow and Yvette Christofilis, who helped make sure this book would happen; and to Peter Selgin for his patient teaching and companionship. The beauty of the story would not have come to life without them. The roughness is entirely our own.

To all our friends and colleagues in the Diocese of Newark, New Jersey, particularly The Commission on Christian Education, with whom Barry did his first ministry. Also to Jack Croneberger and The Church of the Atonement, who recognized Barry's call and who risked much for the gospel of love.

To Art and Bette Miller, whose lives reflected the love of God in Barry's adolescence; Nancy Righter, who cared for us with an unwavering heart; Shirley Redfield, whose joy in life continues to inspire ours; Jeannette DeFriest, whose laughter is often salvation; Tracy Lind and all the out gay and lesbian clergy whose lives are a witness to a gospel of love and liberation.

In countless ways we are blessed by the people of Saint George's Church, whose faith, courage, and generosity of spirit daily nourish hope in our hungry world. With all our heart we thank them for theirs.

Courage
to
Love

Chapter I

For the longest time, he dismissed it
as a vestige of childhood—that evening prayer
he'd faithfully recited, night after night,
alone in bed, until his twenty-third year.

    He'd stopped abruptly. A strange affair:
    one friendly embrace, and the haze
    obscuring his heart had scattered, disclosing
    the abominable hunger harbored there.
He sought godless virtue. He let his heart
lead him to water, yet never drank.
Year after year, he frequented the rank
barrooms, staring, thirsting, standing apart,

    His only lovers he conjured in solitude.
    Miraculously beautiful and wise,
    they were virtuous, as one of flesh and blood
    couldn't be. It shone in their eyes.

Years passed. Then, on a spring night
no different from any other, a benign face
appeared before him, and two radiant eyes.
Fall in love, he fell . . . or so he thought,
 till one day in almost-winter it struck
 like thunder in his breast: not only his flesh
 was taking long-sought nourishment from flesh.
 Quietly, too, his soul had been partaking.
Flesh had come accompanied by grace; the light
in his love's eyes was the love of God.
It was that which filled him, night after night,
in his love's warm arms. And so he prayed.

—*Bruce Bawer,* "DEVOTIONS"[1]

I held my breath with him, instinctively knowing he would be. Kneeling, with his head bowed, he couldn't see the bishop or the hundreds of admirers standing in the silence of a steamy, Indian-summer night. Nor could the praying man see the cameras, the reporters, or the merely curious, who, crushed into the pews, doorways, and aisles of the vaguely Gothic stone and timber edifice, strained forward to see him finally accept the life ordained for him since childhood. Barry Stopfel, the man who held my heart in his hands, was about to be anointed with power, authority, and grace—ordained as a deacon, a servant in the Episcopal Church. It was September 30, 1990.

With his strong arms stretched out before him, Bishop Walter Righter gently bent toward Barry and intoned the sacred lessons in his rich, cathedral-filling voice. Tonight he would charge this one man, alone, stripped forever of privacy, to uphold the sacred calling of the servant.

"Dear friends in Christ," Walter's warm voice reverberated

through the silence, his eyes embracing every person in the hall with a compassionate love born of fifty years of Christian ministry. "You know the importance of this ministry and the weight of your responsibility in presenting Barry Stopfel for ordination to the sacred order of deacons." Bishop Righter let the enormity and moment of the occasion settle over us.

"Has Barry been selected in accordance with the canons of this Church, and do you believe Barry's manner of life to be suitable to the exercise of this ministry?"

In one voice the gathered hundreds proclaimed their faith in this gentle, soft-spoken man's call to ministry. "We believe that Barry has satisfied the requirements of the Church, and we believe Barry to be qualified for this ministry!"

Finally I breathed. Barry did too.

"We believe!" the congregation shouted, their cry of faith echoing over the bishop and bowing ordinand. "We believe!" Faith insisting that the stone was rolled away, and so it was. I held on as best I could until I saw my companion in this life of ours begin to shudder. Set apart for the commitment only he could make, together we wept openly, comforted by the courage and love of a people who dared to dream a new world.

Bishop Righter drew a deep breath, cast his eyes around the congregation, put his hand to his heart and read the charge. "Therefore if any of you know any impediment or crime because of which we should not proceed, come forward now and make it known." He paused.

It was the moment we had joked about earlier, talking like Glenda the Good Witch of the North: Are you an impediment or a crime? But it was a stiletto-edged joke. What were we impeding, what crime were we committing: Faith? Hope? Love? Still bowed and vulnerable, tears fresh in his eyes, Barry sensed a commotion behind him.

Quickly, Bishop Righter tried to proceed with the ordination. He was too late.

"I object! I rise to the question!" a man bellowed from the back of the church.

We had fought so long against so much to get to this day: bigotry, physical threats, hate mail, betrayal by friends, harassment from other Christians. We had just sung Cecil Frances Alexander's exuberant hymn of hope:

Jesus calls us; o'er the tumult
of our life's wild, restless sea,
day by day his clear voice soundeth,
saying, "Christian, follow me."

Now it felt like we were being delivered into the hands of those who despised us. Lee Hancock, my childhood friend from West Virginia, a woman of great, broad faith and the mother of Barry's and my goddaughters, put her hand on the back of my neck. Cool water. I drank deeply.

As if it were happening in slow motion, I watched Austin Menzies, in his late sixties, perhaps older, march down the aisle, flailing a twisted, yellow piece of paper above his head like a banner.

"Barry Stopfel is a self-admitted homosexual!" The disgust in his voice surprised me. Menzies had known Barry for two years, had sat in his adult education forums, listened to his sermons, and had always expressed cordial regards toward him. What had happened?

"Homosexuals are sexual perverts!" Menzies shouted. "Their sexual activity involves genital contact between men which includes . . ." The sanctuary spun around Barry as the most solemn moment of his life was stripped of its beauty and dignity. On the verge of losing what little he had eaten that day, Barry teetered toward Bishop Righter, who steadied him with one arm and with the other forbade the rage to come any closer to the bowing ordinand.

Too late. The sacred moment was poisoned.

What impediment?

What crime?

How did we ever get here?

Chapter 2

Train up a child in the way he should go, and when he is old he will not depart from it.

—PROVERBS 22:6

I saw a handsome man sitting on a stone bench in the Gothic, formal quadrangle of the seminary and walked right up to introduce myself.

He smiled, disarming me, and before I could even think about what I was saying I blurted out, "I've always had a thing for men's thighs." What *was* I thinking? I had stopped objectifying people as quickly as I used to (or so I thought!). This was an embarrassing slip my first day of seminary.

He sat relaxed, easy with his surroundings and with himself. His handsome, now mostly bald but still red head turned toward me in the bright afternoon sun.

"That's quite an opening line," he said, still smiling, relieving the terror that I had just made a horrible blunder. Now that I had entered the sacred sanctum of seminary, I wasn't so sure of my sixth sense.

"My name's Barry Stopfel." He was still smiling. A good sign. "What's yours?" His voice, so gentle and deep, like his eyes, pulled me in.

"Will Leckie."

Our hands reached out and met. He held my hand just that one moment too long and too tender. Sixth sense still intact.

"Haven't we met somewhere before? Studio 54? The Ice Palace?" I was dating myself and surreptitiously trying to date him. Yet something about his square-cut red beard flecked with gray was terribly familiar.

"I don't think so. I would have remembered you." Now, that was a follow-up line if I ever heard one. It worked. I was, as they say, completely taken by this man whose eyes shone like stormy afternoons. I knew that first day at Union Theological Seminary in 1985, as we sat in the cloistered garden crawling with ivy and gargoyles, that there would be more than enough time to learn each other's story.

"How did you get here?" he asked. It was a good question. We were obviously men of a "certain age" for whom a life-changing commitment such as seminary did not come lightly.

I hedged. Too many years spent behind glittering walls of vain chatter left me feeling uncertain about how truthful I could be with anyone, even someone as seemingly sincere as Barry. Yet one of the reasons I had come to seminary was to delve into the cloudy waters of my own, often troubled spirit. Learning to be vulnerable and honest with others was going to be a necessary part of my education. Something about Barry's eyes and his voice made it safe for me to start.

"That's a long story going back into the deepest, darkest recesses of my childhood," I said, laughing. "You sure you want to hear it?"

"I've got three years of seminary to listen," Barry said, looking steadily at me. Handsome and interested. That did it for me! We went for a walk in Riverside Park, where I plunged into my story.

I attended the McCallie School, a southern Christian military prep school in the vigorously evangelical city of Chattanooga, Tennessee. Back then we were required to attend chapel, Bible classes, Sunday school and church, with a Wednesday-night prayer meeting thrown in for good measure. Fortunately for me it was the era of muscular Christianity, with the heaviest proselytizing happening on the athletic fields and in the locker rooms. Most of my free time was spent on the stage, in the band, or practicing the piano. Unlike our athletic classmates, the artists were blessed with an absence of ecclesiastical interference.

As the years passed at McCallie, one by one my friends "turned their lives over to Jesus" and encouraged me to do likewise. "It'll make all the difference in the world for you," they each assured me. Having been raised a proper Presbyterian, where things are done "decently and in good order," I was skeptical about conversion experiences.

Part of my problem was that I never quite understood what it was, exactly, I was supposed to be saved *from*. One Sunday morning, I sat listening to a sweaty preacher rave about God's ability to rescue us from the hidden, perverse desires of our hearts of "like kind lying with like kind." My earliest longings were perverse? I knew my urgings were different from those of most of my friends, but before that morning I had never been ashamed of that difference. I assumed, as did my few friends who confessed similar desires, that some day I would marry and everything would work itself out. The preacher's words laid bare my secret fears that I might in fact be different from other guys, forever. As if that didn't inspire enough self-consciousness and self-loathing, one night less than a week later the school chaplain snagged me on the quad and challenged me about my "cyn-icism," pointing his finger at my tendency to "be that way."

"What way are you talking about?" I asked. I wasn't being fresh. I just wanted someone, anyone, to free me from the now hellish con-fusion of shame and self-loathing.

"Just watch yourself, son," the chaplain shied off the subject. "It'd be very easy for you to go off track with all this music and drama stuff. And those kind."

Ah, *those* kind. I had heard rumors, of course, and lived out thrill-ing episodes in my mind from time to time of what it might be like to have one of "those kind" hold me. So *that* was what I was sup-posed to be saved from—the very longings of my heart. It was salt on my wounded soul.

Years later, in a conversation with Mom and Barry, she said to me, "I think I knew since you were eight or ten that you were going to be gay."

"Why didn't you tell me?" I cried out.

"Well," she thought it over, "we didn't know how to talk about it back then. We didn't have any language for it."

 Early September in Manhattan is still summer, but un-der the leafy elms and maples the air turns cooler. Barry and I sat in the sun on one of the many stone walls overlooking the Hudson River, enjoying the view and the warmth of new friendship.

Barry asked, "When did you know you were gay?" It is a question gay people have asked in all times and in all places. How did you know you were different, how did you cope? The immediacy of our kinship was like the warm splash of sun on our faces, so I embarked on a long reply.

At prep school I fell in love with a beautiful boy, whom I will call Reed. Of course I had no language to express myself, then; men were supposed to fall in love with women, not each other. But I knew I was in love and very confused. By the spring of our junior year Reed had a conversion experience and became quite involved in his Bible studies and prayer meetings. Late one night the beginning of our senior year, he sat up talking with me, witnessing, trying to save me, and praying earnestly that I would accept Jesus as my personal Lord and Savior. The intimacy of Reed's body close to mine, his hands holding mine were so overwhelming I started to cry. He put his arms around me and held me until the fury, along with my arousal, passed.

Reed's touch sprung the rusty latch to my secret. Out of the roaring confusion of its opening I did as he asked and gave in to a conversion experience. Because I could scarcely wrap my mind around all those confusing messages of faith, friendship, love, and arousal, I embraced Southern fundamentalism with the ardor of a true zealot. I wanted to be near Reed, near other men who enjoyed honest, intimate camaraderie with one another. So I clung to this faith with a tenacious self-righteousness all the way through college and a long, chaste relationship with a wonderful woman. My salvation was from the loneliness and shame of desire.

But to stay true to this form of faith I had to deceive myself; my self-loathing about my true feelings grew with each prayer meeting, Bible study, and church service. What, as a boy, I had once treasured as my greatest longing—to be loved by another man—I now considered as pure evil.

A few years later when we were in college, Reed and I were sharing a bed one summer night in a motel room on our way to the beach. On the trip we had talked frankly about our "struggles," as we timorously put it, with our homosexual feelings. We had been lying side by side for some time, unable to sleep, when Reed suddenly asked if he could touch me. I knew exactly what he meant, wanted exactly what I thought he wanted, but my legs were shaking so badly I couldn't utter a sound. Reed touched my thigh under the sheets and started drawing his hand up to my chest. A thousand sirens went off in my head. It was too much for me: too much pleasure, too much guilt, too much terror. I grabbed his hands, flung us both off the bed onto our knees, and started praying for God to deliver us from this temptation.

We only knew to be embarrassed by our bodies and shamed by our feelings, as if human existence was somehow separate from our flesh. We had never been taught that a caring, physical intimacy between loving people is an expression of intimacy with God. We thought homosexual feelings a thorn in our youthful flesh we would outgrow. Or be condemned to hell for.

The tension between my faith and sexuality had its repercussions. Riddled with cramps and internal bleeding, I awoke on Palm Sunday my senior year in college paralyzed from the waist down. Inner conflict had ruptured my body; the result was Crohn's disease.

The body, as my friend and first great healer, Reneé Gorin, would teach me, stores all of our emotions and copes with them as best it can, even when we think we have blocked them out. It took three years, two more relapses, and incessant work with acupressurists, nutrition therapists, regular therapists, Chinese herbalists, and Dr. Samuel Meyers at Mount Sinai Hospital, to rid my body of this dread disease.

 Barry smiled as I told my story, recognizing experiences that are all too familiar to so many gays of our generation.

"I'm afraid the next generation will have the same horror," I said, smiling.

"Maybe," Barry said, staring out at the busy Hudson River. "But don't you think the next generation will have it easier than we did? And each succeeding generation finding it easier to be accepted and accept themselves?"

"Maybe," I said, not so certain.

"Of course," Barry went on with his thought, "it all depends on how well we teach, how well we choose to love our children."

Barry and I were simultaneously walking down the memory lane of my life and strolling by the river. It was fun; I hadn't talked about these times in ages. We tossed a few thoughts back and forth, but mostly he listened (he is good at that). I had hogged the conversation, bad form on a first date, and tried diverting the topic back to him when we happened upon the block-long communal flower garden that runs through the center mall of Riverside Park.

Over the years Barry and I have walked for miles through the city's parks, working through countless misunderstandings, every conflict and pain we have either inflicted on each other or borne from others. Walking in parks, on a beach, or hiking in the woods is how we reacquaint ourselves with the sacred in our lives.

"Faggots!" a biker screamed as he flew past us.

"How did he know?" Barry asked.

"Well," I said, pointing out the cliché, "we *are* standing rather close together, and we *are* admiring a flower garden."

We laughed at ourselves and headed farther south, away from the seminary and all the demands awaiting us there.

"You've heard my story, now tell me about yourself," I urged. "I know you grew up in the Church. What was that like?"

"I want to hear more about you."

No man had ever listened so intently to me before. And now he wanted more! It was very easy to share my past with him, trust him with my story, grow as intimates grow.

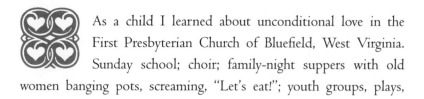 As a child I learned about unconditional love in the First Presbyterian Church of Bluefield, West Virginia. Sunday school; choir; family-night suppers with old women banging pots, screaming, "Let's eat!"; youth groups, plays,

sneaking out with friends to drink Cherry Cokes, smoke cigarettes, and talk about our futures; an organist whose motto was "Less talk, more speed!"; old men who pinched cheeks, and women who smelled of cedar or camphor or rosewater . . . these are the life-giving memories of my childhood. First Presbyterian was a place inherently generous with its children, a place where we grew up knowing that God loved us just as we were. Funny, but as an adult it took me a lot of years to become as a child again and remember that lesson.

"You've absolutely got to come to this dream retreat!" My best friend, Lee Hancock, was on the phone trilling the virtues of doing Jungian dream analysis in her church. Even though Lee and I had grown up together in First Presbyterian and I trusted her implicitly, spending a weekend in a church drawing pictures of God and sharing our most personal garbage with total strangers seemed too strange. Once I moved to New York and began training at The National Skakespeare Company Conservatory, I discarded the judgmental, shaming God of my adolescence. Slowly, tentatively I was coming out to myself and my closest friends, discovering the wholeness and joy when body and soul are at peace with one another. Dismissing God from my thinking had been the key to this new life and I was less than eager to think about things religious.

"Anyway," she blasted ahead, hearing my hesitation, "there's a *fabulous* man I want you to meet." Ah, the hook. "He's young, very handsome, and very well off. I think you two would be perfect together."

We were. The next night Tom and I went to dinner and fell head-over-heels off the Empire State Building in love with each other. I was intrigued that a smart, attractive gay man had somehow reconciled his spiritual life with his gay life. Tom, with his twinkling, boyish good looks, challenged me to do the same. Lee was right. We were meant for each other.

"Isn't it just what your mother always wanted? To meet a nice man in church?" Barry teased me.

"He was a nice man." My bittersweet recollections suddenly choked within me. In fact, it hadn't been quite the scenario Mom and Dad had dreamed of for me. Mom told me as much one day, saying, as mothers do, that she worried I would have a hard time "in this world that's so hell-bent against you. I just don't want you to get hurt, honey, that's all." Meaning broken bones as opposed to a broken heart. My mom and dad cared only that I knew love, and worried only that our world might hurt me for it.

This was more than I had ever told anyone, even after several dates. I was feeling exposed and vulnerable. There is a quiet attentiveness to Barry that encourages openness. But we had just met, for Pete's sake, and so far I knew very little about him.

We were passing by the playground near Eightieth Street, watching a serious jungle-gym competition, follow-the-leader style, with kids hanging from their knees, leaping off the top and catching a bar, hand over hand to the end, with a high kick-jump off into the sand. I took advantage of their play to try and trigger some of Barry's own memories.

"Did you have a happy childhood?"

Barry laughed. "Happy? I don't know about happy," he said, keeping his eyes on the monkey bars. "It looked happy to anyone looking in. I had security, creature comforts, more than nearly everyone else. I had caring and responsible parents, highly regarded by the community and our church." He kicked a stone down the walk and followed it. "But I was a lonely, anxious kid. The world didn't seem safe. I felt on the outside of life, like I didn't fit in somehow no matter how hard I tried." He grew quiet and soon we were walking in silence. I had spilled my guts and now I wanted some gut spilling in return. This strong, silent-type business wasn't going to do. "What'd you do with yourself?" I prodded.

"Oh, I played make-believe a lot. The world I knew was cruel and lonely. It was my way out." More silence.

"Cruel?" *Prod, prod.*

He leaned against a rail and watched the little kids furiously pumping their tricycles.

"Growing up I was a very sensitive child whose feelings got hurt a lot. I'd spin off into these dizzying fits. I think everyone was terrified of me because, you see, my family didn't express their feelings. Any feelings. There was so much under the surface with my dad and my mom and the war and his memories. It just wasn't talked about. A lot of silence in my family. So I guess I was pretty hard to take. As a kid I felt out of place because I didn't know I was having normal, emotional responses to the quiet around me. I thought I spoke or walked funny. Or cried too easily. Or wasn't rugged enough. I couldn't figure out why I was so hard to take, why people walked away from me." He broke off again.

"You were too beautiful to take, that's all," I told him, hoping my truthful compliment didn't sound too much like a come-on. Well, maybe it was, just a little.

"No, I wasn't a beautiful kid," he said.

"I don't mean Gerber Baby stuff. Your interior life was too beautiful, too rich for most people to handle."

"Well, maybe I know that *now*. But then? I just wanted to have a normal life like I thought everybody else had, a Wally and the Beaver kind of life. But I didn't. So no, it wasn't a happy childhood."

It took a lot of years with Barry before I would let him have his emotional memories without trying to fix them or make them all better. I pressed him to say more.

"You didn't know any happiness as a kid?"

He leaned over the rail and looked down at the boats moored in the basin, bobbing gently on the Hudson's strong current. The late afternoon was coming on fast and the glare tried to force our eyes inland. But boats invariably draw Barry and me, so we braved the day blindness that afternoon and dreamed dreams before the wind.

"Happiness in life was something that might happen to you, when you grew up." Was he talking about his childhood, or the ketch two piers out? "But you were never supposed to expect it. If you were lucky enough to find happiness, you never talked about it. That would be prideful, and that was the greatest of sins. Christianity was very serious business: no dancing, no drinking, no pleasures of the flesh."

"I don't cuss and I don't chew," I began, hoping Barry would join in. He did. "And I don't go with girls who do!" We laughed at the hoary old chestnut we had both ended up taking quite to heart.

"The Church has always been important to me." Barry turned from the boat basin and headed back up the river. "I loved the Church; it saved my life and made me feel like I could be somebody in the world. See, I spent so much time hiding who I was from myself and my friends, when I was at church I believed, I mean I *really* believed, Jesus protected me from all those people who just wouldn't let me be me. So I loved being there." He stopped speaking and looked sideways at me for a minute. I didn't have to be a mind reader to know he was thinking about telling me a story.

Chapter 3

Just as I am, without one plea
But that thy blood was shed for me,
And that thou bidd'st me come to thee,
O Lamb of God, I come, I come!

—*Charlotte Elliott, 1836*

"Come here and sit." He patted a space on the bench next to him. "I'm going to tell you something about my mom you'll probably understand." We sat with our feet propped up on the rail, high bushes shielding our eyes from the sun.

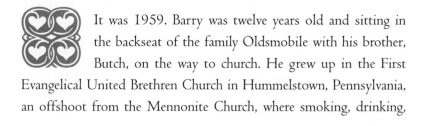It was 1959. Barry was twelve years old and sitting in the backseat of the family Oldsmobile with his brother, Butch, on the way to church. He grew up in the First Evangelical United Brethren Church in Hummelstown, Pennsylvania, an offshoot from the Mennonite Church, where smoking, drinking,

dancing, and fancy adornments were still considered signs of depravity and sinfulness.

Sitting stone-still in their Sunday best, all four family members were hypnotized by the thrum of the heavy eight-cylinder engine. Barry had been called by the elders of the church to speak at a special meeting after worship. Even as a boy he was at the vortex of a heretical controversy, one of his detractors declaring even then that Barry was threatening the life of the church.

The child who was shy about his feelings at school and home was outgoing at church, playing the piano and leading the junior high youth-group activities committee. The post-Eisenhower years being what they were, Barry organized a potluck supper and square dance in the parish hall as a mixer for all the local church junior high youth groups. Given his feelings about the church, Barry thought it would be an ideal, safe place for his friends to have fun.

"The Devil has taken hold of your son, Carolyn," a neighbor warned his mother. "Mark our words, the Beach Boys and the Supremes and all this modern noise is going to replace Jesus at the center of his life. But we won't let it happen to our children. Our youth fellowship doesn't need that kind of worldly influence. You just keep him home 'til he's got right with God." Small-town neighbors can be tough.

"Mrs. Stopfel, this will undermine the teaching and discipline of the Church," another church member complained. "Before you know it boys and girls will be slow dancing, their bodies touching each other, and you know what bodily contact can lead to between young people!"

Carolyn Stopfel remained silent, not yet taking a side in the swirling, small-town controversy. She had given birth to and raised her first son, Butch, alone while Marlin flew with the U.S. Army over Europe in World War II. In return for her war efforts at home, she got back a husband shot down, partially blinded, massively burned, and nearly broken. Three long, agonizing years after his homecoming, and dozens of flesh-restoring operations later, a second son was born: Barry, their silent affirmation of the sheer will to survive.

Carolyn couldn't bring herself to stand against the church and town with whom she had suffered through the war and from whom she had received care. She was a reserved, quiet woman who lived out a self-effacing, mute existence, hanging on to whatever life had dealt her. There were standards to maintain, and Carolyn's personal dignity wouldn't allow her to call attention to herself or her family. In those days, in that place, one trod very lightly around authority and social convention. She would wait and see what the church people had to say.

Two weeks earlier, Barry had met with Reverend Aungst, a stern, humorless Pennsylvania Dutchman, aptly named. That twelve-year-old Barry Stopfel had dared to act without his approval was more than blasphemous, it was infuriating.

"Now, son," his eyes narrowed into slits, "you know the sins of the flesh are legion. And we, who are your elders, know the way to overcome them, saving you from the threat of eternal damnation that your loving Father in heaven has promised if we disobey his commandments."

"If my Father in heaven loves me," Barry responded, "why would he damn me?" Barry's theological challenges to authority had early origins.

Perhaps because he had so few from which to choose, Reverend Aungst was a man of few words.

"God has revealed to us the way to hell and the way to salvation in the words of Jesus Christ," he coldly reminded Barry. "The straight way, the narrow way, the good way has been handed down to us for salvation, and it is forbidden for this dance to occur."

Twelve is a tough age on parents, but wonderful for children, who are just beginning to realize that most adults are jerks. "Did Jesus *really* say it's a sin to dance in the parish hall?" Barry's eyes twinkled.

He was a *very* good Bible student and was pretty sure he had Aungst in a corner.

The entire congregation knew Barry as a quasi-charismatic boy, who had been "giving his witness" since he was nine at the biennial tent revivals, playing the organ and piano in church, diligently studying the Bible. Aungst was up against not just another rebellious adolescent, but the best little church boy in the world.

While the storm was building over back fences and fenders in the church parking lot, Barry had gained the support of the youth-group advisors and several pillars of the congregation, one of whom would eventually become his stepmother. This was his moment, and he let Reverend Aungst know. He could just about hear that square dance caller in the land of the Brethren.

"Reverend Aungst, do you know what happens on Friday nights at the fire hall dance?"

Aungst drew himself up behind his desk, daring Barry to say another word. "Yes, I do! These are things a good Christian does not think about." Shame seldom worked on Barry.

"Well, wouldn't you agree it'd be better for the youth group to be dancing in the parish hall rather than going off to the fire hall?" Barry took a deep breath and, before the reverend could get a word in edgewise, hurled his last stone.

"You know what goes on in the cornfield out behind the fire hall dances, don't you?" All the grade-school boys, who were old enough to be out with their friends on a Friday night after dinner, used to sneak around and watch the fire hall dances. It was a great source of small-town entertainment. And education. Barry had seen Aungst's favorite teenager, his golden boy, an effete, goody-two-shoes universally despised by all the kids for sucking up to any and all adults, get ripping drunk there on a regular basis, often taking some young woman or other out for a toss in the cornfield with equal regularity.

"Of course I know!" Aungst was unstrung. The world had crept into his Eisenhower-led years and he hadn't a clue how to cope. Fear and shame no longer managed children like they used to. "That's exactly why they shouldn't dance at all!"

"They do more than just dance, Reverend Aungst," Barry said. "You should ask your golden boy how he likes the fire hall dances." He was not above using extortion.

The coup de grâce had been neatly executed. Reverend Aungst was, at last, speechless. He called for a congregational meeting, confident that Barry would be intimidated and shrink from his commitment. Intimidation doesn't work well on Barry, either. He's stubborn that way.

Barry made only the briefest reference to the fire hall dance in his speech, just enough to start heads bobbing and tongues wagging. It was all the Brethren needed to hear. *Yessir, there's trouble, right here in Hummelstown! Given the times we are living in, and the multitude of temptations available to kids, perhaps dancing isn't such a terrible concession to make after all. Why, if they're going to dance, where better than in church? Here, at least, we can make sure they're not tempted to further indulgences of the flesh. However: There will be no Slow Dancing!*

Carolyn and Marlin Stopfel listened quietly to the buzz as they watched their youngest boy, born out of the uncertainty of their postwar marriage, sit politely up front as he waited for the vote to be taken. Here was their son, attempting to bring together the emerging sensuality of the new generation with the faith of the old. Barry's life was rooted by an integrity of faith his parents had taught him. They were sure of that, and trusted him. And so, amazed at this child who was no longer their child, in many ways no longer a child at all, Marlin and Carolyn Stopfel voted with the majority.

And the children danced in the church.

Chapter 4

Three passions, simple but overwhelmingly strong, have governed my life: the longing for love, the search for knowledge and the unbearable pity for the suffering of mankind.

—*Bertrand Russell*

In September the sun takes its own sweet time settling behind the Palisades. Barry and I had walked and talked through a lot of history for a first date. Perhaps it was the thrill of starting new lives, strangers on the deck of a ship sailing to unknown lands, that gave us the courage for such intimacy. Within hours of our meeting we were becoming best friends.

We found ourselves at "Fire Island," Riverside Park, a tiny hillside isthmus squeezed between the West Side Highway and the rocky edge of the Hudson River, where grass battles hard-packed dirt for space and air. Our feet knew the way without having to ask our heads: safe places outside of the bars are like that for urban gay males.

"Why did you come to seminary?" I asked as we stretched out.

"The Church was grafted onto my soul. I grew up not only with the usual church activities, but with tent revivals. You know, full of wailing, fanning, fainting; shouts of ecstasy and tearful confessions of sin; and that long, wrenching march down the sawdust trail, bowed by guilt, the piano urging and the congregation singing 'Just As I Am' over and over and over." He smiled, enjoying this.

"I don't mean to trivialize them," he added, "they were thrilling semiannual events, releasing in three days all the emotions we had to swallow the rest of the year."

He gazed out at the Hudson, where a barge fought its way against the current. "The spring revival was the really wild one, because all the preaching and all the songs were about being washed in the blood. For a kid as sensitive as I was, the idea that God would sacrifice himself—and God was always a man—was unbearable. I used to weep about Jesus bleeding when we sang some of the old blood-and-fire songs! So at the height of this one service, the spring of fourth grade, I marched down the aisle, determined not to let God down, and gave my life to Jesus."

I smiled, remembering similar experiences in the deep South.

"I was captivated by the theatre of it, by the absolute abandon we were permitted twice a year. Every year after that I was called up to give my witness. Can you imagine? My mother used to tell me I was going to be a minister one day. It was her way of telling me I'd done good."

"And look at you now."

"Yeah," he said, laughing, "the circle of life is truly something else. But I'm not sure I'm going to be a priest. I'm at Union for the education. The rest I'll figure out when I get there."

We lazed on the hard shore of the Hudson River, the highway buzzing behind our heads, and watched a tanker and a couple of trash barges beat their way to the bay.

The 1960s washed over Hummelstown, Pennsylvania, as thoroughly as the rest of the country. Barry embraced his adolescence with a vengeance, sneaking cigarettes and delighting in the forbidden ecstasies of the Slow Dance. In his junior year of high school, he joined a summer theatre troupe and became a member of Actors' Equity. He was growing up fast, embracing a world of passion only dreamed of in his youth.

When the summer theatre season came to a close, Barry traveled to Estes Park, Colorado, for a nationwide convocation of Methodist youth. In Colorado he found the Church, along with the God it presented to him, too small to embrace the whole of his life, now newly filled with wonders outside its confines.

One evening after a thunderstorm had spent its fury and was passing over the graying Rocky Mountains, Barry hiked alone to a precipice overlooking Estes Park, seeking clarity to the confusion in his soul. The young people here didn't seem as inquisitive about their world as his theatre friends. They didn't question, didn't argue, were content just to be fed information. The night gathered quickly around him, and then, as happens sometimes in sacred places at sacred times in our lives, Barry felt a very personal God telling him to go on and embrace a larger world on his own, to move away from the Church, and find that "something" greater and more supportive of his life and feelings that he was looking for. God was pushing him out of the nest.

This wasn't about being gay; he was sixteen and still several years away from that consciousness. This was about finding a fully embodied, sensual God who lived in the same world as Barry, a God who was hurt and gladdened by the pathos and joy surrounding him. It was about finding a God who could live *with* him in the full range of his inner, emotional life. High in the Rocky Mountains, Barry abandoned any idea of ordained ministry and chose instead to direct his life into the world far beyond his boyhood church.

By the time Barry entered Boston University, the civil rights movement was sweeping a nation embittered by the lies of increasingly cynical politicians. A generation of young men and women believed the dream of the Reverend Dr. Martin Luther King, Jr., and took to the streets to bring about a change in our society. Though basically shy and pacifist by nature, Barry had been taught by his mother to defend the defenseless. It was this conditioning that impelled him into civil rights demonstrations, draft resistance, Vietnam War protests, and the eventual burning of his own draft card. He fell in love with a woman who shared his passions.

Or did he? Barry had feelings of deep affection and respect for her, held her close with sweet, loving regard. But he began to doubt that this combination of feelings and arousal made for a long, abiding, deep love. He was confused that she did not seem to be his soul mate and prayed (he had left the Church but not his faith) that God would bring him someone he could love fully, deeply, passionately.

On the steps of Lowe Library at Columbia University, where he had gone for graduate work in education, he found himself weeping with a thousand other students, stunned by the massacre at Kent State. What happened to many at that time happened to Barry: He grew disillusioned with social activism, seeing little change for the good in America. After graduation he went off in search of the "good life."

He found it in corporate America as director of marketing for Hershey Park and its entertainment complex next to his hometown. Close again to the free-spirited theatre people he loved, he met, was pursued by, and fell in love with a dancer. His name was Peter.

For all its seeming difference from everything he had known so far, it wasn't a mind-blowing shock. Peter rekindled all the passions and loves for life that had been lit when he was a boy in summer theatre.

Oh, *this* is who I am, Barry thought. He was in love, fully, deeply, passionately, and that's all that mattered. At first he wondered if it was just a diversion, a last tribute to youth before settling down to the serious business of adult life. But two weeks into the relationship Barry knew it was more than a phase. He got a copy of John Mc-Neill's book, *The Church and the Homosexual,* and learned again that God is love, love is always a gift of God, and that love is our calling. It seemed Peter was to be no passing fancy; he was an unexpected answer to prayer—the first great love of Barry's life.

In earnest they committed to their relationship, choosing to live as openly gay men rather than in the safety of emotional closets. Barry and Peter were supported and accepted by their coworkers and friends, no small gift for a gay couple in the 1970s. No small gift today.

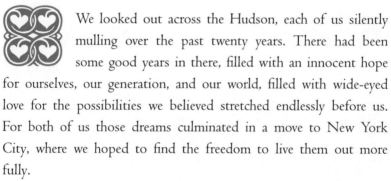 We looked out across the Hudson, each of us silently mulling over the past twenty years. There had been some good years in there, filled with an innocent hope for ourselves, our generation, and our world, filled with wide-eyed love for the possibilities we believed stretched endlessly before us. For both of us those dreams culminated in a move to New York City, where we hoped to find the freedom to live them out more fully.

But almost as soon as we arrived, one year apart and eight years before meeting, we were hit with the pandemic of AIDS. By the early eighties Barry and I were so busy trying to keep up with who was sick, who needed what, where we had to show up in protest, who else had tested positive, when and where the next memorial service was being held, we lost track of whatever dreams we had come here to fulfill. Dreams? Hell, we didn't have time to recover from one loss before the next one rushed in to crush our already broken hearts. Whatever illusion of the good life we came to New York

in search of was wholly trivialized by our friends' suffering and
death.

"Something was missing in the good life." Barry tossed a blade of
grass into the sunset wind. "My childhood God was still working in
my heart, the one that wanted me to actually be my best, not just
settle for something and say it was my best.

"One night, at an AIDS rally, I heard the Episcopal Bishop of
New York, Paul Moore, speak passionately about gays and AIDS
and how Christians should be present, active, and personally involved. I felt something old and familiar shoot through me, almost
like the call to come forward in those old tent revivals. But this time
it was a call to get my spiritual life back in sync with my life in the
world. I was working for American Express at the time, not a particularly spiritual experience. So the following Sunday I walked into an
Episcopal church, Grace Church, in the heart of Greenwich Village."

"It must've been like entering a foreign country," I said, "coming
from a Brethren background."

"Not really," Barry answered. "Grace Church had a strong Protestant sensibility mixed with its ritual, but no smells and bells. The
architecture was beautiful: simple, Colonial, and they had both a
men's and a boys' choir, fabulously old New York. They also housed
the city's first shelter for homeless women, and conducted education
programs for inner-city kids. I felt at home: gay sensibilities and
social justice."

"But there had to be more, or you wouldn't have stayed."

"Oh, there was," he said, growing more animated. "The preaching
there was excellent. My first Sunday the curate preached the most
eloquent, intelligent sermon about unconditional grace I'd ever heard
in my life. Ken Swanson was energetic and youthful with an urbane
sense of humor that called back all of my most powerful, emotional
responses to the Gospel that urged me to be the best I could be. He
kept me on my toes, forcing me to decide whether I was going to be
a man guided by God's grace or by my own initiative. Through his

approach to life and faith I began to integrate my own evangelical prayer life with all the other passions of my life. Ken urged me not to check my mind at the door of the church, but to use all the gifts, simple and sophisticated, God had given me to seek God in my life. I knew I'd come home again."

Barry looked hard at me, deciding if he could, or should, go on. For once I didn't say anything, sensing a turning point in our conversation.

"Something happened one night. I was in a hurry, you know, late from the office, and had to stop into the DDL Food Show on the Upper West Side to pick up some caviar and chocolate truffles for my hosts—my stock-in-trade at dinner parties back then. I'm running up to the store when, out of the corner of my eye, I notice a homeless woman slumped in the doorway. I try to rush past her but end up accidentally kicking her in the face, slamming her head into the plateglass door."

He tossed more grass in the air, testing the breeze with its blades. It was taking some time for this memory to play itself out in his heart.

"I stopped dead in my tracks. Absolutely dead. I looked down at her, down at my feet. I looked at my hands and then, finally, at her face. Out of her silent eyes a question shouted in my ears, 'What am I doing with my life? Where's the boy who wanted to leave the world better off than he found it?' But I choked back the thought and walked past her to buy my truffles and caviar for the dinner party. I think I mumbled 'Sorry,' but I'm not sure. I didn't want to think about what I was doing with my life right then and I certainly didn't want to confront the reality of how callous a person I'd become."

My eyes filled with the tears filling his. Meeting God, I thought, is always humiliating. Quietly the sun slipped behind the Palisades, leaving us in the still, amber hush of twilight.

"Look!" Barry said, his voice strained, choking back the shame.

He was pointing to the lights of the George Washington Bridge, shimmering through the early evening heat. Wordlessly I reached out and took his hand in mine, settling them on the still-warm grass between us. It takes a long time for memories never voiced to reverberate through the heart and fade. Sometimes years. Together we gazed at the bridge forming a gray bow across the Hudson. There was a beautiful soul in this man. I could wait for more.

"Will you go with me to the mixer tonight?" he turned and asked out of the gathering dusk. "I could use someone to slow dance with." I smiled.

We began the long walk back uptown, watching bikers and in-line skaters weave and glide through the sea of baby strollers. We had journeyed a long way with each other this first day, through miles and years, lifetimes and transformations. If I knew nothing else about Barry, I knew I was willing to hold his heart in mine for as long as necessary.

That night at the seminary mixer we danced. Slowly, very slowly.

Chapter 5

If the church or society refuses to recognize or promote any positive alternative in which love and intimacy can sustain a gay or lesbian couple, then those institutions are guilty of contributing to the very promiscuity that they condemn.

—*The Rt. Rev. John S. Spong,* LIVING IN SIN?[2]

I can't say exactly when it dawned on me that we were loving each other. Some fall in love, some grow. Barry and I grew. Maybe we had both lived on our own too long to recognize love, finding restful comfort in being single and swearing to ourselves we didn't miss the dating game. Maybe we were scared to stick a toe in the water again. Maybe we had buried too many lovers, too many friends to believe love was even a possibility. Maybe we carried too much hurt. Maybe we enjoyed deluding ourselves. Maybe all of the above.

I had enjoyed several years of love with Tom, but was devastated when I returned from a tour with the National Shakespeare Company to discover he had become lovers with one of our good friends. I was in such a blind fury about the sexual infidelity, which was merely a symptom of the greater problem, that I didn't realize for months it was the infidelity of his heart that killed the relationship. I loved him when we broke up, still loved him five years later when I entered seminary. Don't get me wrong, I wasn't sitting at home singing torch songs, but I had shut down over the hurt and grown unwilling to give any of the wonderful men in my life a chance at my heart. Once burned, twice cautious. Now there was Barry, and I was aware that the tower I had built around my heart had become unbreachable. I needed my family. I went to see Lee.

"Will," she took my hand in her twisted one, crippled in her twenties by rheumatoid arthritis, "your problem is simple. You've just got to decide if this is the man you're going to inflict your worst self on." We laughed, thinking of everything her long-suffering husband, Mark Rubinsky, had coped with as Lee wrestled regularly with the better angels of her nature. Catching a seriousness in my eyes she hadn't seen there in years, she asked, "Honey, do you love him?"

"I don't know. I think so. Sure. Yes. But I don't know if I can do this and seminary right now." I was looking for a way out, but Lee is very astute.

"Look at it this way," she said, kneading my hand in hers and slipping easily into our common Southern shorthand. "Many of us work out our relationship with God in our relationship with another person. Maybe it's time you learned to love again." Family can be so damned direct.

I had been trying to integrate my reemerging spirituality in an emotional vacuum. For four years now I had been losing friends to AIDS, and had never really wept. How could I open myself to this man? To *any* man?

"I'm so afraid of being hurt," I confessed quietly, hoping to justify my running away from Barry.

"You will be hurt," Lee said bluntly. "If you want to know love then you've got to risk pain." She let that sink in and then spoke of her daughter, my goddaughter. "Hannah is my baby, and every day I love her so much, worry about her so much, it aches. But hurt is not the opposite of love. Hurt is love's companion, its shadow. The opposite of love is isolation."

Thank God I was working with Reneé Gorin, who took on the arduous task of breaking apart my nearly impenetrable exterior. A giant of a healer who stood four-feet-something next to my six-feet-plus, she chiseled and chipped, stretched, snapped, caressed, and loved me enough that I might begin to love myself.

"You can't just shut down one emotion, Will," she encouraged me one day while I continued to move yogalike on the floor of her Gramercy Park office. "Once you shut down one aspect of your emotional life, they all follow. You don't want to feel pain? Fine. Then you won't feel joy. Or ecstasy. Or love. Or compassion. Because our emotional life is a total package. You have them all, or you have none."

All of the ancient religious traditions teach that faith is not something we manufacture in ourselves; it is a gift, some say of the gods. But I know that angels walk among us unawares. Once Reneé had faith in me, it became possible to risk faith in myself, risk love. Now I was going to inflict my worst self on Barry, and he on me, and all the while we would both keep risking relationship because at the core of our being, we knew we had been given a gift: companionship.

Barry had given up a very comfortable, successful career in Hershey so that Peter, his partner of two years, could pursue what would become a successful dancing and modeling career in New York City. The new world they inhabited, albeit more openly gay, was less supportive of their relationship than the one in Pennsylvania. Among their gay friends there were few who believed that Barry and Peter should even remain a couple. They were young and making careers in the Big Apple—they should live with a broader circle of acquaintances, i.e., sleep around.

Seeing relationships crumble all around them, Barry and Peter sought an anchor in that most ancient of traditions in a small, private ceremony at home: They had a Roman Catholic priest bless their union.

But private ceremonies have only a tenuous hold in the very public world we inhabit. Without the obvious symbols of being a couple—rings, framed photographs on the desk, printed, embossed invitations—a gay relationship is easy to keep hidden, which is, after all, the common, social expectation.

As gay men, our liberation is directly linked with the necessity to be sexual beings. Instinctively we sought a kind of salvation from our loneliness and self-loathing that could come only with another man's touch. We survived the exile and critical judgment of our culture with a sexual carnival, drawing no connection between our sexuality and our spirituality. How could we? The voices that might have taught us about such connections were crying in a wilderness of religious tradition that preferred condemning gays to knowing them, and who doggedly believed the body to be separate from the mind and spirit. We had been trapped too long by that kind of irrational doublespeak. The Church became a quaint relic from childhood, something given to Goodwill or the Salvation Army once we'd grown up and cleaned out our rooms.

But this dis-integration of our sexuality and our spirituality exacts a toll. A year after their small, private ceremony, Peter told Barry that he wanted an "unrestricted" relationship; the cornucopia of sexual opportunity beckoned. Peter felt he had a right, if not an obligation, to partake in the freedom of being gay, to express himself and his longings with other men when circumstance and occasion arose. Being twenty-something, tall, and lithe, circumstances arose on a regular basis.

For several months Barry lived with Peter's new convictions. After all, he loved him; Peter was the man with whom he had come out to himself and the world. Barry believed Peter would remain as faithful as he was. But the thrill of the new, the beautiful, and the exotic pulled Peter inexorably away from their relationship and, two years after uprooting his life and moving to New York, Barry gave up the first great love of his life.

Post-Peter, Barry had to figure out how to be a single gay man in New York City. Not a drinker, or given to much idle chatter, the bar scene was out of the question for Barry; the meat-rack objectification of body parts intimidated him, further weakening his already fragile self-esteem. He thought he might meet a nice man in church: a cute, old-fashioned notion, he knew, but he was grasping at straws. Walking with high hopes into a gay church fellowship in the West Village, within minutes he was reeling from the self-indulgent, fussy worship service going on before him, replete with brocaded robes, an incensor intent on choking out the last hope of fresh air, and a fluorescent, stand-and-model coffee hour from hell. He ran screaming, choosing solace in overwork. That, at least, kept the long, lonely nights as short as possible.

Peter would call every few days, seemingly to pour salt into old wounds. But his news was turning bad. He had bouts of hepatitis and then developed a mononucleosis that he couldn't shake. "Gay mono" it was called at first. At first. It was 1983, and the strange killer was stigmatized as GRID: Gay Related Immune Deficiency. The gay communities had no idea what was coming, nor did Peter's doctors, who were at a loss as to how to treat him. We were all at a loss. And then the losses really started.

Barry threw himself into volunteer work at the Gay Men's Health Crisis and became a buddy to homebound men: he went shopping, picked up medicine, got them to their doctors, all the things hundreds of men and women pitched in to do as we tried to get through a presumably brief epidemic with as much charity and grace as possible. Little did we realize the "brief" epidemic would stretch into the next decade and beyond.

One evening in 1984, Lorraine, a spiritual counselor of great intuition and vision, said to Barry, "Your heart is too resilient to be shut down by hurt. Love is your calling in this life. What are you going to do about it?"

As we do with most advice, whether freely given or paid for, he ignored it. For a while.

By then what was officially called AIDS was decimating gay communities, and nearly every institution in this country sat back and watched. Instead of treating AIDS as a health crisis, AIDS was moralized: Gays are immoral, gays get AIDS, AIDS is the cost of immorality. What free time we had we spent being angry at a nation's apparent willingness to choose moral righteousness over justice and compassion. We had no compassion left to give those who seemed not to care or help. Jesus always chose compassion and justice over moral righteousness, often quite angry at those who differed with him. It was a model we clung to because we were so emptied of hope and so filled with pain that we didn't have the energy to try and transform anyone's prejudices. We screamed a lot in the night.

It took gay men and lesbians, outcasts from the mainstream of society, and all of our straight friends, whose compassion drove away their fear, to turn this nation's heart around. But it was too late for too many.

Chapter 6

The first forty years of life give us the text: the next thirty supply the commentary.

—*Schopenhauer*

Sometimes Barry is apt to say it was madness that urged him to enter seminary as a thirty-eight-year-old man. But, when pressed, he will confess that buried deep within him there has always been a desire, a sense of calling to make a difference in his world. As the director of marketing for the Joffrey Ballet, Barry had filled up his life with a dazzling array of glitterati. But nights spent meeting the Reagans in Washington and dinners at the Pierre in New York surrounded by arts dowagers no longer nurtured his sense of self. The era of AIDS was upon us, and instead of successive celebrations of our friends' achievements, we were looking for scraps of meaning in lives too shortly lived.

At Grace Church in the Village, Barry was hearing unconditional grace preached about nearly every Sunday. God has come to us and is present in every one of us, no matter who we are. When we live into that belief, we gain power, as God's people, to effect good in the world.

The growing connection between his reemerging spirituality and his need to be involved in tangible ministries impelled him to volunteer in Grace Church's soup kitchen and home meal program. When opportunity arose to volunteer at Bellevue Hospital's fledgling, overcrowded AIDS floor, Barry jumped in. This was not opening night with the Reagans at the Kennedy Center. Here were teen mothers with two, sometimes three children; street people addicted to heroin, unaware that the needles they shared also passed the deadly AIDS virus; the poor, who had only their bodies left to sell for a meal; people whose lives had been broken by the weight of institutionalized poverty. The Great Society, trickle-down, voodoo economics, and the welfare state were cold comfort to those sleeping on the sidewalks and the steam grates, or in the halls of New York City's great public hospital. Through these ministries Barry felt like he had come home again, living out a thoughtful, Scripture-based affirmation of everything he had learned riding in the back of his mother's Oldsmobile.

Delivering boxes to the poorest of the poor, Barry had learned an awful lot from his mother. She would shake her head at "Sunday Christians" and tell her boys, "If you can't walk the walk, then don't talk the talk." It was a hard-edged compassion born of rural necessity: Community is everyone's responsibility. Carolyn Stopfel knew there was always someone with less than what she had. "So see they get something," she taught; "that way they'll have some to share as well. But," she cautioned, "always give in such a way so you protect their dignity. Never judge others for their misfortune, especially if you don't know them." The Brethren community of Barry's childhood, so often strict and in conflict with the prevailing culture, ingrained in him the truth that compassion is not a warm feeling toward others. Compassion is a responsibility to care for those who have less, who are weakened by life and circumstances.

These were bedrock lessons of the heart, and those who did not live them were a source of grave disappointment for Carolyn Stopfel. Though her life was cut short by the painful debilitation of Hodgkin's disease, she had lived it in hope that her example would take root in her two sons. Barry was far away from home in graduate school at Columbia University and seemingly on a very different path, but Carolyn died believing her youngest son would one day become a minister. Maybe it was simply part of the normal mother/son process of differentiation, but it would be several years before Barry walked into Grace Church, let himself think about his mother again, and re-explore the lessons of compassion she had instilled in him as a boy. By then his father had remarried another woman of great faith and generous heart, Alice Hoover, one of Barry's youth advisors in his hometown church. The circle of love and family is never broken.

Chapter 7

There is no fear in love,

for perfect love casts out fear.

—I JOHN 4:18

When Barry went back to church, he was seeking a source of strength and courage to meet a modern world, nearly gone mad with suffering and apathy, something that would sustain him in his volunteer work. There was so little help, so little known about AIDS in its early days that it crushed both those with the disease and those who walked with them.

He became a regular at Grace Church, forsaking early morning trains to Fire Island or Jones Beach for Sunday services. His friends were stunned by what seemed like a sudden change and chalked it up to a transitional phase in the chronology of a broken heart. True, his heart had been broken, but something much deeper than Peter had broken it; each time he ladled soup or plunged into the caverns of Bellevue Hospital, his heart broke again and again.

The Reverend Ken Swanson, who had impressed Barry with his eloquence and fervor that first Sunday, began meeting privately with him. Barry had been looking at the field of corporate ethics, thinking he might work with boards and business people to help effect systemic change in the business world, so the subject of seminary came up. "Think about it," Swanson encouraged him. "It'll give you what you need to do the work you might be called to."

Weeks later, at a luncheon for Christian businessmen at the Waldorf-Astoria, Barry confessed to Swanson that he was gay. Swanson had suspected it from the first but was clearly relieved when Barry explained that he never talked about his sexuality unless he was asked about it. We all work out our ways of coming out on a day-to-day basis, and unless we have been gifted in the art of drag, and happen to look particularly good in hose and pumps, most of us have to make choices every single day to break down other people's assumptions about us. When we are just coming out, "You don't look gay" feels like a compliment. The older we get, the more ridiculous its presumption becomes, as if queers have a look any more uniform than heterosexuals. So "tell when asked" became Barry's first way of being out in the Church, as it remains for many people throughout their lives. But it is a lonely, uncertain way to live. So long as Barry's sexuality was invisible, it wasn't real. And if unreal, then it presented no obstacle to a life in the Church. Such was the faulty reasoning that both Barry and his priest used when Barry decided to enter seminary.

Since he was wildly popular with both the children and their parents in the church's outreach program for underachieving fourth graders on the Lower East Side, Barry was embraced by Grace Church's leadership as one of their own bright stars. During his first year at Union Theological Seminary, and working with a fellow seminarian, Barry helped establish Grace Church's first AIDS outreach program, training lay people to be friendly visitors to people with AIDS at Bellevue Hospital.

Sometimes in church *grace* is just a nice word. But on the Lower East Side of New York, more often than not it is a bowl of soup, a sack of groceries, or a child learning to read. If people are starving and someone is compassionate enough to feed them, then God comes in a loaf of bread. It is as simple as that. That is grace.

 "I'm working with a wonderful man at Grace Church," Barry told me during one of our now regular, late-night phone calls. Between being full-time students and holding two part-time jobs each, most of our visiting was done on the phone our first year at seminary, with the occasional walk down Riverside Park to maintain sanity. We were both uncertain whether the longing in our hearts for an education was also the call to serve as Christian ministers, and Barry was treading cautiously.

"Swanson seems very committed to me," he told me. "He believes I have a future in the Episcopal Church. But . . ." his voice trailed off.

"But what?" I have never been a big fan of phone silence.

"Oh, I don't know," he said. "The Episcopal Church, like every church, is weird about sex. That's all."

"That's all?" I said in my best hands-on-hip voice. "You mean weird like 'let's pretend you don't have sex' weird? *That* kind of weird?"

He laughed, which is what I wanted him to do. Once one is freed from them, closets are terrifying places to contemplate. "The Episcopal Church has lots of gay and some lesbian clergy," he went on, "and lots of lesbian and gay members in lay leadership. But it doesn't have a lot of integrity in the way they deal with their gay clergy. Most of them I know are in the closet, or else marginally employed."

That afternoon Barry and Swanson had met, beginning with prayer, as was their custom. Swanson held Barry's hands in an easy, brotherly familiarity that Barry found awkward at first, but shrugged off as his own internalized homophobia about public displays of affection from straight men. They talked at length about Barry's involvement in the church, how what he was doing in the AIDS ministry was the best example of lay ministry Swanson had ever seen, and how Barry saw himself fitting in as a priest in the Episcopal Church, perhaps with a specialized AIDS ministry.

"But I don't just want to be a gay priest," Barry had confided in Swanson. "If I'm going to be a priest, then I want to be a priest to the whole Church." To define himself as a "gay priest" seemed as ludicrous as telling a heterosexual to be a "straight priest." The labels, and their accompanying attitudes, made no sense. Either we are priests to all people, or we are not priests at all.

"That's great!" Swanson finally said. "I believe you're ready to proceed with ordination. Shall I set up a meeting with the rector?"

I could feel Barry's elation as he related the story over the phone. "Swanson has agreed to present me to the rector as an aspirant for Holy Orders! He's going to sponsor me!"

"Does he know you're queer?" Until I knew exactly what we were dealing with, I was holding my enthusiasm at bay.

"Yes. He's known all along."

"And he didn't choke?"

"No. He's very excited about my proceeding with Holy Orders. I'm meeting with the rector, Harold Barrett, next week. I'm going to become a priest!"

When he finally said it out loud, our two voices froze. For a long minute we listened across the telephone line to each other breathing, the sheer enormity of the revelation marked by silent awe as we experienced the Deity passing by. We both knew Barry had spoken the truth. But the following night, when we celebrated his clarity with a round of hot fudge sundaes, we had no idea what that truth would cost.

All of Barry's friends at seminary told him he was nuts if he thought he would get anywhere in the Church as an openly gay man. Advisors suggested he keep his cover until he got ordained, then little by little he could come out, if he felt it really *necessary.*

Barry was at sea; none of this advice rang true for him. "What kind of priests could these men be?" he wondered out loud. "How can they preach about truth if they're living a lie? That's not the kind of priest I want to be."

"You're not going to be that kind of priest," I reassured him, "because you know deep down inside God's got a hold of you. God picked you up from the hell of your own fears, your own closet because she has a job for you."

The hour for his meeting with the rector at Grace Church was upon him, and we were wandering through the cloistered walkway to the seminary gates. "What am I going to say to Harold Barrett when he pops the big, queer question?"

"Barry, sit down," I said. We were on the same stone bench where we first met. "I'm going to give you a mantra a friend once gave me." We both meditated as part of our prayer discipline and knew that having a centering thought in times of stress was invaluable. "Take a deep breath, love yourself, and tell the truth."

"What?" he asked, amazed I had been so brief.

I repeated the mantra. When he still looked puzzled I went on. "First you breathe in, filling your body with air, with life. Then tell yourself you're wonderful, marvelous, fabulous! Love yourself, just as you are right now. And then you tell the truth, because truth comes from love and, besides, that's what we do here.

"Take a deep breath, love yourself (don't leave this part out), and tell the truth."

He was off.

Chapter 8

Integrity is not in and of itself a sense of right and wrong; rather, integrity is the faculty that enables us to discern right and wrong. Integrity is not by itself a guide. It is a guide to being guided. It does not so much tell us right and wrong as it helps us to see the truth of right and wrong. And at the center of that integrity lies a willingness to be open in our discernment of the right.

—*Stephen L. Carter*, INTEGRITY[3]

Thanks to our hellacious job and class schedules, it was after midnight when I caught up with Barry after his meeting with Harold Barrett. We were both churning out meaningful papers due the following day.

"Well, how'd it go?" I wanted to be excited, but something about the tension in his shoulders made me hesitate.

"You want to go for a walk?" As we headed to Grant's Tomb, he said, "They won't sponsor me." I felt the earth slipping away beneath us. As we plodded up the hill in silence I reached out for him and took his arm in mine.

We were standing before the monolithic memorial to a cigar-smoking war hero surrounded by ecstatic, loose-jointed concrete benches covered in a riot of mosaic, glass, and enameled and mirrored tiles, dancing the Dance of Life around the staid tomb of Death.

"Can you tell me about it?" I asked.

"It was a disaster," he began slowly and simply. "You remember me saying to Swanson that I didn't want to be a gay priest, but a priest to the whole Church? That I didn't want to have my priesthood defined by who I am as a sexual man, but by who I am as a spiritual man?"

I remembered.

"Well, I can't believe this. He heard me say I didn't want to be gay! And after he heard me say that, that's when he said, 'Great! You're ready to be a priest!'"

"No!" My stomach did an instant boil.

"Yes. It gets even better." Barry shook his head. "I walked into a land mine, into a flippin' land mine. Swanson said nothing to Barrett about my sexuality, because he assumed I was going to be an ex-gay priest! Whatever that means . . ."

Harold Barrett was the definition of a lanky, Anglican vicar, half-glasses set just so on his nose, an understated reserve permeating his terribly proper enunciation of the King's English. He professed great affection for Barry and the work he was doing at Grace Church. They were friends, Barry thought.

"So Barrett asks me if I'm married," Barry said, nodding his head and remembering the scene.

"What'd you do?" I asked.

"I did what you told me to. I took a deep breath, loved myself, and told the truth."

A chill ran up my spine. Of course I was proud of Barry for being honest, but on second thought, seeing the pallor of his face and the stoop of his shoulders, maybe it had been foolish advice.

Barrett was only temporarily stunned by Barry's honesty, going to great lengths to assure him that some of his best friends from college and seminary were gay and that they remained devoted to one another.

"But," Barrett amplified the allusion in a conciliatory voice, "human sexuality is a deep, dark pool that we have to be very careful of." Barry wondered what it was about human sexuality that moved Barrett to use such a harsh phrase.

"In fact," Barrett continued, "I would not hesitate to hire you once you are ordained." Now Barry was thoroughly confused. What about the deep, dark pool of Barry's sexuality? Would that be overlooked if Barrett needed a good priest? Barrett was pressing on.

"But given what Grace Church is, we could not possibly sponsor you for ordination under these circumstances." What Grace Church "was" was biblically based in a nearly literal interpretation of the few Scripture passages that have tenuous allusions to homosexuality. The unspoken message was clear: If Barry was going to be honest about who he was and his struggle to integrate his whole life and his desire for intimacy with the Gospel of Christ, Grace Church wouldn't be the place to do it, even though they knew he would be a fine priest. He felt nauseated; the betrayal cut deep.

"You have all the qualities any church would want in a priest," Barrett mollified Barry as their meeting drew to a close. But Harold Barrett would not ordain him, "Grace Church being what it is." For that to happen Barry would have had to become something he was not—either an ex-gay or a closeted homosexual.

I was sick for Barry. Sitting on one of the kaleidoscopic mosaic benches I wondered if Barry would have been better off without my advice, and maybe without the "truth" altogether.

"Maybe you don't tell *all* of the truth," I said. "Maybe you have to keep some of it back so you can win the prize. Maybe you hold out for a greater good?"

We knew plenty of religious folks who did just that, telling Barry,

while they served up compromises on silver platters, that until liberation came, deceit was a political expedience. Jesus promised that the
truth is what sets us free and that truth always comes at a great
price, greater than we can imagine. However, the cost of deceit is
unfathomable.

"Can a greater good be built on a lie?" Barry asked, poking his
finger in my heart.

He had me there. He had learned some things about deceit, especially deceiving oneself. He had spent years believing he could love a
woman fully. He could not. He had deceived himself in his job,
hiding his true identity in order to "pass," to get along. Then when
Peter left him, the compassion and understanding every colleague
would give freely to a heterosexual suffering the same feelings of
abandonment in divorce were not available.

Barry knew firsthand that subterfuge is corrosive and insidious,
taking tiny, delicate bites from the edges of our souls, until one day
we no longer recognize our true selves and collapse. Someone or
something will always strip the veil off our portraits in the attic.
Someday we always face ourselves. Love is a matter of the heart, and
any time we have to close a part of our hearts off, love and soul
shrink because they live in our hearts. He heard his mother's voice in
his mind's ear—*There's no greater good that lying will achieve*—and knew he
had turned a corner with his life.

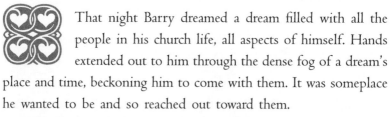 That night Barry dreamed a dream filled with all the
people in his church life, all aspects of himself. Hands
extended out to him through the dense fog of a dream's
place and time, beckoning him to come with them. It was someplace
he wanted to be and so reached out toward them.

Suddenly he was looking at Ken Swanson with Harold Barrett
smiling next to him, both in full priestly vestments. He looked over
at Swanson and saw a glimmer in his eyes, a question seeking an

answer. Barrett was laughing as if he knew Barry would answer rightly and join them in what had now become a game.

In the dream's swift shift of logic and person, Barry was now looking at himself, standing on the other side of the unspoken, unclear question. The man he was looking at was himself, but not yet. That much he felt right away. The man he was looking at had answered the other men and been embraced as one with them.

Barry looked harder at this man who looked like him. His eyes were blank, and, looking deeper into the man's face, Barry saw himself, wasted and empty. Alive but dead.

The terror jerked him awake and he prayed, reflexively, "Please, God, never let me die on the vine like that."

 A place of worship stirs heart, mind, and soul. It is a place filled with mysteries, where one finds meaning in the present and hope for future life. The longing for communion with God stirs in that place. The womb, the cradle, the grave are made holy there.

Barry's faith was renewed at Grace Church. But it was a new spirit in an old body. No matter how awkward or uncertain he felt in the territory of faith, he kept asking God to grant him the will and wisdom to be faithful about his choices. In time he understood this early faith development as a great moment of being remade, that mysterious thing God does in our lives when we say yes, we will walk in the ways of God.

But it was still hard to leave his family at Grace Church. This is the way of faith—being always ready to leave home so that God can lead us into a new land. He thought this family would never reject him, would risk something new with him because they had grown to love him as he had them. He believed God would use their love and respect for one another to begin a new vision for gay clergy in the Church. It was an odd kind of hubris; none of us ever truly knows where the hand of God is moving until it has passed us by, gone before us, as it were. God was shaping Barry in one way, Grace Church in another. But that is the business of God—building up and tearing down, getting rid of the old and making something new. It is no wonder that a life of faith, like a life of loving, is so painful. Life, death, and resurrection don't happen without a personal, emotional cost. Faith is always both gift and burden.

After Barry left Grace Church, Harold Barrett wrote that he was certain Barry understood the church's long-standing intolerance of homosexuals as biblically justified and theologically consistent with tradition and reason. He assured Barry that he would always be welcome at Grace Church, and ended with "Please, don't take this personally."

Four months later, Barry asked Ken Swanson to meet him for lunch. He had not heard a word from his mentor, advocate, and friend. He was starting to take it personally.

Seated in a split, red vinyl booth at a favorite neighborhood hamburger joint in the Village, Barry spoke his mind. "Ken, you've known me for two years. You know the depth of my faith; you nurtured me in it."

Swanson sat bowed and mute.

"You know the nature of my relationships with people, my sexual ethic. You know I'm a good role model for children; I've gotten raves at the Grace Opportunity Project. Ken!" Barry slapped his hand against the back of the booth. "The Church ordains alcoholics, adulterers, pederasts, wife beaters every day. Do you mean to tell me my whole character as a Christian man is nullified by being *honest* about my sexuality?"

"Yes," Barry remembers Swanson answering, "because we don't ordain *confessed* adulterers."

Barry's mouth fell open. Swanson seemed to be equating queers with alcoholics, child molesters, spouse abusers, and adulterers, the man whose depth of preaching and thought had reawakened his own spirit. Through the din of betrayal, Barry remembers Swanson saying something about one day knowing perfect love and all fear being cast out; that he personally loved Barry but, as a priest, he had to hate the sin.

Hate the sin but love the sinner? How could anyone live with such an incongruity in their compassion? When we divorce physical expressions of love from our heart's expression of the same reality, our spiritual well-being disintegrates. The mind, body, and soul are a sacred whole created by God. Barry was speechless.

He was desperately struggling not to sit in judgment of this man, but he had neither the strength to suffer Swanson's justification nor the faith to forgive him.

"Well, Ken," Barry finally spoke, "all I know is that perfect fear casts out all love."

"You're right, you're right. Help me work through this," Swanson pleaded.

"It's not my job, Ken." Barry was on his feet and very quiet. "Homophobia is a straight person's disease. You go work with straight people to get over it. And, please," Barry turned back to Swanson, "stop trampling all over us while you figure out whether you're supposed to love everybody or not."

God was reshaping Barry out of Grace Church, and in true form, Barry was not ready. One moment he would be filled with trust in his call, the next overwhelmed with doubt. "Oh, Lord, why can't it be all one way?" he called out more often than he cared to. But that is the way of faith—a stew of doubt, fear, and trust. And it was going to be that way for a long while.

Chapter 9

It is our conclusion that by suppressing our sexuality and by condemning all sex which occurs outside of traditional marriage, the Church has thereby obstructed a vitally important means for persons to know and celebrate their relatedness to God. The teachings of the Church have tended to make us embarrassed about rather than grateful for our bodies. As means of communion with other persons our bodies sacramentally become means of communion with God.

—DIOCESE OF NEWARK, NEW JERSEY, TASK FORCE ON
CHANGING PATTERNS OF SEXUALITY AND FAMILY LIFE[4]

"I'm leaving seminary at the end of the term." Barry dropped the bomb as we sat at Häagen-Dazs eating hot fudge sundaes, our number-one indulgence. "I want to stay, but it's costing me a fortune. And anyway, I'll never work in the Church." I stuffed in another bite of hot fudge to keep quiet. He needed time to think this through.

Disillusioned with the Church after his betrayal at Grace, Barry thought he had found a home at All Angels' Church on the Upper West Side of Manhattan, where the rector was very welcoming and eager to sponsor him for Holy Orders. An evangelical, Episcopal community committed to an expansive program of feeding the hungry and housing the homeless, All Angels' was serious about their Christian mission. Barry jumped in.

But a few months after Barry's arrival the church called a new rector who was compelled to stop the feeding and housing programs. He made it quite clear, as if his actions hadn't already, that he would not continue to sponsor Barry for ordination. It made a perverse kind of sense.

"Look," I encouraged Barry, "this isn't the church for you," unsure whether I meant that with a small *c* or a capital *C*. "You will never work in a community that comes down on the side of comfort over commitment or compassion."

"I don't think I'll be working in any community at all." He was pretty resolute.

"Jesus was betrayed, some say by his best friend. He taught that following him was hard. Are you going to back out now?" I hoped to taunt him into changing his mind.

"Don't lecture me about making personal sacrifices," he pounced, his face turning red. "I'm full up to here with the institutional Church's sadomasochistic insistence on sacrifice." His voice snapped in anger. "I don't see the people with power leaping into the pool of self-sacrifice. No, they're too busy pushing the queers in the pool, and the poor and the homeless and the starving!"

Barry pissed and moaned about the sorry state of Christians and the Church, then followed it up with a delicious few minutes of congratulatory, self-righteous wound-licking. Halfway back to seminary we collapsed on a bench in a sugar coma, put our feet up, and watched the Hudson River's dark progress.

"You're sure God's using these institutions to renege on your call to ministry?" I asked. I was going to miss my friend something fierce if he left.

"No," Barry answered, "but I am sure my life in the Church won't be as an ordained priest. I've been thinking about this a long time, Will, and it's pretty clear to me that I'm not supposed to work in the Church."

"Really?" I looked at him. He didn't sound clear.

"Yes, really!" He thought awhile before going on. "It'll be very easy for you to be ordained in the United Church of Christ. They have a written commitment for including gays and lesbians. But in the Episcopal Church I have to be ordained before I'm even considered for a job." The sugar blues were crashing fast. "I have to be ordained to the Priesthood, capital *P*. There are hoops to jump through before I'm even allowed to think about working: psychological testing; finding a sponsoring rector; interviews with my bishop, whoever that might be; meetings with the church vestry; meetings with diocesan committees. A lot of hoops, and most of them ringed with fire for gay people. It doesn't look like this Church wants to ordain or employ me as a priest." His dreams were turning to ashes around him.

"I'm tired of being a queer warrior in a battle nobody asked me to fight. I'm tired of being broke all the time and tired of being exhausted from my job, my chaplaincy, and a full academic load. I'm just sick and tired of it all." His voice was up in his throat somewhere now. I kept quiet, growing familiar with the rise and fall of his passions and hurts. Soon enough he would be ready to say what he had to say without my butting in, trying to cheer him up by lying to him about how it really wasn't so bad.

"Maybe I've just been deluding myself. Maybe the voice I heard wasn't God's at all. Maybe I was just having a crushing midlife crisis."

"Maybe it was gas," I couldn't resist.

"Stop it!" He backhanded my chest and laughed. "I'm trying to work this out. I'm confused, and I'm hurt."

"I'm sorry, Barry. I'm hurt for you too, but I don't do hurt too well. Sorry."

He was in the midst of a crisis of faith, feeling abandoned in hell. A place I was terrified to visit.

"Maybe I don't really know God yet," Barry thought out loud. "I need more time to think about this seminary thing."

Barry's leaving felt like a death blow to me, even though we hadn't talked about what was happening between us.

"So what will you do?" I asked, hoping he hadn't worked it through.

"Start to look for another marketing job. I have friends in the business I've talked to. They're very excited about me coming back. I'll have a job in a few weeks." Obviously he had worked this through. Barry has a serious, stubborn streak; once his mind is set, it's set with a "Do Not Disturb" sign hung over it. I let it drop.

We walked on up the hill to seminary. "Think about it some more," I ventured. "I'm very fond of you, you know. I'll miss you. And," I linked my arm through his, "I think you're one of the finest men I've ever known." I was getting into some pretty intimate territory here, new ground for me, for us, but I plunged ahead, hoping he would reconsider.

"The Church is in desperate need of people with integrity and faith," I told him, tugging him a bit as we hiked the hill. "That's you, Barry. You have a calling and your heart's urging you on to this work. You think it's hard now? If you quit you'll never be able to live with yourself, you'll never have a moment's peace. You want to wrestle with angels the rest of your life? God has touched you, Barry Stopfel. You're not going to turn away, *are* you?"

"Your Southern roots do pop out when you get all cranked up, don't they? Your accent even comes back!" He laughed at me, referring, I suppose, to my sometimes overwhelming need to rescue, my semi-scriptural allusions, and frequent alliteration.

"All I'm saying is," I pressed on, unwilling to be sidetracked by this gentle poke at my upbringing, "if you quit for just these few reasons you've told me, then there is no hope for change. If New York won't have you, try another diocese."

"Where? New Jersey and Bishop Spong?" he said, pointing across the Hudson River. "He's the most outspoken advocate we've got in the Episcopal Church. But I don't know anybody in New Jersey, let alone how I'd even start the process there." Was his hot fudge depression wearing off? This topic was suddenly not as closed as it had been. I leapt into the opening.

"It is an awfully long way away, isn't it? Don't you need a passport to cross the Hudson?"

"Yes, I think you do." He laughed. We stopped on a parapet and faced the chilly breeze off the river, soothing the fires inside.

"Bishop Spong is a courageous man," Barry told me. "He's been out front for women's ordination, and then for gays and lesbians. He and a diocesan task force published a fantastic document on human sexuality and family life, declaring queer families as vital as straight ones."

Barry turned and looked across the river at the cliffs of the Palisades. "It might be a place for me. But I don't know him. And, well," he said, now gazing south at the industrial waterfront, "it's never been a dream of mine to live in New Jersey."

"Oh, I know, it's a dreadful thought, isn't it? But there are worse places," I assured him. "Aren't there?" I asked him to think about it over the weekend, while I was away at the shore. "Okay?"

He turned, took my hand, and looked right into my eyes. "Okay," he said.

Chapter 10

What if: the primitive perspective is as true as the scientific perspective and the world is filled with signs, messages and miracles?

What if: everything addresses me—if I only have the eyes to see between the phenomena and the ears to listen to the silence?

What if: everything that is purely natural is wholly magical?

What if: novelty is more fundamental than law?

Of course this is all foolishness. When we call someone mad we mean they see the world differently than the other voters. Sanity is the virtue of the masses. Those who are saved from simple sanity become fools. But if sanity locks us into a goose-stepping world of explanations, and laws, it might be worth the risk of foolishness to live in a free and surprising universe.

—*Sam Keen*, Beginnings Without End[5]

April is an uncertain month at best, but New York suffers especially from a bipolar affliction every spring, tossing her urban sky dwellers between bouts of manic birdsong and spirit-numbing cold. Having been cooped up for too long, Barry risked the afternoon's weather swing and took a walk in the park. Many friends were encouraging him to pursue his ministry, recognizing in him a calm, sure faith energizing a generous spirit. He loved the patient work of building faith, delighted when both children and adults had "aha!" experiences. He treasured the body at worship just as he loved the traditions of history rooted in the Episcopal Church. He felt impelled by something, or some One, outside himself to do this work, no matter the cost. These and other reflections were on the plus side of his deliberations that spring afternoon.

In the second column of his mind he listed all the financial and heart-numbing reasons for leaving seminary: This last year's endeavor was breaking the bank; he wouldn't be employable in the Church unless he lived a lie; he would be three years away from his business contacts, further impoverishing him if the Church wouldn't employ him, which didn't look promising; the Church's continuing condemnation of queers gave tacit approval to the wholesale genocide of friends to AIDS; his heart was breaking; he was in danger of losing his faith. This was a pretty heavy column.

He had journeyed through many Episcopal churches in Manhattan in the last few months and found a chasm between what is preached and what is practiced. Too many churches were professing love for the sinner and hate for the sin, benignly fostering contempt, intolerance, and, ultimately, rage toward those who do not repent from a perceived wickedness. So many who called themselves Christian had forgotten the greatest commandment of all: Love your neighbor just as fiercely as you love yourself. Stand for your neighbor, Jesus taught, and work for their well-being as righteously as you would work for your own.

Barry had no time for the twentieth century's idolatrous warm, fuzzy, we-feel-good-in-the-Lord kind of love dished out by mediagenic and, not coincidentally, enormously wealthy evangelists. Comfort in a time of uncertainty is big business in America. But church was not about comfort to Barry. Church was about our commitment to one another, the stranger, the ones who are not like us. Church was supposed to be about doing justice, loving mercifully, and walking humbly with our God. Jesus didn't die for our velvet hats and pew cushions.

There was work to be done all over New York, and if the Church could do without his heart and his hands, he would turn his back once again on the Church in order to do the ministry he believed every Christian is called to do.

Barry was already in the trenches against AIDS, along with tens of thousands of other gay men and lesbian women; there were community organizations tutoring children left behind by the city's school system; and he had his personal discipline of study, prayer, and meditation. He had learned academic honesty and rigor in his first year at seminary, opening an exciting world of theological inquiry; his studies could continue on his own. His body warming in the sun high over Riverside Park, his lungs full of new spring, he began to believe he was ready to leave seminary.

He was just this side of certainty, just shy of saying out loud to himself that his life was taking a new turn, when a bright, orange-bellied robin soared past him. Chirping furiously it landed not three feet in front of him. Barry stopped still in the shadow of Riverside Church and looked down at it. He didn't move. The robin didn't move. He took a step toward the bird. Still the robin refused to budge. Barry took another step, now nearly on top of the bird. The robin still wouldn't flee but cocked its head first this way, then that, staring up at him, talking a blue streak.

Anyone happening upon Barry that afternoon might have thought he was just another madman staring dumbly at a chattering bird. But Barry grew up knowing that what seems to be purely natural is also purely mysterious, and thus of God. This robin's insistent fury was not to be ignored, not right at this turning point in his life.

No visions of angels, no voices, no scrolls in the sky. A robin stopped him from putting up his "Do Not Disturb" sign, and released a deep-seated awareness that he must rethink his life once again.

Omens are what we make them. Perhaps our insistence on feel-good religions has stripped us of the necessity to take omens seriously, for if we believe that God is alive and living in the world, incarnate, then we must accept our personal responsibility to listen for and then obey God's urgings, which usually don't feel too good up front. This is the costly grace Dietrich Bonhoeffer speaks of in *The Cost of Discipleship*, "that which must be *sought* again and again, the gift which must be *asked* for, the door at which a person must *knock*."[6] In blinding moments of honesty with himself, Barry accepted the fact that the only thing he really knew how to do was to look for and trust in God's gentle guidance. Even if that guidance came from a bird. Even if God meant him to be a priest in the Church.

"I have to tell you what's happened," he greeted me Sunday night when I'd returned from my own soul searching in the Hamptons with some old friends. I wasn't too sure about this man called Barry, or more to the point, I was freaking out thinking about the *C* word: *Commitment.*

"You seem very full of yourself." I poked at his good humor. "You look like a man who's had a vision!"

"No. Well . . . sort of. I'm going to finish seminary." My face froze in the half-smile, half-open-jaw look of the demented. He pretended not to notice.

"I figured out I was letting the Church's fury about who I am make me enraged at the Church and at, well, everything. I couldn't really hear God through all that until I took a long, quiet walk I'll tell you more about. But I believe I have to stick with this. And I believe I have to pursue this in New Jersey with Bishop Spong before God's through with me."

I gave him a big hug. Of course it was the answer I had been hoping for.

"I have a gift for you," I said, unsticking my grin and reaching in my pocket. "I was walking on the beach thinking about things. You know, seminary, the future, what we'll be doing, stuff like that. You," I finally whispered. Barry looked up at me. "Right when you first filled my thoughts I looked down at the sand and saw this." I pulled a stone from my pocket, pummeled and worn smooth by the sea into a heart. "And I knew you were my heart." He forgot to tell me about his omen bird for nearly seven years.

Chapter 11

Turning out the light, I take
three steps to our bed, climb in,
and pull the covers over me,
making certain you're covered too.
In the dark, I lie facing you,
nearly touching, hearing you breathe.
Gently I reach out, stroke
your back, and you sigh softly,
happily, still asleep. Can this
be my life? It's almost been
a year, yet this bed, these bare
walls, still seem sheer bliss,
undeserved by me, a cosmic blunder
let pass for another blessed day.
Like the émigré breathing free air,
I fret even as I weep with wonder.

—*Bruce Bawer*, "BEDTIME"[7]

The bed I was to sleep in was covered with a plastic mattress pad. Barry had brought me to his hometown, Hummelstown, Pennsylvania, for the Fourth of July, 1986. Central Pennsylvania is farm country dotted with thousands of small towns whitewashed in civic pride, where folks take their time, look you in the eye when you ask a question, and weigh the rightness of their answer. Thoughtfulness is not lost on people who live close to the rhythms of the earth, who, even though they might now work in town, know planting and harvesting, and keep an eye on the weather rolling up through the valleys, mindful that all their futures are in the rainfall. This July was blistering hot. The plastic-covered bed would not do.

"You can sleep in here with me," Barry offered. "But we're going to have to talk."

I'll say, I thought. Sex was usually assumed for two gay New Yorkers, the standing joke being if we wanted to talk, we would call our girlfriends. Sharing a bed didn't necessarily mean we were going to have a sexual relationship, but we had been dancing around that flame for a long time, deciding early on not to add that element to our relationship. Barry and I had become the best of friends, looking out for each other, talking about everything and everybody in our lives, inevitably sparring about each other's dates: *He's too young for you; He's got awfully big teeth; Well, he certainly is blond!*

We had talked to death the esoteric minutiae of our religious differences, fruitlessly chasing the greased watermelon around the pond of theological inquiry. We debated whether being a disciple of Jesus of Nazareth meant actively pursuing social and spiritual freedom for those on the margins of society or just for ourselves. Jesus acted on behalf of the weak, the outcast, the ones dangling off the edges. This sort of discipleship we understood and talked about. But sharing a bed . . . well, that was something new.

It had been the best of companionable weekends: We watched the fireworks below high from the Moorish, flagstoned balcony of the grand Hotel Hershey; played a late-night round of miniature golf with some of Barry's oldest friends on a gnarled and hilly grass course in Mount Gretna, home of the United Methodist Campground, where he had spent so many childhood summers; sat beneath ancient oaks and towering pines strung with Chinese lanterns at the best ice cream stand in Pennsylvania, slurping down their "world-famous Jigger," a narcotic confection sprinkled with a secret mix of nuts, chocolate bars, malt, maple sugar—everything a child would ever wish for in an ice cream sundae; and I listened to him talk with his friends about their youth and, of course, their church, inextricably bound together as one.

Moving easily among family and friends, we began to recognize a growing intimacy of soul between us. We had both grown up in small-town church communities, enjoyed being back in them, a welcome respite from the din of urban demands. We had always found each other attractive, but now that spark flamed a little hotter with my ease around his "kin." This is a critical test for any relationship—being gay only adds an interesting twist—because if we can meet each other's extended family with the same open heart we meet each other, chances are pretty good we are going to grow fairly old together. Extended families show *all* the traits of the clan, all the possibilities I might have to live with if I made a commitment to Barry. They were strong, fine people of faith and goodwill who embraced me as one of their own. I felt ready to throw my lot in with Barry.

Barry was uncertain about making a commitment to me. After my first breakup I had resolutely turned myself into the "unmarrying kind," and Barry found the walls I hid behind awfully thick to get through.

We talked late into the night. Could we survive two more difficult years as adult students and the enormous change of vocation before us while nurturing a relationship? Would a physical relationship destroy the spiritual camaraderie we already enjoyed? Would it deepen? Would we begin to take each other for granted? Would we lose our sense of humor and playfulness with each other? On and on we talked, gingerly sticking our toes into the waters of our new relationship. The overseriousness of our self-analysis really became quite silly and, around two in the morning, we were laughing at our stupidity and our fear.

How can one see into the future of one's heart? Love is a leap of faith. All love. Not knowing what is down the road is part of the adventure. Ultimately we choose the hidden path based on the imponderable, illogical guidance of our heart, believing, equally illogically perhaps, that it is not good for us to be alone. With the lights finally out, logic nodded off and left our two hearts to reach out and discover each other all over again. It was the Fourth of July, 1986. And every year there are fireworks on our anniversary.

 "My, you two look awfully happy after your weekend in Hummelstown!" our best buddy and classmate, Ann Evans, wryly observed a few days after our return. "Something happen I should know about? Are you boyfriends yet?" Were we really grinning that much?

I introduced Barry to Ann our first day at Union Seminary. She and I had become immediate, fast friends the summer before at a conference on Creation Centered Spirituality led by the great liberation theologian Matthew Fox. Matt was a good primer for Union Theological Seminary's probing questions about the validity of meaningful expressions of faith lived outside the ancient orthodoxies. The whole of creation is the embodied expression of God's loving, creative heart, every color, stripe, orientation, and belief. And it is all created good.

That first day of seminary, before Barry and I had taken our first revealing walk together, Ann was on us like white on rice. Tall and dark, with a big, spirited smile just looking for an excuse to burst into one of her signature belly laughs, she was sinewy testimony to the fully embodied goddess she embraced. One minute in Ann's enfolding aura and I knew, without a doubt in my mind or my body, that God is definitely a woman.

"So, who's your boyfriend?" She slid up to me in her terribly satisfying tank top, raising the autumn heat a few degrees. "Uh-oh. Don't tell me, I can tell. I've hit a nerve." Ann adores conversations on the edge. And since I was smiling stupidly at her, she knew she had hit a home run. Barry and I had just met, we weren't even through the preliminaries of "Where'd you grow up? Why'd you come to seminary? What'd you do before?" and Ann was reading the signs.

"Hi!" She grabbed Barry's hand. "I'm Ann Evans, since your friend here's being so rude. What's your name? You look very hot in those shorts. Are you available for the dance tonight? Oops, silly me! Where are my manners? You're going with *him!*" bouncing on the last word and staring right into Barry's face. The dance hadn't even come up yet, but Ann has an earthy prescience that sees deeply into people, encouraging them to live in their bodies what they know in their hearts. Inside of an hour she was also Barry's best friend, the kind of friend you want to grow old and cantankerous with because she will forever poke fun at your most stubborn longings for the past and make you laugh.

Ann always knew we were going to end up as "Significant Others," capital *S*, capital *O*, but had the grace of a good friend not to say so. For eleven months she watched us never admit that what we were doing was taking a very, very long time to fall in love. She knows that muscles knotted by time do not release quickly; they need a careful hand touching the rhythms and soothing the emotions carried within them. It was Ann we sought after our first Fourth.

Chapter 12

The inability to love is the central problem, because that inability masks a certain terror, and that terror is terror of being touched. And if you can't be touched, you can't be changed. And if you can't be changed, you can't be alive.

—*James Baldwin,*
in response to a question about
the core of our society's tensions

After graduation from Union in the spring of 1988, we were look-ing for some place cheap to live, when we took a wrong turn off the interstate in New Jersey, bumped down the western side of the Pali-sades, and found ourselves in a single-stoplight town on a street called Main. Lined with 1930s and '40s houses transformed for business in the 1950s and '60s with aluminum, commercial fronts now faded in the afternoon sun, it felt comfortably familiar.

"It reminds me of Hummelstown." Barry looked around at all the fifteen-year-old cars, and people in white shoes getting out of them. "Let's look around."

The oak- and maple-lined streets soothed something within us we didn't even know needed soothing, so long we had lived among concrete and steel. Barry stopped in front of an aqua and white tin house with a "For Rent" sign in the open door.

"You never see that in New York!" He laughed and led me in.

"It has a backyard! We can garden," I whispered while the owner fussed over the mess the last tenants had made of the burgundy nylon carpet in the bedroom.

Barry wanted the tonier neo-Tudor high-rise sublet in Englewood, definitely more upscale but, for the same money, the backyard and washer/dryer hookups in the basement won out. Without benefit of a ceremony and civil license, gay people frequently experience major-appliance purchases from Sears to be among the singularly defining moments of their relationships. With one "Charge it!" we were the proud owners of a Lady Kenmore washer/dryer combo and were as hitched as any couple in America.

It was so hot that day in July, 1988, when Pete, Jackie, Michael, Scott, Andi, and Alan moved us in that our thoughts evaporated before we could speak. We were reduced to babbling, grunting, and pointing.

"This place is great." Jackie was admiring our aqua and white bathroom fixtures, which, to me, looked for all the world like an old Nash Rambler. She had laid out the garden in her head while stuffing vintage knotty-pine kitchen cupboards full of everything two gay cooks just have to have. If it didn't fit or she couldn't decide what it was for, she carted it to the basement. It took weeks to find the ricer.

"This yard'll get a lot of sun once you cut back that heap of honeysuckle and forsythia," she encouraged Barry. "Put your flowers all around the edges and your vegetables in the back. Perfect!" And the next year, when we did just as she told us, it was.

Neither of us had what we could call real jobs. Barry was working part-time as director of the Christian Education Resource Center in the Diocese of Newark, and I was starting Clinical Pastoral Education work in a month at Overlook Hospital in Summit, New Jersey. The Reverend W. Joel Warner would walk with me through the valley of the shadow of death and forever change my experience of grace as he led me in the way of hospice ministry. At the same time I was working with some wonderful people starting a lesbian and gay church in Manhattan we called Spirit of the River. The CPE program at Overlook had a hefty tuition fee, and Spirit of the River was strapped to pay me fifty dollars a week. Barry and I were squeezing dimes.

What with eight hundred dollars due every month on our student loans, then the rent, phone, and utilities, then the credit card accounts we used to buy clothes, food, and more credit, we lived in perpetual terror of stumbling under the weight of our financial debt after seminary. And just in case this wasn't nerve-racking enough, leaders in both of our denominations were not hopeful about our prospects for employment. We were "too out." (Like we had an option to be only a "little bit out"? Is that like being a "little bit pregnant"?) Life in the closet wasn't an option for us. We were too old and had journeyed too far to play psychosocial parlor games about our sexuality, and we had definitely buried too many great friends and lovers to pretend to be other than we were. That much we agreed on. But juggling our minuscule cash flow was crazy making.

"We have to pay the landlord. Right?" I asked Barry when we were sitting down for our monthly checkbook slugfest. No answer.

"Do you agree we have to pay the rent?" My voice was rising rapidly.

"No. He can wait. He's got a deposit," Barry answered in his discussion-numbing voice.

"Barry, that's a load of bull!" I had gone from zero to sixty in five seconds. "We get behind in the rent, we'll never catch up!"

"Look, *I'm* working as much as I can!" he shot back with his now familiar accusation. In Barry's eyes we owed our financial plight to all the time and money I was spending on Spirit of the River, as well as my study and work at the hospice chaplaincy. This always punched my buttons.

"Look, we agreed when we made this move I'd be doing Spirit and Overlook."

"Yes, but we didn't agree that you'd give half your money back to the church!"

"I don't give half of the money back!"

"You do, too! I look at the checkbook! I see!" He had me there. Spirit of the River was a struggling, start-up community of folks working to integrate a faith life with their already proactive commitment to social justice. I carried a great deal of personal responsibility for its success, perhaps too much.

"You have to stop giving away so much of our money," Barry was lecturing me now. "Tithing doesn't mean giving away fifty percent, for God's sake! It doesn't even mean giving away ten percent. Tithing is a spiritual discipline, giving what you can on a regular basis. You give time. That's enough."

I undercut his mounting anger by nodding my head, lowering my voice, and offering a compromise. "I have to give something, Barry."

"Of course. Okay," he deflated a little, "give them ten percent of what you earn. Give them five dollars a week. Not twenty-five! I want to eat too!"

"Barry, the issue here isn't money. It's faith. Don't you believe we'll have enough?"

"Faith isn't the issue here, Will." He leveled his gaze in preparation for the attack. "It's cash. Lots of people with plenty of faith collapse under the cost of seminary education and poorly compensated work in the church. God isn't in the financial services business!"

My old friend Lee Hancock, in her wise way, had warned us this would happen. "I'm embarrassed to say it, Will," she told us over dinner a few nights later, "but the worst fights Mark and I have are about money."

"But it's not really about money," Barry insisted. "Money's the thing we use to fight about because everything else is going wrong."

She laughed at the two of us looking hang-dogged and bedraggled; we were still exhausted from our last go-round, tiptoeing gingerly past each other's moods and tempers. "Of course it's not really about money," Lee agreed. "But money is a finite entity, a tool, or really, a very convenient weapon. We always fight over something tangible. You can't fight with each other about the pressure you're living under. You can't fight about the church's prejudice against you as gay men or as a gay couple. And since it's so hard to fight systemic evils, you fight with each other. Over money."

"Everything breaks down when we fight," Barry admitted, "and I mean everything. I just shut down. I don't feel anything, can't feel anything. And he," indicating me, "just goes away."

"What do you mean, goes away?" Lee asked him. "Does he walk out of the house?"

"No, he doesn't walk out," Barry wouldn't look at me, "but he might as well. He gets a look in his eyes and I can tell he isn't hearing anything anymore. He's gone."

"The lights are on," Lee asked, "but nobody's home?"

"Something like that." Barry laughed half-heartedly. "But I feel it's just about me. The phone can ring and he'll be right there with somebody from Spirit or the hospice. But when he hangs up, he's not there for me."

"Wait a minute!" I jumped in, never comfortable being made invisible, especially by my best friends. "I'm sitting here; talk to me. That's just how I deal with my own emotional garbage. I shut down." I felt ganged up on and struck back. "It may not be the best way to cope, but it's cheaper than breaking up the crockery!"

"Ssh, the girls." Lee nodded toward their bedroom, calling a timeout. She reached over and put her hand on mine. "Honey," she said,

drawling the familiar endearment, "it's not how you stay in relationship. You've got to be willing to go through the bad with your
partner as well as the good. And wide awake."

Barry and I settled down and sat in our temper for a while.

"Rage is big in a relationship, and especially big in one like yours,
where there are so many social pressures you can't do anything
about." Lee was loving me, and us, as well as she always did, talking
slowly, deliberately, taking care I heard her even though I had shut
myself down five minutes earlier. "Will," she shook me kind of hard,
"you can't take your rage at the world out on each other, or they'll
win. The world will kill the one thing you've got."

"What's that?" I asked, looking down at my hands.

"Your love, silly!" She shook me quite violently this time. "Your
love!"

"I love it when you shake him that hard." Barry was clearly enjoying this. "If I tried that I'd have to wear boxing gloves!"

As if to prove it to Lee, he reached out to take my hand and I
instinctively jerked away. "Don't gang up on me and then try to
sneak a cuddle to make it all better! I'm not playing."

Lee was laughing at me! Not a compassionate smile, or a knowing
affirmation in her eyes. Laughing!

"Lee's right, Will. We can't let those people who want to hate us
win." Barry cornered me on the sofa and put his arms around me.
"We're good men, faithful men. We try to live with some level of
integrity. We can work this out, and anything else that gets thrown
at us, if we just remember this."

"I wonder if the people who love to hate so much," Lee asked
after letting the intimacy reroot between Barry and me, "I wonder if
they could live with the kind of intolerance you've lived with your
whole lives and still find the courage to love?"

I hate to lose a fight, but I had to admit it felt pretty good to be
in his arms. Barry was right: We should have been hollering at the
queer bashers, not each other. If we grew to hate ourselves as much

as they seemed to hate us, then we were in danger of becoming another notch in their belt, another statistic for those who believe gays can't or won't maintain loving relationships.

We sat in silence for a while. We rarely remembered to blame our anger, or at least a part of it, on the public nature of our work and the accompanying pressures of swimming upstream day after day against a flood of institutional intolerance and financial and professional insecurity nearly guaranteed by that intolerance. We came of age in a generation overcharged with anger and rage, a staple in the psychic lives of all gay and lesbian people, emotions Barry and I found difficult to deal with. But public life on the edges of broad cultural awareness does not afford the luxury of avoiding either the culture's rage at our visibility or our own rage at having a light shined up every nook and cranny of our lives. We were living in the suburbs eight years before newspapers started reporting about gays and lesbians moving out of the cities and into suburbia, many to have or adopt children and raise families, "just like everybody else."

But we are not just like everybody else. Oh, in all the community, neighbor sort of ways, of course we are: We keep house; some raise kids who play soccer and need orthodontia; we are active in our churches and communities, just like everybody else. But we do not enjoy the same civil protection under the law as our married neighbors; many of us cannot receive each other's pension in the event one of us dies; our children can be removed from our homes; without a fistful of legal documents and a combative spirit, we can be denied next-of-kin rights in hospitals. Regardless of how entwined our lives become, just like every other couple's, we cannot file joint tax returns, take advantage of family leave if one of us grows seriously ill, share in Medicare benefits, or, in most cases, health coverage. We live out our relationships and raise our families with a great deal of uncertainty about our civil rights. It makes us different: edgy, politically active, often angry, and very visible, which we can't avoid. In this country, at least, discrepancy in the administration of civil rights ultimately increases the visibility of the minority until its difference as a class or status is incorporated with the majority. As a nation we have righted this wrong concerning interracial and interfaith marriages. Right ultimately wins, but it is a painfully slow process for the millions of Americans who are waiting; and apparently not slow enough for millions of others. So we live in the tension of our times, just like everybody else, and try not to take it out on each other.

Barry and I sat with Lee, gaining strength for the next day of being a couple. We were still responsible for the way we treated each other; no whining that the culture made me this way! It didn't, and wouldn't as long as we kept choosing honesty in our rage and intimacy in our love.

"Jeez! You guys look terrible!" Mark Rubinsky, Lee's husband, blew through the door, finally home from his work on Broadway as a stage manager. He laughed and hugged us. "Having a fight, are we?" He was still laughing as he bent to kiss Lee. The three of us just looked at him.

"Oops. I've stepped in something, haven't I? Sorry." He's a quick study and shifted his high, post-performance energy into low for the mess he found dumped in his living room. He is a good friend. "Well, that's good. I mean, not that you're fighting. No, I mean . . . Well, yes, it is good that you're fighting." He laughed, getting all tangled up in his thoughts. "I thought you guys never fought and I was really beginning to resent the hell out of you for it. So this is great! Thanks. And, well, sorry that you're fighting." His merry glee was spoiling our funk and in half a minute we were all laughing.

"You think we never fight?" Barry was flabbergasted.

Mark shook his head. "Not like Lee and I fight. I mean, we fight about everything!"

"Mark!" She held onto that *r*, screwing his name right down his throat. It's a charming, Southern way of telling someone to shut up. "We do not fight about everything," the smile was plastered on now, "just some things. Usually money, which is what Barry and Will were fighting about. Well, mostly." She deftly shifted the direction of the conversation, all of us too tired to replay it for Mark.

"Oh that." Mark sagged. "Oh God. Well, it's good you're starting now. You'll have a lot of years to work out the finer points of that fight! We have."

"Mark!" This time she didn't hold anything, just reached over and slapped him on the shoulder, hard.

"Well, it's true!" He laughed and tickled her. "You have to admit it's one of the things we've gotten really good at. Right? Right?" He was poking her in her ribs.

"Stop! You'll wake up the girls!"

"Right?" Poke, poke. "Say I'm right!"

"You're right! Now stop!" On cue a cry rose up from the girls' room. Lee groaned, "Damn! See what you did?" and pinched her husband's thigh.

"I'll get 'em!" Mark jumped up from the sofa and in two seconds swept back in with Hannah on his neck and Sarah in his arms.

"Uncle Will!" Hannah cried and reached out for me.

"Hey there, beautiful girl! Sorry we woke you up." We were nuzzling nose to nose. "Uncle Barry and I were having a fight, and then your daddy was tickling your mama, and we just got kind of silly."

"Uncle Barry!" Seeing him for the first time she immediately crawled across everybody's lap to get into his for a snuggle. Sarah plugged onto her mama's breast for a midnight snack, her daddy smoothing her hair back, talking soft. These are our goddaughters, the children in our lives who call us "Uncle," who light up when we visit, whose lives mean more to us than our own. Lee used to tell us there were lots of ways for gay men to have children in their lives; we just had to be willing to envision family. Hannah and Sarah trade in the coin of the commonwealth of God that Jesus talked about, where trust and love and acceptance are given with no economy of deserving. Somehow, whatever it was that had fired Barry and me up didn't seem quite as hot anymore. Children do that, put things in perspective. Hannah cared only that we were here, singing her back to sleep in the middle of the night, being family. We would work out our problems. Maybe tomorrow, maybe the next day. Right now unconditional love had crawled into our arms and needed our attention.

Chapter 13

Do not neglect to show hospitality to strangers,

for thereby some have entertained angels unawares.

—HEBREWS 13:2

"Guess who?" He came up behind me and put his hands over my eyes.

"Let's see. Richard Gere?"

"Nooo." He shook my head. "Guess again."

"John Travolta?"

"Nooo." He shook me a little more insistently. "Try harder!"

"Harder, eh? Well, is it Brad Davis? No, can't be. He's dead." He was really getting into the shaking thing now. "I get another guess!"

"Try harder!" One brain-wobbling shake on each word.

"Well, if you're not Richard or John or Brad, then you must be my other lover, Barry."

"Wrong!" He flipped me around into his arms, laughing. "You're looking at the new lay assistant at The Church of the Atonement in Tenafly, New Jersey! Jack Croneberger has given me a job!" This was too good to be true. For the longest time we just stared at each other. Finally we hugged.

"Did you come out to him?" I asked the all-important question.

"Yes, of course."

"And he didn't care?"

"No." He smiled and then hedged a bit. "Well, we made a deal, but I'll tell you about that later. He's willing to take some risks and to sponsor me for ordination!" He was on his way!

A generosity of spirit urges a person to do the right thing and say to hell with the cost. But a generous spirit doesn't come naturally to our species. No, it is something we glean from parents and teachers who are themselves generous people, seeing, more than hearing, that a generosity of spirit is its own delight. Jack Croneberger had just offered a hand for Barry's priesthood when most people were turning away and passing by on the other side. Jack must have had generous parents. We were instant fans.

"I really like him. He was raised in Pennsylvania and is easy to talk to. He seems down to earth, wise, and has a great sense of humor."

"He's going to need it with you around," I butted in.

"Don't be wise! He's well liked and highly respected in the diocese. That's going to make him a formidable advocate for me in my ordination process."

"Well, well, well," I hugged him again, "this is quite a turn of events, wouldn't you say? How many hours? What're they going to pay you?"

Barry laughed. "You know, I don't remember!"

"Okay. Is it a flat salary, or are you working for credit in your heavenly account?"

"No, no," he laughed, "there's a salary. I just can't, for the life of me, remember what it is!"

We were both laughing and poking at each other, calling out numbers: "Twenty dollars?" "Thirty dollars?" "No? Fifty dollars!" For the moment a future of financial solvency outweighed any thought we had about the future of Barry's ministry. If it was fifty dollars a month it would be fifty more we could eat on. A hundred more and we would live like kings. We celebrated with a meatloaf dinner, but made special tonight with beef, veal, and pork instead of ground turkey, and lima beans swimming in butter and rosemary. My man makes a mean meatloaf when he is happy.

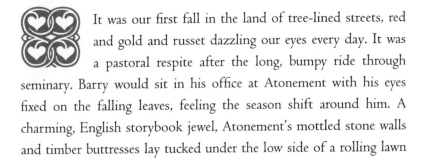 It was our first fall in the land of tree-lined streets, red and gold and russet dazzling our eyes every day. It was a pastoral respite after the long, bumpy ride through seminary. Barry would sit in his office at Atonement with his eyes fixed on the falling leaves, feeling the season shift around him. A charming, English storybook jewel, Atonement's mottled stone walls and timber buttresses lay tucked under the low side of a rolling lawn cooled by ancient blue spruce and oak.

It was only a couple of weeks before he met two women so filled with a generous spirit of life that for his whole time there the tiniest fix of their good company would get him through the toughest spots.

"Barry, I'm Bea Branfuhr and this is my sister-in-law, Marie Branfuhr." An effusive, matronly sort of woman overflowing with cheer extended her hand for his. Bea Branfuhr enfolded people in her great spirit and good humor. Her sister-in-law, Marie, thin and regal with steel-gray hair pinned up in back, matched her sister-in-law in twinkle and exuberance.

"We're so delighted you're here—" Bea started.

"—and wanted to welcome you with a little token," Marie finished. Bea lifted the linen towel to reveal a phantasmagorical basket of home-baked goodies.

"Now these," Bea's eyes shone with the telling, "are made by Marie, and—"

"No, dear," Marie interrupted, "you made these."

"Yes," Bea was not to be deterred, "but you usually make them, dear. And they *are* your recipe."

"My mother's," Marie corrected.

"Yes, well, anyway . . ." Bea had lost her train of thought and poked her finger through the basket as if her touch would call back their story. "We bake," she finished.

"Bea does most of it now. My eyes," Marie apologized.

"You do plenty, sister."

"Well, not like I used to."

"This is so wonderful of you." Barry broke into their private conversation, certain he would get the full story another day. His mother baked and their gift pulled him back to a childhood filled with good people freely sharing the savory richness of their hearts. And larders. "Won't you sit?" he urged.

"Oh, no." Marie edged toward the door.

"No, no," Bea echoed. "We don't want to keep you. We just wanted you to have a little something."

"Please do sit," Barry cleared boxes from two chairs, "and let's taste these."

"No, dear, those are for you." Marie chuckled. "You can see that we eat plenty." The sisters-in-law sat anyway and smiled at Barry. It was his cue.

He picked out a tiny, flat confection with a thin chocolate icing and popped it in. Bea and Marie folded their hands in unison on their laps and waited.

Barry's mouth exploded in sweetness. "Oh my God," he mumbled, struggling for air. Caramel, butter, walnut, more butter, and just a hint of chocolate shocked through his mouth to the top of his head and halfway down his back. He had to sit.

Bea and Marie were gleeful. "So glad you like them," Bea cooed and stood up. "Well, we're off. Glad you're with us. God bless you."

"Thank you. They're marvelous!" he sputtered, getting to his feet as they made for the door, then remembered to return the blessing. "God bless you as well, and thank you so much!"

"You're very welcome. We'll see you on Sunday. Oh!" Bea remembered something she meant to tell him and rerouted herself back to his office. "Some of the others aren't so sweet. They're on the bottom." And with that they took each other's arm, steadied themselves down the stairs and out the door.

Was she talking about the cookies or the people? After sifting through layers of people, many as generous as Bea and Marie, the ones on the bottom were truly not very sweet.

"Barry, can you come in for a minute?" Jack was at the door. "Oh! I see Bea and Marie have been here."

"Please have one. They're unbelievable!"

"I never say no to their baking. They're legends at Atonement, you know." Jack quickly chose his favorite and pointed Barry to another. If we are what we eat, they had just turned the corner to bliss and let its enjoyment linger.

"I'm afraid what I have to talk about won't be as sweet." Jack ushered him into his study all ajumble with books and papers stacked every which way. "I've just had a long conversation with one of our older parishioners. There's not a problem, but I think you should know the range of folks at Atonement. They're not all Bea and Marie."

Jack sat heavily with his arms braced against the cluttered desk, his shoulders weighed down by ten years of easing his people from contentious squabbling to a more compassionate concern for one another. Congregations of Christians do not herd easily in new directions, and the task told in Jack's body and eyes, now sometimes dimmed by exhaustion and heartache.

"This man has been a member of this church for many years. A brilliant man, sharp and sharp-tongued. But he's tough. He absolutely destroys any group he's in, monopolizes it. You know what I mean?"

Barry nodded.

"Well, he wanted to know all about the new guy, your education and background, that sort of thing. Your age." Jack shuffled an impossibly high stack of phone messages in front of him, looking for the words to ease his tale. "And since he'd heard you have a partner, he wanted to know what *kind* of partner, what did that mean."

Barry sat, silently seizing up inside, and nodded for Jack to go on.

"So I said that yes, you have a life partner, and that he's a man, and yes, you are homosexual. That was part of our agreement, to tell the truth when people asked. And anyway, I saw it as an opportunity to do some pastoral work with him." Jack laughed at himself. "You'd think after all these years I'd know better, but I keep trying."

Barry smiled a polite, strained smile.

"Well, anyway, he asked me then if you were to administer it, wouldn't the Communion be contaminated."

What little air there was left in Barry flew out of him. "What did you say?" Barry whispered.

"I know how to deal with him. He likes things concrete. So I pulled out the Articles of Religion in the Book of Common Prayer and quoted him Article Twenty-six: 'Of the Unworthiness of the Ministers, which hinders not the effect of the Sacraments.' " He read to Barry from the book, still open on his desk. " 'Neither is the effect of Christ's ordinance taken away by the priest's wickedness, nor the grace of God's gift diminished.' This seemed to satisfy him. As I said, there's not a problem, but I just wanted you to know."

"There's not a problem, Jack?" Barry began very quietly, all too aware he could be dismissed as quickly as he was hired. "But you just left me hanging out there as a wicked, unworthy person." Jack's face dropped. "You've got to decide real soon whether you believe I'm unworthy and wicked or not. Because if that's how you feel about me, and about your son, then I can't stay here."

"Wait a minute." Jack put up his hand. "Nobody here knows about my son." Only three or four of Jack's close friends in the church knew that Tim was gay. Jack told Barry during their interview, but also said it was not something he wanted talked about at the church. Everybody was keeping the secret while Jack worked through his personal issues with his son. And now with Barry.

"I'm not ashamed of my son," Jack promised Barry, "I love him. I admit, it was hard at first. I was ashamed, felt it was my responsibility, that somehow I'd failed and all that. He got me over myself, I guess you'd say, and we've come a long way together the last few years." He looked hard at Barry, not mentioning Tim's attempt at suicide.

"And I am not ashamed of you," Jack went on. "I guess I didn't think it through with this guy, what I was saying about you. Sorry."

Barry smiled but was weary. Being a semi-sane gay person while straight people work through their homophobia is hard work. But then, extending ourselves to anyone who is very different from us always is. First we have to learn each other's language, then what it means, and finally what it feels like to be the other. Hard work for both.

"Thanks for understanding, Barry." Jack patted him on the shoulder and let him out of his office.

The problem Jack underestimated was that with Barry around as an out, gay man, it was going to get harder and harder to keep secrets—people would become more open, stories would be told, fears would thaw, and people would begin to trust one another with a little more of their truth. Healing was going to touch the deepest of secrets.

Barry relished his work of bringing a defunct church school back to life and relevance, as well as his new responsibilities at the worship service and Eucharist, and dove in, hoping this early heating of the water was a fluke. I wasn't so sure.

I parked at the top of the hill on Barry's first official Sunday and sat watching the congregation assemble. Did fathers still use Bryl-creem to hold their son's cowlicks in place? Did mothers still threaten their babies with sudden death if those starched white Sun-day-go-to-meetin' clothes arrived at church in less than pristine con-dition? We knew our parents weren't too serious about the sudden death thing and dashed on anyway, skipping blithely across the lawn, getting our white shoes nicely stained in the grass, picking up a quick game of tag before settling down to learn another story we would forget for many, many years until one day, sitting in a parked car watching children file into church somewhere, the love and inti-macy and hope and longing would well up within us and we would know we must come home again.

But my heart was still reeling from last week's service when Jack introduced Barry from out of the congregation as his new assistant and completely ignored the man sitting next to him. Jack and Barry had made a deal: Barry's sexuality would be discussed only on a need-to-know basis, and the less known the better.

"Look, I've got to do this," Barry reasoned with me. "This is the first step for me if I'm ever going to be ordained."

"Okay, I understand," I lied. I did not understand at all. "But don't tell me I've got to like being invisible. I don't like it."

"You can't fly off the handle every time we have to compromise. We won't get anywhere, and nowhere near my ordination."

"Barry, listen to yourself. This little under-the-table, need-to-know tactic doesn't have a lot of integrity, if you ask me."

"I'm not asking you."

"Well, I'm telling you! Be careful. If you keep going this way it's going to cost you more than you're really ready to pay." I was fum-ing and hurt. "I am not an 'inconvenient situation.'" I took a deep breath and tried to get a hold of myself because Barry turns me off when I get loud. "Does anybody else know you're gay?"

"Jack, the wardens, a couple of others. We're not going to lie," he urged me to stick with him on this one. "Jack's son is gay. His family's very supportive."

"Oh, right. Isn't this the son that tried to kill himself when he found out he was gay?"

"Yes," Barry eyed me sideways, "what's your point?"

"Well, if they're so supportive, why'd we almost lose another gay youth to suicide?" I didn't know why this child had tried to kill himself and knew nothing about the family. I only knew Barry had to open his eyes a little wider about his maiden voyage in a church that had signs of becoming the *Titanic*.

"You're hard, you know? You don't give people the benefit of the doubt."

"Look, we're queer and we're here in the suburbs. Just keep your eyes open, honey, that's all."

"I've got my eyes open, I know what I'm getting into. I won't lie, Jack won't lie. We're just not bringing it up until someone else does. Please, trust me."

What is love without trust? What companion, or lover, or parent, or friend has not had to swallow their own fear in order that their beloved might fly on their own? I didn't believe he knew what he was in for; I had no idea, either, but of course I said I would support him in whatever choice he made today or tomorrow or the day after that. I would always stand by him. (Thank you, Tammy Wynette.)

Walking toward the church I was chewed up worrying about how to introduce myself. Was I Barry's roommate, lover, companion, spouse? We had always used *partner*, so why not now? I took a deep breath, loved myself, and vowed to tell the truth, however obscure the language. I sat in the back of the church.

I am not an Episcopalian. Raised Southern Presbyterian, ordained in the United Church of Christ, and founder of a gay and lesbian community of faith that freely and unabashedly reinvented its worship liturgy every week, I am uncomfortable fumbling through two books and a bulletin, searching for arcane paragraphs that seem as relevant to my life as songs about sheaves. I felt like I had stumbled into a private club and didn't know the secret handshake. But when Barry stood with Jack Croneberger at the altar, their backs to the congregation, and assisted him in preparing the Eucharist, I cried.

This was a deeply sacred moment for Barry, and I watched in awe as the simple task of holding out hospitality and fellowship transformed his tensions into a posture of grace. It wasn't the relics, not the polished silver and starched linens, but the moment of sharing bread and wine, remembering that we are but here as receivers of every good and perfect gift from God, who brought us into being for her delight. I whispered the first article of the Westminster Shorter Catechism of Faith I had memorized as a child for my own first Communion: Man's chief end is to glorify God and enjoy Him forever. So I wept. And forgave the Episcopal Church for its resilient wisdom in holding on to its ancient poetry. For what language better reveals the life of the soul than the poet's?

I stood on Barry's side to receive the cup from him and looked up when it was my turn to remember the richness of our life together in faith and love. My eyes had resolutely refused to obey my will and were still full.

"Sorry," I whispered when he bent toward me with the wine.

"It's okay, honey," he whispered back, tilting the cup toward me and saying, "Will, this is the blood of Christ, the cup of salvation." He watched me as I drank deeply, knowing all the reasons I had sat in the back and so had come last to the table. Like the lives of those who had gone before us, even Jonathan and David, and Ruth and Naomi, the richness of our life together overwhelmed us in that moment and together we caught the shadow of God moving past us like the Spirit. He wiped the cup, put his hand on my shoulder, and whispered, "Peace, my lover."

I walked back to my pew keeping my head down. It looked a bit reverent for me, I know, but really I didn't want anybody to see my eyes. And for a few, precious minutes I forgot all about the dreaded coffee hour to come.

Unless one is blessed with the demon of gregariousness, coffee hour in a new church is a torturous experience. If one is of average height, comfort can be taken in blending in below the sight line of most people. I am well over six feet tall. I do not blend.

"Hi! Welcome to Atonement!" One after another cheerful congregant greeted me. "I'm so-and-so." And then the inevitable question about tribal association, "How did you come to Atonement?"

Barry was nowhere in sight. *Okay, breathe deep, love yourself, tell the truth.* "I'm Barry Stopfel's partner."

Now, there were a variety of intriguing responses to this innocuous statement ranging from "Oh, really?" accompanied by a blank stare to "How nice" and a quick turn to greet a seemingly long-lost friend. But my favorite was from a tall, gray-suited gentleman who asked in all seriousness, "Partner. What business are you two in?"

Well, he had me there! "Love!" I wanted to shout. "We're in the *business* of love!" But my mama raised me right so I explained further, using even more obtuse metaphors.

"No, no business," I smiled. "I'm Barry's companion. We live together." Why the hell did I not just say I was his lover? Need-to-know, I kept reminding myself.

"Oh, yes," Gray Suit nodded sagely, "you're roommates. How nice that you came to his new church."

"Do you know where coffee hour is?" And with that I was directed down a hall, around a corner, up some steps, and sent on my way. Nice segue, I thought.

Now, for a religion founded on its expansive table fellowship for the stranger, I found it unsettling that the hospitality of this particular church was meted out in such a claustrophobic cell. Perhaps strangers were not supposed to come back here? I wedged against the wall and answered the same two questions over and over for a thousand years until Barry finally appeared beside me.

"How's it going?" Barry touched my arm.

"Like Sisyphus pushing his stone up a hill in hell."

He laughed. "Good. That's good. You're still pushing. Sorry it took so long to get here. I got caught in the hall talking to parishioners." He was simply glowing, enjoying his new position as assistant and the congregation's mostly enthusiastic welcome. Many folks worked their way through the horde and introduced themselves to Barry as we stood together, gamely balancing their doses of caffeine and sugar in one hand, extending the other in greeting. Others spoke to Jack, turning their heads toward us, discreetly checking us out, inquiring about us. I caught a few eyes and smiled boldly before they could turn away. But I was exhausted with the ritual dance of evasion and desperately needed out of this constricting room. I wanted to shout, "This is my lover! We love each other! And God has been made known to us because of our loving!" Alas, I am way too Southern for that sort of public outburst, so I let my stomach do its own little anxious dance of death. Oh, it is a tangled web we weave when first we practice to deceive.

"Honey," I whispered in Barry's ear after I caught his arm, "I'm beginning to feel like scum on a pond here. I'll see you at home."

"Don't say that," he laughed, "you're doing fine. Really. People like you; they're introducing themselves."

"Barry," I had my don't-even-think-about-discussing-this smile on my face, "it's time for me to go. I'll see you at home." My own discomfort relieved, I whispered, "You're doing great! Stay and schmooze. I'll see you later." And with that I headed for the door.

Well, it was a door, but it let out onto a dark backstage area.

Now nearly desperate for air, I rammed my way through a maze of giant plastic playthings.

"Are you lost?" a small voice pleasantly inquired from somewhere beyond the dark.

"I'm afraid I've taken a wrong turn!"

"Oh, I hate that room. It's so hard to get in and out of. And there's no air! Here, dear, come this way."

I did battle with a heavy maroon velvet curtain and emerged in a cavernous gymnasium.

"The stairs are over here. You know, it's really dreadful that they make us go in that tiny room for coffee hour." She laughed. "Look at all this unused space! Oh, hi. I'm Shirley Redfield." Five-feet-something, silver haired, with a grip like iron, she had one of those purposeful, lean figures that resolutely sloughs off anything unnecessary. Her eyes were full of a rich history, brimming with stories to delight and awe.

"I was just on my way out the back. I live over there, behind the church. Were you leaving?" No niceties, no coffee chatter, just direct and straightforward. I was revived by her freshness, and very nearly seduced by her warmth after the chilly coffee hour.

"Oh, thanks, I'll walk out with you."

"You're new, aren't you? Did you come with the new minister?" She was direct!

"Yes, I did. I'm Barry's partner, Will."

"Oh," she stumbled for words, her momentary look of absolute confusion endearing. Something about my tone told her we weren't in business together but she wasn't going to go through the categories of her life experience right now to unpack it any further than courtesy demanded. "That's nice." She smiled up at me as I held the door open. "I'm very glad to meet you. Barry seems like such a nice man. Just what this church needs. Well," she parted with a low, dry laugh, "I've got to run. I'm meeting a friend to go painting. Hope you won't be a stranger." With that this slight, spry woman strode swiftly up the hill and into her more important afternoon. The delight with which she saw the world around her attracted me. Would that I might reach my seventies or eighties with her kind of spirit! She hadn't blanched at the word *partner*, just stumbled across something new she tucked away to examine later. She was charming and I was seduced.

Chapter 14

And Jesus took a child, and put him in the midst of them; and taking him in his arms, he said to his followers, "Whoever receives one such child in my name receives me; and whoever receives me, receives not me but the one who sent me."

—MARK 9:36–37

Bishop Jack Spong wears the authority of his office easily. An austere, graying man possessed of a towering Virginia Tidewater charm that belies his unsettling, resolute directness, he sums up people and issues with a quick, penetrating mind grown comfortable with translating theological tomes into the language of contemporary relevance. He holds a high regard for scholarly priests and thrives on these conversations.

Barry was working two floors below the bishop at Cathedral House in downtown Newark and gradually became acquainted with him around tables at lunch, where the bishop would invariably introduce a theological problem. He is not a man given to light conversation. Undaunted by the bishop's stature and authority, Barry frequently rose to the bait.

Jack Spong orders his physical world through intellectual concepts with the same rigor he orders his spiritual life and faith. Neither are static, finite entities fixed in tablets of stone. God is the wellspring of life, and the essence of life is change. The gradual turn of his heart about gay and lesbian people (he was not always an advocate) came about as he lived into his changing Church and world, applying the foundations of Anglican study—Scripture, Tradition, and Reason—in an effort better to comprehend all that God has wrought in the world. When science taught him that gay and lesbian people do not choose a lifestyle but, rather, are given a disposition in the miraculous stew of genetic fabrication and socialization, he found himself reordering his world by virtue of his Reason. As years passed and he knew more and more gay and lesbian people, working closely with many, embracing some as friends, his Experience, often added as a fourth leg to the Anglican school of study, moved him more deeply to examine Scripture and Tradition. To sit at lunch with such a bishop can be a terrifying experience for the unready.

The bishop, having met me on several occasions, was fully aware that Barry was gay and soon had him in for a private conversation of things certain and uncertain, the very stuff of faith. Jack was three months away from ordaining an openly gay man, Robert Williams, to the priesthood, determined to do in the full glare of the media what so many of his peers had been doing in secret for too many years. He knew Barry was next in line and wanted to test the mettle of his faith and commitment, and see whether the two of them could come to a mutual understanding of the risks and process involved in what had become, for Jack, a crucial and important witness to his Church and his world.

"Barry," the bishop asked, drawing him into the heart of his thinking with characteristic directness, "do you believe human sexuality is determined or a choice?"

"Well," Barry laughed, "I don't believe anyone would choose to be gay given the culture of fear and animosity we live in right now." The bishop nodded his head thoughtfully, indicating that he should go on. "I didn't wake up one day after a long-term relationship with a woman and say, 'Hey! Wouldn't it be fun to be one of the most despised people on earth? I think I'll try being gay for a while!' "

The bishop smiled. He had experienced quite a bit of animosity himself for standing with minority races in this country, and with women and gays in the Church. "When did you realize you were homosexual?"

"I fell in love with a man," Barry answered simply. "I hadn't planned on it, wasn't looking for it. I'd been in a relationship with a woman for some time."

"Did it shock you?"

"No," Barry answered him unequivocally, "it was not a shock. I was in love for the first time in my life and felt like I'd come home."

Bishop Spong stretched his long legs out in front of him, settling down with his thoughts. "And this woman? Were you not also in love with her?"

"After I met Peter I realized that what I thought was love was only a deeply felt, genuine regard. With Peter my whole body and soul, my spirit, the whole of who I was as a man sang out with joy. And I knew, to further answer your question about determination, that this was the love I was supposed to have."

"But you're no longer with this man." The bishop leaned toward Barry.

Barry saw his error. "It wasn't about being in love *with* somebody, it was about the experience of love's power to free and transform. Falling in love with Peter had the same transforming power in my life as my early childhood experiences in the Evangelical United Brethren Church. I was loved, and loved in kind, wholly and deeply, spiritually, if you will. All of me." He stopped, aware in one horrible moment that he might have gone too far. "What the hell made me say all that?" he chastised himself. The bishop was staring a thousand yards away, comfortable with the ever lengthening quiet in the afternoon's conversation. Barry watched the dust motes dance through a narrow shaft of light beaming through the leaded-glass window.

"I, too, believe it is the quality and integrity of our relationships that reflect our Christian commitment," Jack affirmed Barry's experience, "not the gender or orientation of the beloved. We will work well together. Now, on to the business at hand.

"It doesn't look good for gay people right now," he came right to the point. "I can ordain you, and I will if you meet and pass all the requirements of this diocese. I depend on a tough Commission on Ministry and Standing Committee to oversee this process of ordination. I believe a call to the priesthood is best discerned in a community, and I trust these people implicitly. The process will be rigorous and thorough, but you will know at the end of it whether you are truly called to be a priest." He got up and went to his desk.

"Jack Croneberger's a very lucky man to have you, but you won't be there forever. Just because I ordain you doesn't mean you're going to have a job." His eyes betrayed a weariness of fighting uphill for too many years. "There are no jobs in this Church for openly gay people. None. So there are no guarantees." He turned to the window, looking out over a portion of his diocese.

"I have ordained a number of highly qualified people," he went on, "who were known to me to be gay or lesbian." Jack turned back toward Barry. "Known to *me*, you hear?" Barry nodded.

"They found getting through the ordination process and getting a job grueling enough without having to constantly defend their sexual orientation." He was driving home a lesson in ecclesial ethics that confirmed what gay and straight people had cautioned Barry about all along.

"I appreciate your being candid with me," the bishop said; "that's good, and you need to continue to have an honest relationship with

June Leckie, 1944 WASP
(Women's Air Service Pilots)
class portrait.

Bill Leckie at sea, 1982.

Carolyn and Marlin Stopfel, circa 1943, before Marlin went overseas for World War II.

The Rt. Rev. Walter C. Righter embracing Barry after ordaining him a deacon, September 20, 1990, at The Church of the Atonement, with the Rev. John Croneberger (right).

The Rt. Rev. John S. Spong addressing the congregation after ordaining Barry a priest, September 14, 1991, with the Rt. Rev. Walter C. Righter (right).

Butch Stopfel, Marlin Stopfel, Alice Stopfel, and Polly Jordan (Barry's aunt) at our home with Barry after his ordination as a priest, 1991.

Feature story photograph in *OUT* magazine that saved two lives.

Hannah, Will, Sarah, Barry, and Spirit, on vacation with the family at Nags Head, North Carolina, 1996.

At Saint George's Church, being marked as Christ's own forever is a family value. Barry baptizes Grace, the adopted daughter of Ulysses Dietz and Gary Berger, with the Rev. Anne Bolles-Beaven assisting. Lay Eucharistic Minister Jack Hart assists (right).

The Oldsmobile.

Barry with Mark Polo before the Gay Pride March, New York City, 1992.

Mark Rubinsky and Lee Hancock atop East River Mountain in Lee and Will's hometown, Bluefield, West Virginia, Thanksgiving 1990.

Barry's Spiritual Journey group at The Church of the Atonement, 1992. Edie Lauderdale and Shirley Redfield are on the sofa (right).

Barry (far right) at his cousin Charlene's (rubbing her eye) birthday party in 1953, Oberlin, Pennsylvania.

Rhea Grill

Barry, the Rt. Rev. Walter C. Righter, and the Rev. Anne Bolles-Beaven celebrating the Eucharist at Saint George's Church, October 1995.

Rhea Grill

Children have the keys to paradise. Barry and the children of Saint George's celebrating the "glorious impossible," Christmas 1996.

your bishop. But you do not need to be that candid with everyone in order to have a career in this Church." They held each other's eyes across the room for a long moment, knowing a bridge had to be crossed, if not now, then very soon.

 Preachers tend to talk about issues that are personally hot for them. Ambition was Barry's topic the following Sunday in his second sermon at Atonement.

"My goddaughter Sarah had just learned how to haul herself up onto a lawn chair, but hadn't yet figured out the mechanics of getting down. Giggling and delighted with her new game, she asked me with outstretched arms to get her down.

"Who can resist, right? She's a child, and our delight as parents or friends or godparents is in helping our children, serving their needs.

"When I lifted her up she hugged me and shined one of her pure, joyous smiles that just knocked me dead. Her thanks was so immediate and genuine, so unencumbered that I laughed right along with her. Of course she climbed right back up and we had it to do all over again, passing a lazy afternoon with Sarah's game. Later I realized that Sarah was teaching me in the vulnerable way of Jesus.

"The way of Jesus teaches something contrary to our comfortable, clichéd social Darwinism of dog eat dog, everyone for themselves, survival of the fittest. If we are to be followers of his way, then our greatness is measured not just by our service to the powerless, but by our total identification with them. We are to become one with their feelings, their thoughts, their reality. When we do this, we become as little children: open, vulnerable, and trusting, a terrifying prospect for any of us raised to survive as the fittest. But it is our call, our task as Christians.

"I believe we are commanded to stand squarely against our culture's definition of greatness. We are called by this Jesus of Nazareth to be a servant people, a servant church, like children in our openness to others, like children in our vulnerability to others, like children in our trust in others: We are to become like the ones we serve.

"And the promise is that when we live like this, we will release something very deep and personal, something that has been within us from our own childhood: We will release the God within, transforming the world with our vulnerable greatness."

He was preaching to himself. Two weeks later Barry accepted Jack Spong's counsel and did not reveal his sexual orientation in his formal papers to the Commission on Ministry. The topic hadn't come up so he didn't raise the "issue." He had been vulnerable enough in his life and found that it hurt. It might be the way of Jesus, but Jesus didn't know our world today. For now Barry would seek the meaning of his call by dint of his own ambition. For now.

"I've been outed to the Commission on Ministry," Barry announced after his postulancy screening weekend, a first step in discerning his call to the priesthood.

This was not what he had planned and I swallowed hard, knowing the consequences might blow him out of the water. We made no secret that we were living with an elephant in the living room; Barry had just not talked about it on paper. "So what happens now?" I asked. "Are you out of the process?"

"Well, they're going to treat me as if I were just another married, straight man."

"What does that mean?" I was getting on my horse again.

"Calm down!" Barry commanded; he wasn't up to dealing with this and my attitude. "It means you have to write a letter to the Commission on Ministry describing what my ordination and ministry mean to you and how you see yourself in support of my calling."

By the time Barry explained the details for a letter written by all spouses of potential clergy, I was stunned dumb. Well, nearly dumb.

"How many other gays do you think have written a letter like this?"

"I don't think any, so far. And that's the point. As far as I know we're the first. So it's important. You've got to think about it, about what it means to you."

Of course, meaning is what we bring to our lives. Meaning is the soul, the spark of life within us; it is not an external absolute. Meaning is an illumination for our way in the world that comes from within, from our experiences and our loves in life. We were walking over a new mountain here; my gender, as Barry's partner, was no longer an issue. The Commission on Ministry had come to recognize that sexual orientation is morally and ethically neutral, and what they needed to concern themselves with were Barry's qualifications for ministry and how they are informed by the quality of his relationship with another human being. It was time the two of us became one: both of us seeking meaning for a journey we thought only one of us was taking.

Chapter 15

In this life Barry and I have been given to one another as partners. Our days and weeks and years are filled with the hundreds of transfiguring moments known to all loving companions, moments that continually re-create us in the image God has for us. These are the personal, intensely private moments that encourage us for our "exodus"—our going out from one another into the world in service. . . . I believe that to the extent that any of our relationships encourage, nurture, and sustain that service, they are ordained and sanctified by God.

—*Will Leckie*
to the Commission on Ministry, February 1989

"In the second chapter of Genesis we hear the writer declare that God's response to our aloneness is to create another who is worthy of us, another with whom we can be in complete and utter relationship." Along with his work with the children, Barry was preaching regularly at Atonement. Following the lectionary cycle for the

Church year, it was Barry's turn to preach on a portion of the biblical creation story.

"Two become one. We miss the deeper meaning of this gift of relationship if we assume it only refers to an intimate, physical relationship between a man and a woman. This verse has been used to support, and in some ages enforce, a compulsory heterosexuality that the writers of this creation story were not even thinking about. They were not talking about sex.

"They were revealing the most profound difference between their God and the gods of the world around them: God is not distant. The God of the Hebrew people is a God who is with us in relationship.

"The whole sweep of Hebrew and Christian Scripture teaches us the good news that we are not alone. God is with us. God is with us in the companions we are given in this life; God is with us in our acts of mercy and compassion to one another; God is with us when we break bread and eat together, because God decreed that it is not good for us to be alone."

Barry went quickly "from preachin' to meddlin'," as one terminally disgruntled parishioner complained. Some people found Barry's more inclusive experience of Deity to be the tonic of renewal they had been seeking, while others complained he just enjoyed being controversial. They were both right because it is controversial to believe that God is truly with us, whoever we are, whatever our circumstances.

"We want to keep Jesus neat and tidy," Barry preached another Sunday, "looking very much like us, protecting the values that we cherish. But Jesus was not a champion of the status quo, and the religious elites of his day scoffed at him for preaching that whores and tax collectors were of equal worth to God.

"It's hard for us, comfortable in our cushioned pews, to remember that Jesus was born to homeless parents, his mother an unwed, teenage peasant taken in by an older man, a rough carpenter, who was either still single or widowed. Jesus was an illegitimate child. We gays and lesbians are illegitimate members of our culture. We and this Jewish teacher understand something about each other."

By his fourth month Barry really alienated his gathering adversaries by preaching a sermon on compassion and the Gospels' demand that if we really want to follow Jesus, we must be seeking justice for all people. To underscore his point, he quoted fourth-century Roman Emperor Julianus Augustus: "No wild beasts are such enemies to mankind as are most of the Christians in their deadly hatred of one another." It was, perhaps, a trifle zealous, but was meant to help make the lighter side of his point. No one laughed.

"There's nobody out there like me!" he wailed after church.

I waited an eternity for him to expand his thought—sometimes it takes him a while to wind up—but he had already finished thinking it through. All I got was the summation of his personal journey. I suppose all partners, spouses, and lovers go through the same dynamic from time to time. If one of us is thinking long and hard about something, we assume the other is thinking right along with us.

"You've got to tell me what you're talking about, honey. I'm in the dark here."

"Right. Sorry." He smiled, knowing full well he'd done it again. "I look out at the congregation and there's nobody there who's gay. I spend so much of my time preaching and teaching about common humanity, about how straight and gay folk have more in common than not. And yet I'm different. Along with all the commonalities we like to celebrate, my life is shaped by a constant barrage of intolerance, hatred, and sometimes violence. In one way it makes no difference that I'm gay. But on the other it makes all the difference in the world. I just wish I could look out from the pulpit and see someone out there like me, someone who's shared the same exile."

"But a lot of people there support you, even love you." I tried to put the best face on his growing despair.

"I know that, and it's great, believe me. But some days I feel like I'm from Mars and no one has a clue, or even cares what that's like!"

Friends raised in loving homes as racial or ethnic minorities in this country tell stories of being taunted or shamed or beaten while they were growing up because of who they were. But a common thread through their stories is that they could go home to a family of people who were just like them and there would be someone to clean up the bruises and the hurts, hold them, encourage them, and brush off the pain of ostracism. As gay men we had no such homes to come back to when the pain of being gay turned real. We learned strength and courage in other ways, in other places, and generally moved to those communities as soon as we could, defining and creating family as best we could.

"We're queer!" I joked with him. "You can't piss and moan about not fitting in and people not liking you because you don't fit in! That's just part of the glamorous, gay lifestyle!" I thought a minute and said, "Anyway, *everybody*'s different. *Everybody*'s alienated. *Everybody*'s lonely. Gays are a living reminder of everyone's alienation in one form or another. No one enjoys feeling isolated."

"Isn't it strange that the Christian Church should be so vehement in their condemnation of us?" Barry asked, rather rhetorically. "After all, the Church was established on the teachings of the man who preached that we're all alienated. It's when we *receive* each other that we break through our isolation and become children of God, become community—God with us. That's the good news. And you know what Jesus got for his efforts." I knew.

"All the same, I've been praying for God to bring someone to the church. Someone who understands the tension of living and working on the edge, where the stakes are so high. Someone like me. I'm praying for God to bring some gay people into the church. A few queers, more people of color, and at least we'd start to *look* a little more like the world. Next thing you know, we'd have to start figuring out what it means to be a Christian in a world packed with so many different sizes, shapes, colorful hues, and varieties of alien-ation. This church is too homogeneous!"

"You need some pink people in your church, I think." Barry laughed, remembering our oldest goddaughter's identity crisis that fall. Hannah came home from her first day in first grade distraught, absolutely undone. Lee hovered and petted, her own day-long sepa-ration anxieties soaring through the roof at the sight of her weeping daughter.

"Mama," she finally managed to choke out through crocodile tears, "I don't have any color!"

Well, after confirming that Hannah had not missed out on art class and that she had the Crayolas she went to school with, Lee figured it out. Hannah was in a class with Asian, Indian, African, and Hispanic-American children, whose vibrant hues unleashed a despair over her white blandness. After a long conversation and much empirical observation (Lee processes with her children as in-tensely as she does with her friends), Hannah hit upon a solution: She was not a white person. She decided she was a pink person. Crisis averted, she returned to school confident that she, too, was a person of color. Pink.

Prayer is a powerful force that many have written about, many more experienced. In my own work at the hospice I had seen prayer transform people absolutely. Rather than changing the way of God, prayer is the process of putting ourselves in the way of God, opening ourselves to the divine will. Barry was praying about his loneliness and terrible alienation within his congregation, opening himself up to God's will. Having just preached about God working through relationships, Barry could be forgiven for expecting God to show up in his church as a queer. God would understand his desire.

Most of the time he prayed for strength and courage to continue in his work and his journey toward ordination. He prayed for hope and health in the relationships that sustained him, as well as in the relationships that sustained his parishioners. And if health came, if courage came, the question he asked was, did it come because I prayed for it, or did it come because it was the Deity's will? He didn't have the hubris to believe he could control the Deity, and so accepted that his prayer and meditation life served to place him in the way of God.

In the way of God is a dangerous place to be. Most of the Hebrew Scriptures we read rarely refer to this as a quiet, restful place: waters rush, mountains quake, heavens thunder, bushes burn, the earth breaks open when it is in the way of God. People are blinded. The fear of the Lord, the Proverbs tell us, is the beginning of wisdom, and Barry was pretty wise.

"It's what I need," he insisted when I chided him once for being so specific about his prayers. "Believe me! Isn't it bad enough what we've had to give up so far?"

"What's that?" I asked, as if I didn't know.

"Come on, Will. We're giving up any expectations for a comfortable, secure future. The Church tends to treat its ministers very badly, particularly economically, and gets away with it because it's all done in God's name. But gays in the Church, well, we're another cross. They need us around as a goat they can load up with sex negativity and chase off into the mountains."

"Who put a quarter in your slot?" I teased him, but there was no stopping now.

"The Church is too comfortable sacrificing its children to a vengeful God. The religious elite want to keep somebody out? God must want that, too, and next thing you know, *wham*, you're out." Barry took a moment to settle down and went on.

"I don't want to be a martyr. I don't want to be maimed or killed to be a priest. It's not worth it. This Christian sadism is evil." My ears pricked up. Barry is very cautious about using absolutes like evil. He knows firsthand their murderous power.

"*Evil*'s a pretty big word, don't you think?"

"No, not at all," Barry said reasonably. "When the Church became an institution, it took the way of love and grace and beat it into an idol of rigidity and conformity. Then they masked the tyranny of the majority by sanctifying it as 'the unity of the Church,' in effect creating another idol to worship rather than God. When has the Christian Church *ever* been a unity? Jesus' own followers were of several minds about him. And they lived with him!" He was getting wound up again, green eyes flashing silver, color rushing up his cheeks past his beard.

"Yeah," I egged him on, "one even thought so much of him he had him offed."

"Right," Barry laughed, "the moral being, watch your back and settle for eleven friends!"

We sat in the comforting glow of self-righteousness, watching late-afternoon sunlight angle past bare maples and oaks. Why is it we, at least the Christians, are all so afraid of one another? Maybe the answer is too huge to grasp. So be it; let us be afraid of one another. But must we keep trying to destroy one another? An itinerant, irascible Palestinian Jew who was filled with as much love as God could ever put into a human being is really tough to sign on with. In the heat of rage we tend to forget his great commandment to love, and his great promise that we can have the faith and courage to do so.

The following Sunday Barry was back in the basement chapel with his kids, his favorite place in the church. He had spent a lot of time creating a carpeted worship space for them, filling it with pillows on the floor and boards to show off their art. And they loved it. Barry was "their" priest (of course, he wasn't a priest at all, but children don't sweat the details and are often far wiser about these things than adults).

Twenty or so kids sat close around him and showed him their project.

"Barry!" the red and yellow and orange and green and blue poster shouted. "You help us catch the Spirit!"

"It's *beautiful*," he told them.

"No!" a couple of them cried out. "You have to *look* at it, Barry!"

"You have to *read* it, Barry!" a very insistent five-year-old demanded. So Barry sat down in the middle of the floor and started reading. What he thought were paper leaves, maybe doves, he now saw were tracings of their hands, cut out and glued to the poster. Each of the children had turned their hands into an image of the Spirit, written their name and a message on it, and given them to their "priest" as a gift. His whole ministry to them was one of love and acceptance, of themselves, of one another, and of the Spirit that helps us walk more in the ways of Jesus of Nazareth. They got it. And gave Barry an image of their hands, the hands and spirits that would reshape the world, one kindness after another.

Chapter 16

The light shines in the darkness,
and the darkness has not overcome it.

—JOHN 1:5

"A dinner party?" I asked, exasperated at having to spend yet another night alone in our three rooms in Leonia.

"Yes, I've got to go. It's a church thing, you know."

I was getting to know all too well. These weren't meetings he was attending, they were social occasions in people's homes. Hospitality was being extended. To Barry.

"Who's going to be there?" I asked, doing nothing to hide my exasperation and hurt.

"The rector, his wife," and then he listed two other husband-and-wife duos and a single woman, gathering for some post-Christmas cheer.

"But not *your* wife?" Man, if poison didn't drip from my tongue.

Barry turned and busied himself with a suddenly very dirty glass in the sink. "We've been through all this before, Will." He dropped the glass onto the rack and grabbed another. "If they extend hospitality, I accept. That's their gift to me. I have to accept."

"I'd like to accept it, too, you know. Sometimes."

"I can't make up a guest list to someone else's party. Anyway, the deal we made with Jack—"

"The deal *you* made!" I sliced into his defense.

"This is a church event!"

"It is not!" I shot back at him. "These are people you call friends. What kind of friends ignore each other's companions?"

I wasn't making it easy for him to enjoy tonight's dinner party. That wasn't my job. It was one thing to be dismissed and ignored by anonymous church people, quite another to be hidden by my own lover. Since Bishop Spong had recently crossed the barrier by openly ordaining a gay man to the priesthood, I didn't understand why we were maintaining our ludicrous, semi-closeted charade.

"Will," Barry pleaded with me, "the rector and I agreed that we wouldn't talk about my sexuality unless the issue came up."

"Right! You've made that perfectly clear to me!" I hollered, turning my back and walking away. "So now I'm not your lover? I'm your issue?"

Barry dried his hands, sensing the hurt I had wanted to mask with anger, and took my face in his hands. "This is so hard on you, so unfair to you."

"You got that right!" I wanted to keep the fight going but he had changed the battle lines. I gave in to the two tears betraying my real feelings.

"I just can't take this lie we're living," I confessed. "If Jack Spong's being up front, why are we playing patsy with Jack Croneberger? We're not fooling anybody!"

"This isn't about Jack Spong. It's about our agreement with the rector at my church. This is how we said we'd do it, for the sake of his congregation, and we're honoring that commitment."

"But it's costing us too much, hiding our love, hiding who we are."

"I know," he held me close, "I know. But I don't know what else to do."

"We knew this would happen, Barry. Remember? We knew the cost would be high. I just didn't think it might cost us our relationship."

"Don't say that!" He buried his head in my shoulder. "Don't even think that! I'll quit this whole thing before I let that happen."

I rocked him close to me, afraid of the isolation seeping through the cracks of our own internalized homophobia. "But will you see it in time? Or will we just drift apart, one inhospitable dinner after another, until some morning we wake up and find out we really are just roommates?" I felt his tears, hot through my shirt, and we clung together, suspended in time. "We have to be careful, lover boy, or our own fear will encourage everybody else's fear, and our love will be killed. Which is, after all, the goal of those who loathe us, isn't it? To stop us from loving? And the hell of it is," I laughed a little, wiping the tears from his face, "if we let any more of their fear and hate into our hearts, we'll do their job for them. We'll murder ourselves."

"We won't let that happen. I promise." He held my head again.

"Pray God we don't." Slightly chastened that I had wrecked his dinner, I watched him leave and settled down to the *New York Times* crossword puzzle, *Wheel of Fortune*, and scotch on a rock.

"Buy a damn vowel!" I screamed at the functional illiterate on the screen, neatly filling in a twelve-letter blank on my own puzzle and reaching for the phone.

"Will, it's Lee!"

"That's it!"

"What's it?" her alarm ringing through the line.

"Lea & Perrins!"

"Uh-oh. Not a good sign. You're alone again and watching *Wheel of Fortune.*"

I shut it off—well, just the volume—and turned most of my attention to my oldest, childhood friend. "What's up?"

"Did you see the paper?" she asked. The world was still a mess, the infrastructure was still crumbling, politicians still lied; I had gone straight to the puzzle, too full of care for some of my dying patients to worry about the world. "Can you believe what happened to Robert Williams?"

I flipped back and scanned the article, while on the other end Lee washed dishes and battled with Hannah to pick up her room.

Robert Williams had been ordained by Jack Spong to serve as executive director of The Oasis, a mission in the Diocese of Newark designed to reach gay and lesbian people and nurture them back into the Church. As an openly gay priest to the first such ministry in the entire Episcopal Church, Williams was pushed, ready or not, into a very public arena of political tightrope walking. People who are called to the ramparts, to live at the edge of cultural change cannot afford to make even one mistake, one slip of the tongue. Women, people of color, queers—we have all had to bear the pressure of being impeccably perfect pioneers in order to break through the boundaries of prejudice. Unfortunately Williams wasn't very practiced in the art.

"Oh my God!" A new horror flushed any previous ones down the drain. "He said Mother Teresa ought to get laid?"

"What was he thinking?" Lee cried out, sensing that the repercussions on Barry would be catastrophic.

"I'm sure I don't know! I hardly know the man. It must be taken out of context," I prayed, hoping the bishop could fix this with a terse press release. Lee promised she would call around, talk to some friends who had been Williams's professors, and get the skinny on what was real here.

"Thanks, honey. The phone lines'll be burning now! Nothing like sex and church to set tongues a-waggin'!" I couldn't believe this assault on one of the world's living saints, and tried to laugh off my dread at what was bound to come our way. Williams must have been misquoted.

I left the paper open on the kitchen table for Barry and turned in. I was beat and had an early morning date with the dying, who no longer labor over the banal missteps of their species, turning their energies toward the uncertain door before them.

"Oh, man," Barry woke me when he crawled into bed. "The fat just hit the fire." And the phone lines were popping.

This is what reportedly happened. Williams was addressing questions at a symposium in Detroit when he said "There is no way celibacy can be justified apart from a sex-negative philosophy. As long as the Church continues to romanticize celibacy, it works against those of us who are working for sexuality being an inherently good thing."

"Do you think Mother Teresa of Calcutta's life would be substantially enriched if she took to herself a lesbian lover?" a priest in the diocese asked Williams.

"If you're asking me do I think Mother Teresa ought to get laid, the answer is yes."

According to one news account, the audience froze and several gasped. I guess they would!

The fat that hit, as Barry so delicately put it, was swift, vicious, and most vitriolic among the closeted gay clergy in the Diocese of Newark, who went after Williams tooth and nail. Having called him to lead an openly gay ministry whose bylaws permitted anonymity about board members' sexual orientation (a duplicitous insanity that rightly infuriated Williams), they were terrified he would blow their closet doors open. The board couldn't talk about internalized homophobia because they couldn't talk about being gay. They couldn't talk about Williams's distinctions between monogamy and faithfulness because they couldn't talk about their own relationships. What they could talk about was sacrifice: Robert Williams in exchange for their closets. Why is it the Easter people just can't seem to stop hanging out with Pilate?

Internalized homophobia isn't a simple sort of self-loathing. No matter how long we've been out, all gays or lesbians experience fear about how out they can be in any given situation; we fail to correct a gender assumption about our orientation because we are at work or in a charged social situation; we don't speak of our partners or lovers or companions in conversations with associates, or slide over gender-specific pronouns when talking about our families and home life. It's a terrible, schizophrenic way of surviving in a world that mostly wishes we would just vanish. We knew. We had accepted crazy-making conditions for Barry's employment at The Church of the Atonement and fell into the same trap of playing a game whose rules are written by a heterosexual majority, and all because we wanted the prize of Barry's ordination. We were naive.

Bishop Spong had gone way out on a limb, putting diocesan money where his mouth was, and chose a man he believed to be strong enough to handle the job. He was wrong and found himself thrown to the lions along with his first openly gay priest.

In a matter of weeks, in January 1990, a number of Spong's colleagues in the House of Bishops were calling for his head on a platter, with no dance of the seven veils to soften the blow. They were wary of his public striving for the marginalized of our society: women, gays, lesbians, divorced men and women, the poor. They were sick of his dogged struggle to mainstream a broader interpretation of the Bible than what was offered by more fundamentalist teachers, and now angry that he dared them to state publicly what many of them were doing in secret: ordaining queers. Yes, Jack

Spong had forged himself into a lightning rod for all the charged-up members of the House, who seemed to see no greater good than maintaining an appearance of unity about their cherished traditions. But he was judged by his peers not for his advocacy on behalf of the weak nor for his theological writings, but because he did it all in the public eye, writing books on controversial issues, speaking out wherever he was invited the world over.

The Church has always preferred secrecy, a kind of gentleman's agreement, when conflicts arise between received tradition and cultural transformations. Its theological musings are lugubriously debated until a majority gains enough power to publish an opinion as Truth. Usually the issues are tempests in teapots, harangues enjoyed far longer by churchmen (sic) than the generations in which they arise. People unencumbered by dogma are generally quicker at getting on with their lives. Exactly how long did it take for the Roman Church to declare Galileo free of the charge of heresy when he agreed with Copernicus, correctly, that the Earth revolves around the sun? In the ensuing centuries, millions agreed, also correctly, that the Church was becoming increasingly irrelevant to lives now deepened and enriched by the arts, the sciences, and a growing ability to communicate new ideas. By clinging to cloistered traditions and not embracing the totality of human experience as it unfolded before it, the Church left the people to figure out their own spirituality in more meaningful, relevant symbols and religious systems. The people didn't leave the Church. The Church left the people. "People are leaving the Church in droves," comedian Lenny Bruce remarked in the 1960s, "and finding God."

In ordaining Robert Williams to the priesthood, Jack Spong only did in public what the Church has always done in secret. Well over one hundred bishops in this country and abroad have knowingly ordained well-qualified but closeted and semi-closeted gay men and lesbian women to the priesthood, including Lord Runcie, the former Archbishop of Canterbury. Their actions, albeit just, have done little good. By acting in secret the Church does not take a stand against the prejudice, hatred, and subsequent violence enjoined on gay and lesbian people. By acting in secret the Church nods its charitable head toward the intolerant and turns its back on her children fallen among thieves.

Jack Spong challenges Christians to walk the walk if they are going to talk the talk, a living echo of Barry's mother's voice. From their first meeting Barry knew they were men cut from the same cloth and knew Jack would always do the right and just thing. The cost to Jack for his social justice was escalating rapidly.

 "Well! Tell me what's happened! What did I miss?" Mark Polo breezed in for dinner a few weeks later, swiping his strawberry-blond hair out of his eyes and giving our apartment a quick, professional once-over.

"You never stop looking, do you?" I teased him about his inability to relax his sharp designer eye.

"Nope!" He laughed, poking his toe at the wished-it-were-wool nylon wall-to-wall. "Someone's got to keep up the standards. It's my job!"

Mark walked into Atonement by chance on the National Day of Prayer for People with AIDS. By chance? We know there are no accidents. Having long since abandoned his Roman Catholic up-bringing, he didn't know churches might occasionally pray for peo-ple with AIDS and found himself shedding years of resentment and agony over the tundra of loss in his life. Carefully built walls that protect us from all manner of callousness crumble suddenly when we expose our hearts to life's depths. These are sacred, fragile moments of the spirit, times of personal transformation swaddled in mystery, and for his care Mark found Barry. And of course, Mark was Barry's answered prayer for "someone like him" at his church, someone whose faith would nurture his own and help him bear the loneliness of being a gay Christian in a straight church.

"Uh-oh, you're sagging." Mark pointed to Barry. "Something's up. Tell me."

"Take a look at this." Barry handed him a stack of news articles, letters, and faxes about Robert Williams.

"Oh my God!" In one minute Mark absorbed as much as he could bear and tossed them back on the table. "I guess he's blown in and blown up. Too bad. What happens now? Is he going to be blown out? Any fallout? What's Spong's response? Does this affect you?" He was still in work mode, gathering information like he gathered facts about materials, cost, and delivery.

"Rough day?" I laughed at him. "Want a drink?"

"Yes and yes. What're you drinking?"

"The same thing I always drink."

"Me, too. But with more ice." I poured us both a couple fingers of scotch and Barry a seltzer. Glasses clinked all around, we ordered pizza and settled down for a long winter's tale.

"Well, yes, there's going to be some fallout," Barry started in, "some major fallout."

"You mean major-minor," Mark asked, "like Robert just shot his career in the foot? Or major-major, like he just shot *your* career in the foot?"

"Major-major," Barry answered.

"Damn." Mark sank into the sofa and immediately popped back up, his mind working fast. "All right, what do we do? Who do we write?" Mark fixes problems; that's his job.

"It's up to the bishop." Barry sighed, his right eye drooping under the worry he had amassed the past few weeks. He trusted Jack to do the right thing but had not heard any word from him or his office for too long—not a good sign.

Barry plunged on. "The closet queers in the diocese have been trashing Williams at every turn—what's the popular term?—*distancing* themselves from him and running for deep cover. Jack Spong has asked for his resignation."

"Wait a minute!" Mark halted the Earth's rotation. "I'm on the board of directors! I don't know about this!"

"No, you're not." Barry laughed at him. "You work with me. On the board of chaplains. And you've been in Miami."

"Oh," he looked at me over his glass, "never mind. You mean the *board* board."

"The board of directors wanted his head on a plate," I explained to him, "and they got it." There were some good people on that first board, straight advocates who believed in the ministry. But with so many board members incapable of openly presenting their own lives as an alternative to Williams's, one insensitive, flip comment and all the queers were painted with the same brush.

"What's happened to Jack?" Mark raged. "Is he turning tail and running? He started all this!"

"Jack Spong is beset by the House of Bishops, queers in his own diocese, and a Commission on Ministry that went way out on a limb for this ordination. All his support's been blown away by a thoughtless comment about a living saint!" I was in high dudgeon. "Now Spong's stuck stanching the wounds to save the cause."

"Robert didn't get much help, either," Barry told us. "Nobody's talking to him, providing pastoral care, guiding him. Everybody's trying to pretend he doesn't exist and hoping he'll just disappear." He laughed a little, mirthless laugh. "Christians just adore sacrificial offerings."

"Right!" Mark jumped in. "Robert angered the Episcopal gods of good taste and propriety. Now he must be offered up to appease them!"

"I think it's too late," Barry said. "The Presiding Bishop and his council of advice in the House of Bishops have moved to disassociate from Spong."

"What? They won't eat with him anymore? Won't play cards with him?" Mark chided. "What's that mean, *disassociate?*"

"Right," Barry laughed, "they don't want to play with him anymore. It's a vague term, but the fact is they'd really like to silence him." Mark looked puzzled, so Barry went on. "Basically they're trying to put as much distance between Spong and the rest of the Episcopal Church as they can, isolating him, making him a nonentity in the House of Bishops. Since we don't excommunicate or try for heresy, disassociation is as severe a punishment as he can get. It'll destroy the power of his voice in the Church. And that's bad news."

"Okay. I'm getting the picture, but what's it got to do with your ordination? You're not Robert Williams," Mark insisted.

"No, but I'm another queer in the Diocese of Newark." Barry sighed. "All the bishops who work hard at undermining Jack Spong are painting every queer in New Jersey with the same, broad stroke. You know, if one's a loose cannon then we're all loose cannons. They're having a field day with this one. They're going for blood. Jack's, and consequently mine. If he ordains another queer any time soon, his career is over."

"But that's not fair!" Mark hollered, nearly sloshing his scotch on the wall.

"Fair doesn't have anything to do with it. Fair is not what this is all about." Barry's ire was up. "The House of Bishops is not interested in fairness or justice. They are interested in carrying out a petty vendetta against Jack Spong and I'm caught in the crossfire. 'Sorry! Stray bullet! Didn't mean to hit you! No offense? You understand we have to maintain collegiality and, of course, our sacred traditions.' " His sarcasm was cut short by the phone.

"Oh God!" I wailed. "The pizza guy can't find the house again. And I'm starving!" I picked up the phone, dropped my jaw, and handed the receiver to Barry.

"What?" Mark asked.

"Shh!" I hissed. "It's the bishop's office."

"Oh, damn," Mark editorialized for us all.

"Double that."

"Triple that," Barry said as he hung up from the very brief call. We had been summoned to the bishop's office. The three of us sat staring at one another. Finally somebody asked if the missed pizza delivery was a sign.

Chapter 17

Dear Barry:

I am deeply concerned about you and believe that you and I should talk as soon as possible. The present mood of the Church, I think, makes it almost impossible for me to proceed with ordination of someone who is honest about his sexuality. I do need to discuss this with you and find a way, if one can be found, that we can proceed. But unless we find some way to alleviate the anxieties sweeping through the Church at this moment, I do not believe the Standing Committee will approve your ordination. This comes with my best wishes.

—*John S. Spong,*
letter to Barry Stopfel, March 12, 1990

"It's over, isn't it?" Barry sat while Jack Croneberger finished reading the bishop's missive.

"It might be," Jack admitted. "There's a lot going on here, a lot of fallout from the Williams thing. A lot that has nothing to do with you."

"But it does have to do with me!" Jack sat quietly, knowing Barry was facing an overwhelming loss, and waited for him to say whatever he needed to say.

"I'm leaving," Barry announced, "I can't stay here any longer," and got up to go.

"Barry," Jack laughed a little, "tell me one thing before you go. Are you leaving for today or for good?"

Barry rounded on him in the door. *After nearly two years and the man still doesn't know me!* He checked his rage, remembering to keep the issues and people here separate. Jack Croneberger was not the bad guy. Hell, he wasn't even sure Jack Spong was, but he would do for now.

"I'm leaving for today, Jack," Barry sighed, "just today. Maybe tomorrow, I'll see."

Jack shook his head in understanding.

"Why the long face?" the parish secretary asked. Barry handed her the brief letter. "Oh. That's unfortunate." She handed it back to him, professionally detached. It was one straw too many.

"Unfortunate?" His voice rose on each syllable. *"Unfortunate?* This isn't some dinner party that's gotten canceled! This," he was shouting now, "is a damned tragedy! This is my life! I've just been hit by a semi on the New Jersey Turnpike at seventy miles an hour! This is a disaster!" The secretary sat dumbfounded. She had never seen Barry lose it like this and kept very still.

His head shook, along with the rest of his body as he walked away. "Unfortunate?" He was laughing now. "Jesus Christ! *Unfortunate.*"

"Barry," Jack reached out "go home, friend. Go home." Barry flew out, knowing he would apologize later, and went to sit with Shirley Redfield, who had rescued me from my first coffee hour.

It was one of those very warm, early March days that gives one just enough hope to survive the last four weeks of winter sure to come. Shirley's yard is a wooded wonder of ancient oaks, elm, and birch towering over a long reach of yard islanded with perennial flower beds and a smorgasbord of bird feeders.

"Shirley, I think I'm going to have to quit," Barry confessed as he sat with her in the welcoming warmth of her back porch. "I just don't think it's worth this kind of torture and harassment."

"Oh, Barry," she cried with him, "this is just terrible. Just terrible," she repeated, at an utter loss for words for the man who had become her dear friend. Her Sundays were filled with the life-renewing activities of hiking in the woods, reading, caring for the county's nature preserves, and always her beloved painting. That is, until she first heard Barry preach.

"I came back to Atonement because of what you give us from the pulpit, what you give us in your classes. Barry," she reached over and took his hand, an unfamiliar gesture for this friend, steeped in the protocol of her generation, "you can't quit. You mean too much to so many of us. And anyway," she took her hand back, "you know you have to go on. I've never known a man who should be a minister more than you."

"Shirley," Barry laughed at her, "how many ministers have you known?"

"Enough. Like Will teases me," she laughed with Barry, "I'm an old lady and I've been around the block. Does he know?"

"No, and he's going to be a wild man when he finds out! I'm not looking forward to that." They laughed as friends do who know the best and worst about their partners, and are grateful for them. Sitting with the unexpected warmth of a midday sun on their faces, they fell quietly into their thoughts of loss and betrayal.

"What happened to Bishop Spong?" she asked after a pair of jays entertained them with a very noisy ballet. "I always regarded him as a crusader, committed to gay and lesbian people. What happened?"

Before she met us Shirley Redfield had never once said the words *gay* and *lesbian*. She had never known one before us and so never had a need to use the words. When she helped me out of the curtains that first Sunday at Atonement, she had a hunch we might be a homosex-ual couple. This was something new, and it piqued her innate curi-osity about life. Within weeks I was included in Shirley's invitations to lunch, for a swim, to sit with her friends, who were of every age but all delightfully young in spirit, and to talk, talk, talk.

"I don't know what's happened to Bishop Spong," Barry told her and related the brief history of Robert Williams, the House of Bishops' move against their bishop, and the possible disassociation. It still made no sense to her.

"If people like that are coming after Spong, wouldn't you think he'd know he was on the right track?" Shirley asked in her clear, innocent voice. "That he was doing the right thing? I'm surprised at his, well . . ." she looked for a delicate way to put her thought, ". . . his humanity. I always thought he was such a tower of cour-age."

There was no answer. No one can ever know what transpires in someone else's mind, what fears overcome them, what doubts sing in their ear. Alone at night the voices of our past compete with our vision of the future, waging a holy war in all people of conscience. Do we hang on to the life we know or dare for a new and better one?

Later Barry went for a run, hoping to clear his head and maybe hear what counsel God had for him. But he wasn't hearing anything. He was screaming.

"Where are you, you masochistic bastard! How dare you trick me into believing? Where are you now? Some God! Life in the Church, you said. Like hell! You just dumped me. Hung me up to die! How could you, you son of a bitch!" He screamed and screamed at the heavens, his body shaken by a psalm of rage. "Do your job! Talk to me! Tell me what the hell's going on! Talk to me!" He collapsed with his doubts, hearing only his sobs, feeling only the hard winter earth beneath his fists. Today, God was silent.

Chapter 18

Gamaliel, a Pharisee in the Sanhedrin, a teacher of the law, and held in honor by the whole people, stood up and said, "Men of Israel, take care what you do to these people. I suggest you leave them alone and let them go. If this movement of theirs is the work of men, it will fail; but if it does in fact come from God, not only will you never overthrow them, you may well find yourselves fighting against God."

—FROM THE ACTS OF THE APOSTLES, CHAPTER 5

"Would you just slow down some? And clean the windows!" Barry snapped at my driving.

"I can't drive any slower," I barked right back at him. "We're on the damn turnpike. What? You want to get rear-ended by these cowboys?" The New Jersey Turnpike is not a particularly attractive or user-friendly highway. But it is never more unattractive than on those cold, drizzly days of late winter when crusts of melted scud are flung over your windshield by racing eighteen-wheel behemoths.

Not knowing what was hiding behind the door to Bishop Spong's office, we were taking out our anxiety on each other. In the three days before our appointed meeting we had fought about the laundry, a dripping faucet, whose turn it was to make the bed, how knives should be stored, and which direction the toilet paper should roll. And my driving. Tension does wonders on a relationship.

We were now entering the institutional Church world of intrigue and politics, a new world for us. We didn't have a strategy, not a clue how to proceed. We assumed the great "they" had one, but we didn't know who "they" were. If we were not to be included and heard in the decision-making process, then we were sure to be squashed like tiresome gnats. If we battled with each other at home, gained advantages over each other and the petty minutiae of our lives, then we might delude ourselves into believing we were still in control of a world spinning wildly away from us.

Meanwhile the power players were working everything out, turning the two of us, our relationship, our faith, our lives into an abstract concept to be battled over "for the good of the Church." We were perceived as not only causing an irrevocable split in the Episcopal Church, but setting the cause of gay and lesbian liberation back an entire generation. For goodness's sake! We were just two guys who loved each other. We had no revolutionary ax to grind, we had no access to people in or out of the institution. Barry wasn't even a deacon yet!

It all happened with uncanny speed. Within days Barry, and I because I loved him, became the line drawn in the sand for opposing sides of a battle. We were stripped of our humanity and turned into an issue, just as "those Jews," "those blacks," "those women's-libbers," "those welfare mothers" have been and too often still are. The two sides in the battle over human sexuality in the Christian Church were now officially at war, and Barry was to be the number-one casualty, perhaps even sacrificed by our own side if it would save a bishop, or the "unity of the Church."

The day Jack Spong forced Robert Williams's resignation, his adversaries in the House of Bishops smelled blood. Seeing his action as a sign of vulnerability, a chink in Spong's shining moral armor, they rushed in for the kill. Knowing he was planning to ordain another out gay man to the diaconate was all the justification his enemies needed. Spong must have seen it coming, for he joked that Christians tend to eat their wounded—a point of view no doubt nurtured by his confrontational years in the House. If his antagonists were successful, they would bring Bishop Spong's episcopacy down around his heels, expel him from his position of advocacy for the weak, and cut off his voice to the world. The future of his ministry was hanging in the wind with Robert Williams. And Barry Stopfel.

For years Jack Spong had been critical of his peers' lack of courage, chiding the lesser of them for their insensitivity and inaction on key social crises of our time. He and his diocese were constantly in the news with one charged issue or another: reproductive rights, science and religion, human sexuality, race, assisted suicide—any issue demanding moral and ethical responses. Whatever the issue, Jack Spong would put his considerable mind, voice, and body into it, belying the assumption that Christian fundamentalists are the only voice of morality for this country. For all of this, Spong's critics were wrong in calling him a "loose cannon." Jack Spong was as firm in his convictions as those with whom he disagreed.

Bishop Spong had spoken to his colleagues, announced at their annual meeting and informed the Presiding Bishop that he was planning to ordain, publicly, an out gay man to the priesthood. Jack believed that if acceptance of a healthy ethic of sexuality was ever to happen, the Church had to have openly gay and lesbian role models. The crimes of the closet would stop only when humanity no longer needed closets to hide in. Williams's youthful opinions and public expressions about human sexuality had done a good deal of damage, but Jack wasn't about to let one mistake deter him. Several times he said to Barry, "I wish it had been you. I wish you'd been the first one ordained." So did we.

Many in the House of Bishops failed to grasp the implication of Jack's stated intent to be honest about a practice that had been kept secret for centuries. Truth not only sets us free, but also unleashes the hounds of hell.

By March 1990, not twelve weeks after Williams's statement about Mother Teresa, Jack Spong's adversaries had seized upon a 1979 nonbinding Resolution in the House of Bishops in order to "disassociate" the House from Spong's ordination of Williams. The 1979 Resolution stated that the ordination of noncelibate gay and lesbian persons was "not appropriate." The Resolution was counterbalanced the next day by a Statement of Conscience and signed by twenty-one bishops. By 1985 the Statement of Conscience would be signed by over seventy bishops and said, in part, "Taking note . . . that this action . . . is recommendatory and not prescriptive . . . we cannot accept these recommendations or implement them in our Dioceses."

Statements of Conscience are common in this democratically governed body of diverse and opinionated people of faith. There were still several men who refused to ordain women in their dioceses, based on the authority of their Statement of Conscience. Of course, the ordination of women is, in fact, a canon law, but the other members of the House, one supposes, simply turned their heads in the spirit of collegiality.

Many bishops, guided by their consciences, quietly ordain gay and lesbian people as deacons and priests. But an act of faith is only an act of faith when it is held up as a light to the world. Jack was not well liked, even by those who agreed with him, and his courage and public faithfulness were often derided as forms of grandstanding, narcissism, and self-promotion.

A troubled Bishop Spong beckoned us into his chamber. His office tumbled with books, wedged onto the shelves and piled up on his desk and every table in the room. I was impressed with the breadth of the bishop's reading.

"Great library, Bishop Spong," I said, shaking his hand.

"Sit down, sit down." The bishop rubbed his long hands together and plunged in, bypassing the usual niceties. "We have a dilemma that you both can help us solve." He recapped the latest attacks on him, giving Barry and me a clear picture of the very real threat he faced. As he spoke he seemed to become less sure of himself and the efficacy of his past actions, specifically his ordination of Williams. The political tide in the House of Bishops was working its vengeance on him.

"Barry, I know you're doing excellent work at Atonement, and I believe you're going to be one of the church's finest priests. I look forward to the day when I can ordain you. And I would sacrifice my episcopacy to do what is right. But given the strife in the House of Bishops and the dissent in the broader church about homosexuality, I do not believe the Standing Committee will approve your ordination at this time." We had read it in the letter, but to hear it spoken by the great advocate made it all too real. We sat mute. If he ordained another gay man, Jack Spong believed the House of Bishops would resolutely move to depose him.

The three of us searched for a solution that would effectively defuse the crisis, saving both his episcopacy and Barry's priesthood. Perhaps Barry could voluntarily withdraw from the process for Holy Orders until the whole Church was of a single mind about the issue through a binding convention resolution. In other words, wait until the canons of the Church were changed—not a likely prospect in our lifetimes!

Barry was stunned. Were Jack and the Church really so terrified? How could one man's ordination, this little ol' country-boy queer, schism the Church, set back the cause of gay and lesbian people a generation, and destroy an episcopacy to boot? Did they not know that it is God's church? If God has an interest in keeping it alive, nobody can destroy it, not even Barry.

In the anxiety of the moment Barry thought he heard the bishop asking him to sacrifice himself and his ministry in order to save Jack Spong and the "unity of the Church." But was Barry not a part of the Church? Are gays and lesbians not a part of the Church? A "unity" that included us obviously had not occurred to the House of Bishops.

Barry was stunned. For thousands of women and men, straight and gay, John Shelby Spong had been one of the very few bishops out front and fighting for an inclusive, just Church. Barry knew that if we lost Bishop Spong there would be no one left to speak for us. But his own calling was before him, as was the labyrinth of political duplicity necessitated by a Church that seemed to want both Barry and Jack to lie: Barry about who he is, Jack about who he ordains. But neither man is a liar.

With a controlled, gentle voice Barry told his bishop, "I cannot voluntarily quit the process. It would be dishonest when so many people of faith, yourself included, have encouraged me to continue. We have to find some other way."

For quite a while we sat, breathing heavily as the implications of Barry's choice threw the bishop's mind into overdrive. Jack's chancellor was being a good friend to him, one of the few, and counseled him to get as far away from Barry Stopfel as possible. He made it very clear that, in his opinion, if Jack ordained Barry, it would be the end. But Jack Spong does not back away from controversial issues of justice. A complex man of conscience, he is also a brilliant political animal.

"Barry, there is one idea out there I want your counsel on." The

Furies raged across his face. "You understand I am not asking you to do this. I would never ask you to do this. It's an idea that has come to me from a friend. Actually you know him, too. I just want you to know the kind of advice I am getting."

What in the hell could be coming? Jack pressed one thumb into the palm of his hand and rubbed as he continued. "What if you wrote a letter to the Standing Committee? In it you say, yes, you're gay, but you're celibate. Then I would be able to proceed with your ordination without raising the stakes in the national Church." Still rubbing his hands he explained further. "There are no canons forbidding a celibate man from Holy Orders. At least not yet!" He smiled briefly, knowing how quickly political expediency can shift. "Then, once you're ordained," he finished telling us about the advice he had been given, "you write another letter to the committee and tell them you're unable to maintain your celibacy. It was," he looked back at his hands, fumbling for words, "one . . . solution offered by a friend of ours. He thought it very clever: you'd be ordained and I'd be able to do it without drawing a lot of unwanted attention to this diocese." He had floated the idea. Now he waited.

If I had had anything to eat that day I would have thrown up on the spot. I couldn't believe this was the counsel Jack Spong was getting! Barry, who is redheaded and already fair, paled visibly. Jack didn't look at either of us, so I looked hard at Barry, willing him to look back at me. When he turned his head the earth fell away beneath me. I didn't recognize my lover. I saw him dead. His mouth was ajar, his cheeks pulled down, and his eyes . . . well, his eyes weren't there. He was looking at me but didn't see me. I put my hand full on his arm, bishop's office be damned, really to see if he was still pumping blood. His was the face of a man dead on the vine—the man in his dream not so many years before.

Just as I was about to move closer to him, a very tiny light went on somewhere inside and Barry put his hand on mine. He licked his lips, turned his head a little to one side, blinked a few times, and then saw me. He shook his head in that nearly imperceptible "I'm okay" gesture known to lovers the world over, and let out a deep breath. I got up and dragged myself to the leaded-glass window. I needed to see out of this room, see daylight, maybe a sign. The March drizzle fell steadily over the gray slate roof of Cathedral House.

"You see," the bishop broke the long, long silence, "I would never ask you to do this. I just wanted you to know the kinds of ideas people are offering." He shrugged his whole body. "I guess they feel that since it is a sometimes duplicitous institution, then we must use duplicitous means to get what we want." He stopped and looked at Barry. "I'm sorry. I shouldn't have even mentioned it. It's just," he faltered for words again, "I'm at a loss right now. People say all kinds of things to me. I wanted to make sure we felt the same way."

"No," Barry said, his voice welling up deep inside.

"No, I'm sorry," the bishop said. "Don't think about it."

"No," Barry repeated, overwhelmed with a confusion of sympathy for Jack and rage for whomever had given such life-threatening advice. "If I denied my relationship with Will, what would we have left? There is no job, no calling worth that price."

"No, no, there isn't." Jack looked over at the picture of his wife. "We'll find a way through this. A right way."

We moved down the stairway, bumping into each other, stumbling back into the winter gray.

 "Barry!" a white-haired man with smiling eyes called out. "Come in for a minute, won't you?" his deep voice rumbled in invitation. I followed Barry in, too battle-weary for another assault to matter. "You must be Will. I'm Walter Righter." He grasped our hands, sat us down with a glass of water, and asked, "How'd it go?"

"Thank you," Barry answered the gift of a drink. Somewhere in the recesses of my mind I remembered Barry telling me about this sage, retired bishop who had become a gracious chaplain and advisor to him.

"It was bad, Walter," Barry began, and for several minutes outlined our conversation with Bishop Spong. "I don't think he sees a way that he can proceed."

"That man is paranoid," I finally blurted out. For all I knew Walter was Jack Spong's closest friend, but it had been a tough day and the words just flew out of their own volition.

"Well," Walter laughed, "I don't know about that, but he's been through an awful lot in the House of Bishops. No one, and I mean no one, has ever been subjected to as much abuse in that House as Jack Spong. They're gunning for him, you know. It does something to a man when even the people you think are your friends betray you. I don't understand why they're being so vehement, but it'd be a damn shame for them to get him."

Down to earth, thoughtful, with a rough edge: I fell in love with him right then. I like a bishop who can cuss a little, makes the collar a little more human, a little more real.

He and Barry chatted, Walter asking about his work at Atonement and what the people there felt.

"It's a very supportive community, Walter, all in all." He looked over to me as if asking permission to tell a familiar story. I had no idea what story he wanted to tell, so I just stared back dumbly.

"I guess the biggest problem is Will. One of the vestry members told me they didn't have any problem with my being gay, but commented that they'd just learned Will wasn't an Episcopalian. 'You're living in a mixed marriage,' they said. 'That's what bothers me!'" Walter laughed gently with us, enjoying the grace of good humor in the midst of stress.

"They've never had to deal with something like this and would probably prefer not to. But Jack Croneberger and the vestry believe I should be ordained and are standing with me. I'm very grateful. But now I don't know . . ." Barry's voice trailed off as he became lost in thoughts of an uncertain future.

With the counselor's sure instinct Walter let the hurt sit while Barry's eyes did their own tearing up. After a couple of minutes Barry wiped his eyes and laughed. "I don't think he'll ever be able to ordain me."

Walter had journeyed with Barry for many months, guiding him through the machinations of diocesan politics, praying with him and for him as he discerned his call to ordained ministry. "Barry," he smiled like a grandpa seeing only the promise in a favorite grandson, "it's not a matter of *if* you'll be ordained, but *when* you'll be or-dained."

We drove back up that abysmal highway in the rain, Walter's compassion and reassurance buffering Jack's uncertainty only a little. Numb beyond words, with a hollow ache chilling us both, the smeary *slap, slap, slap* of the windshield wipers and my heavy foot on the gas didn't seem to matter anymore. Barry's priesthood was surely gone.

That night I held my grieving lover close, laughed at the religious pleasure haters, and caressed the fury away.

Chapter 19

Our faith imposes on us a right and duty to throw ourselves into the things of the earth.

—*Teilhard de Chardin*

Driven by circumstances outside their control, Barry and Jack Spong became pitted as adversaries during the late winter and early spring of 1990. In acting out of his love for me, Barry set in motion circumstances that would eventually put him in the eye of the national Church's storm over human sexuality, the very place Bishop Spong most wanted to avoid for now. We weren't looking for controversy; we were just being honest about our relationship. "No," we told the Church and its leaders, "thank you very much, but you may not make us over in your own image of God. We worship a God for whom nothing is outside the possibility of love." The Church seemed terrified of our loving. Why? Is the tree of love so big that any of us dare lop off a single branch?

Barry and I are rarely certain of most articles of faith in our lives save one: Jesus told those who wished to follow him to practice acts of love. Not to *feel* love, mind you, but to do love. Which is never easy or simple. Now I had to ask myself, had Barry failed to act in love toward Bishop Spong by acting to defend the integrity of his love for me?

Many whom Jack Spong had long thought his friends and allies were siding against him in favor of the disassociation being considered by the House of Bishops. He had always had the vocal support of a minority of his peers, together with the voting support of a majority of like-minded, but less outspoken, allies. Now, however, in the name of preserving the "collegiality and unity of the Church," that support was virtually disappearing.

"Unity without justice is hardly worth preserving!" Bishop Douglas E. Theuner of New Hampshire's thoughtful voice cried out in the Presiding Bishop's Council of Advice and the House of Bishops. But by early spring 1990, his voice was all but drowned out by those who had decided they had been shamed and betrayed by Jack Spong's forthrightness and public honesty long enough.

Bishop Spong's next meeting with Barry was brisk. He believed Barry couldn't grasp the political pressure he was under as his bishop. But Barry did grasp it. What he couldn't grasp was the sacrifice he felt he was being asked to make.

"Of course I'll ordain you, if the Standing Committee recommends you," the bishop told him. "I will have to. My integrity would demand it of me. I will not participate in the Church's duplicity. But the Standing Committee is uncertain whether their recommendation of you for ordination will cause my being deposed."

So that was how it was going to be, was it? "Jack," Barry reasoned, setting aside his own anger, "as long as they believe you'll be ruined if you ordain me, the Standing Committee is sure to vote against me. Integrity won't have anything to do with it. They'll have to protect you."

"I'm not convinced of that," the bishop countered. "They're very independent, committed to their own process. They're good people and I have never known them to change their mind on any issue because we were not in agreement. No," he said, running his hands over his cluttered desk, "they'll do what they believe to be right. And ask me to do the same. I count on them for that."

Several times during their meeting Barry reminded the bishop of his vision and courage, which had meant liberation for a generation of people, people far beyond the doors of the Episcopal Church.

"We're going to find a way to move ahead with this ordination, Jack," Barry told him hopefully. "The day you ordained Robert Williams, you set in motion something that can't be turned around. The question, as I see it, is how will we do this with justice and integrity?"

"You know, I suppose," Jack said with a sigh, "that Walter Righter has asked me to let him ordain you?" This was news to Barry.

"Well," Spong went on, now running one hand then the other over his fists, "I can't let him. I don't feel comfortable asking Walter to take this kind of abuse in his retirement."

Barry was feeling desperate and tossed a bomb.

"What about the fact that you are going to ordain a closeted lesbian in my class of deacons? Aren't you worried Williams might sabotage this ordination by outing her?" The bishop let the question pass. For a moment Barry wondered what his open struggle with ordination must mean to this woman. What was happening to her spirit? Barry knew that, ultimately, the price she would pay for the Church's duplicity would be far greater than his.

But Jack was rushing on, stringing out one possibility after another that might get Barry ordained without bringing the wrath of Jack's enemies down on his head.

With a jolt Barry caught up to the bishop's thinking. Perhaps the best solution would be for Barry to come to the diaconal ordination—Jack would see how much press attention, if any, it would get—and then proceed at his discretion. On the other hand, Barry might vest and process with the other candidates, then stand to one side in protest. Or maybe not vest at all but sit in the congregation as a silent witness to the Church's continuing hypocrisy. Bishop Spong kept balling each hand into the other as he tossed out idea after idea, none of which ensured Barry's ordination.

While Barry and the bishop were trying to hammer out a solution in the chamber upstairs, I was on the first floor of Cathedral House praying in the chapel with the Reverend Norman Mol. Norman is a hulking Teuton of a man with a twisted sense of humor and a very expansive concept of prayer. Perhaps it was being a single father that had so expanded his prayer life, having to pray when and where he could, often touching grace on the fly, with the radio blaring in the station wagon on the way to a soccer match.

Through that tense, cold winter several friends met frequently with Barry to pray at Atonement. People of all stripes met together, getting themselves in the way of God, listening for that discerning, wise voice in the wilderness. Some nights Barry would look around the small circle, at the closeted gay and lesbian people praying with and for him, and find their motives troubling. In a way they were asking him to pay a price they were unwilling to pay, to put his life on a line they didn't want to walk themselves. Yet there they were, praying, laughing, crying with him. God! he thought on more than one occasion, it's hard to stay committed to the needs of brothers and sisters who are so opposite from me! They hide safely in their sacristy closets and meanwhile I'm out here being strung up for my honesty. And for the sake of their closets! But he couldn't condemn them for their choice. Once you accept the fact that life is not scripted like a nighttime television drama, responses to other people and their issues become very, very complex. God creates and accepts each of us as individuals and asks us to do the same. Tough job, being human.

When Barry came down to the chapel after his hour-long meeting with the bishop, he looked beaten, drained.

"Well?" I prodded, a partner's prerogative.

Barry spoke slowly, calmly facing the altar. "I think he's upset that I'm not clever enough to find a way through the elaborate maze of Episcopal politics."

"So?" Norman asked. "Jack's very good at all that. You don't have to be."

"No." Barry sat down, bone weary. "It's something more. I feel he's fighting something he's not telling me about, or can't tell me about. There's more at stake here than just his job, his episcopacy. I think . . . I'm not sure . . . but I think he sees my ordination, or nonordination, as the case may be, as some kind of turning point, not for himself but for the whole Church."

"Small *c* or big *C?*" I asked.

"Big *C.*" Barry nodded. "Big, big, big *C.*"

"But, honey, that's crazy! Bishops ordain queers all the time. It happens at all times and in all places."

"Maybe even one going on right now," Norman said.

"Yeah," Barry agreed and thought a second. "But those bishops aren't hated like Jack Spong is." We could only nod in agreement.

"Besides," Barry went on, "Jack's not the one turning me into the keystone for gay and lesbian liberation in the Church. It's the ones who hate him that're doing it." More thoughts raced across his eyes. Norman and I waited for him to gather them together.

"You know, he told me everybody knows my name now," Barry said with an ironic smile. "Everybody. *Both* sides. I laughed, but it wasn't really funny. I'm not even a deacon and the whole House of Bishops knows who I am."

"Do they know where we live?" I joked.

But it wasn't funny. This whole thing was getting a little scary.

Chapter 20

Week after week we witness the same miracle: that God is so mighty he can stifle his own laughter. Week after week, we witness the same miracle: that God, for reasons unfathomable, refrains from blowing our dancing bear act to smithereens. Week after week Christ washes the disciples' dirty feet, handles their very toes, and repeats, It is all right—believe it or not—to be people. Who can believe it?
          —*Annie Dillard*, TEACHING A STONE TO TALK[8]

Barry's ordination was in trouble. The rector at The Church of the Atonement knew it; so did the vestry. Without Barry's knowledge, they wrote their bishop in March of 1990.

At our regular monthly Vestry meeting, we learned of the possible postponement or cancellation of Barry Stopfel's ordination to the Diaconate in June . . . We urge you not to lose sight of the goal of opening the ordained ministry of the Episcopal Church, both in the Diocese of Newark and the Country as a whole, to all people who are called and who qualify. We appreciate the difficult situation in which you find yourself and acknowledge your pain, hurt and reticence to continue on your chosen leadership path. . . .

We are proud that Barry has been open and honest with us about himself, which has made it possible for all of us to know him as the real, caring, loving, supportive and nurturing man that he is. It has helped us grow. . . .

We strongly believe that you should proceed with Barry's ordination as originally planned and fully support him in seeing that this happens.

Barry had begun his career at Atonement with a set of crazy-making rules, telling people about his sexuality on a need-to-know basis. But eighteen months later the vestry had found the courage to unanimously support him in his call to the ordained ministry as an out gay man. It was an unexpected affirmation he would cling to in the coming, brutal weeks.

Letters were arriving with unsettling regularity on the bishop's desk. He was not amused.

Richard and Joan Hennig wrote with their daughters, Marissa and Kristina.

Barry has become an integral part of our parish life and proven over and over again that he is indeed a "Man of God." Postponing his ordination will serve no purpose other than to play into the hands of those who wish to destroy the progressive and important leadership that our church deserves . . . We couldn't help but think back to your sermon given at Atonement in January, the Sunday we celebrated Confirmation. We suggest you look over your notes for that occasion and reaffirm your own beliefs! A person's sexuality should not determine what his chosen profession should be. IF GOD GIVES A CALL, WHO ARE WE TO DENY GOD'S WILL!!

"Dear Bishop," Edgar K. Byham, president of Integrity, Inc., the national Episcopal gay and lesbian advocacy organization, and friend to the bishop wrote, "Having sought my counsel, I hope you won't mind my sharing a few additional thoughts now that the Standing Committee has approved the ordination of Barry Stopfel to the Diaconate. This places the decision solely on you about whether to proceed."

This was April 1990, and the Standing Committee had approved Barry for ordination, believing they and the bishop would find a way to proceed in the great march to full inclusion and justice in the Episcopal Church. They had taken the prudent step of writing to the presiding bishop and his Council of Advice, asking this august assembly to respond to their letter and tell them if there was any canon expressly forbidding their decision. Having received no response, they recommended Barry to the bishop for ordination.

Byham's letter continued:

I don't suggest going into the closet about this ordination. It is important that the integrity of all concerned be maintained. The fact is, however, that it won't be newsworthy and so the press won't cover it. . . .

The lesbian and gay community in and beyond this Church has almost uniformly rallied to your defense. We want you to remain an effective bishop. There's virtually no chance you'll cease to be a bishop. What our opponents want is for you to stop being effective in that role. I fear that if you don't follow through with this ordination, it may be the beginning of a diminution in your effectiveness as Christ's Vicar in the place you have been called to minister.

"Dear, dear Barry," Shirley Redfield wrote. "Right now my thoughts are one continuous prayer for you. These nights the stars are particularly bright, what mystery and strength! Take courage,

Barry, and remember you are so necessary to us and we love and care for you deeply."

Barry's ordination might be delayed, but, sooner or later, it *would* happen. Too many good people, including his beleaguered bishop, wanted it to happen.

 "Honey, you've got to read this!" Barry called out to me as I tumbled in the door from a hospice funeral a hundred miles away in Pennsylvania.

"That's nice," I mumbled, weary and sad. "Can it wait? I've just got to go to bed."

"All right. Lie down. But read this," he insisted.

I read:

TO THOSE WHO DETERMINE POLICY AND ADVISE THE PASTOR OF THE CHURCH OF ATONEMENT . . .

Do you really think that parents with young children, or pre-adolescent teenagers, will look forward to joining The Church of Atonement that has a homo-sexual [sic] priest on its staff?

"Oh, for God's sake!" I jumped off the bed, fully awake and loaded for bear. "Who wrote *this* garbage?"

"It was anonymous. And," Barry went on before I could say a word, "it was sent to the vestry and a few members of the church. We're not sure how many."

"This is sick!"

"Oh, it gets better! Read on."

I did:

I wonder how many parents who had children in the Sunday School the past year would have kept them attending it had they known that Barry was "gay"? Obviously, many of the women who attend The

Church of Atonement are utterly naive as to the true nature and personal lives of homosexuals (both male and female). TV shows smiling, lovable homos, arms entwined, occasionally kissing each other on the cheek, as they march down Fifth Avenue at periodic times during the year. It wasn't sheer caprice that, since the earliest days of Christianity, the Church has condemned homosexuality as a sin. All physical perversions against the natural functions of males and females with regard to their sexual activities have been regarded as crimes against nature.

"Who mined this filth?"
"Read on!" Barry laughed. "It gets better."

I challenge the leadership of The Church of Atonement to take a poll of its members as to how they feel about having an avowed homo-sexual on the staff. Why not re-print the following, attach a ballot, and get a *Yes* or *No* verdict from the membership?
  LOVE MAKING BETWEEN HOMOSEXUALS

What followed were three graphically detailed summaries of what the writer thought a gay man does with his "penus," and two less detailed but equally pornographic summaries of what he (it *had* to be a man) thought women do with their "sexual organs."

" 'Penus'!" I shouted. "He spelled it *p-e-n-u-s!*"

"It's really very funny." Barry had been waiting for me to get to that part. "Jack Croneberger also thinks it's funny, which is good. It'd be trouble otherwise."

"Who *is* this person, and how does he know this is what gay men do with their *p-e-n-u-s-e-s?* Hmm?" Barry was laughing. "I think the lady protests too much here! Has someone been doing a little empir-ical research? My God! *P-e-n-u-s!*"

"Since Jack's away, he asked me to respond to this with the ves-try." What response could there be but howling laughter—or tears?

"Don't you dare respond to this illiterate trash!" I donned my very best high-and-mighty hat.

"You know how you get sometimes?" Barry asked. "Well, you're getting that way *now!*"

"Listen." I took a deep breath and calmed a decibel or two. "You never respond to this kind of filth. You don't give it any credence by acknowledging it. You know that."

"I know."

"Listen," I said, "one time at First Presbyterian Church, someone sent an anonymous letter around about something. I was too young to remember what it was about, but I remember my dad standing up and saying that people who send anonymous letters are the same people who write on bathroom walls, and we should pay as much attention to one as to the other. It was sage advice, if slightly graphic, for a church community."

That night Barry composed his letter to the parish.

Dear Friends, I shared your misfortune in reading an anonymous letter from someone in our parish regarding my ministry and my human sexuality. . . .

What is obvious to me is the author's sickness regarding their own human sexuality. Besides anger and disgust, the only other decent human response is one of compassion for an individual who must be deeply troubled. . . .

As a Church we have been unwilling to help folks deal responsibly with the physical and spiritual complexities of human sexuality. Our unwillingness as Christians to affirm the nature of God's gift of sexuality has done much to wreck the lives of too many of our sisters and brothers in Christ. The author of the anonymous letter is a case in point. . . .

I believe we are all bound by the same sexual ethic. . . . Whenever human sexuality is self-serving, oppressive, demeaning to oneself or another, or is compulsive and impersonal, it exists in a state of sin. . . .

The anonymous letter proves that in so many ways in our teaching, we have missed the mark and failed to reflect God in our lives. There is much work to be done . . . I am honored to be doing it with you.

The author of the "penus letter" hoped to disgust the vestry and the church into withdrawing their support of Barry. He did not. For, when justice is planted and watered by faith in action, hell itself cannot prevail against it.

Chapter 21

I don't know about you, but I got a lot of mixed messages about sex from the church.

On the one hand sex is dirty: save it for the one you love. On the other, sexuality is a gift from God, just don't talk about it in church.

It's a wonder any of us is the least bit healthy about our sexuality.

—*Barry L. Stopfel,*
IN A LETTER TO THE CHURCH OF THE ATONEMENT

Someone had kept the furnace running all night, conscientiously taking the early spring chill off a cavernous sanctuary that now sweltered in mid-April.

"His name was Ray Roberts," Bishop Spong began his remarks to the packed assembly of friends, priests, and parishioners, already overheated and not halfway through the memorial service.

Now that Barry and Bishop Spong had come down to the wire on his ordination, they weren't getting on well. It appeared that the presiding bishop's Council of Advice would successfully vote to disassociate itself from the Bishop of Newark, now beleaguered by an almost daily diet of advice from priests, parishioners, friends, and his peers urging him to proceed with Barry's ordination. Perhaps out of his feelings of abandonment and uncertainty he had floated a last-minute suggestion from a mysterious someone that Barry might go back in the closet, the very closet in which Ray Roberts had languished. The closet Jack was now preaching against.

"He was forty-eight years old," Spong's voice echoed through the sweltering hall. "He was a priest. He graduated from the Episcopal Divinity School in Cambridge, Massachusetts. He had been both married and divorced. He was the father of a twenty-year-old son. . . . He had a quiet pastoral manner that created confidence. He also had the ability to calm troubled waters.

"In 1987, in a routine naval reserve physical, he was diagnosed as HIV positive. He died of AIDS on April sixteenth, 1990. He was a homosexual person. His final request to me was direct and intense. 'Bishop, when I die, please tell my congregation that I died of AIDS and that I was a gay male. I want to be honest in my death in a way that I could not ever be honest in my life.' I promised Ray I would be true to that request."

As the bishop paused a wave of realization rolled through the sanctuary. To be sure, most of Ray's colleagues had known the truth about him for several years, but out of deference to a man not yet capable of self-acceptance they had kept it to themselves. Barry had not really known Ray. Their casual diocesan meetings had been strained since the two men lived on opposite ends of the homosexual spectrum, one in, one out. Barry had been asked by a closeted lesbian to be a pallbearer. In fact, several of the pallbearers turned out to be queer, some in and some out of the closet, an eerie metaphor for a conflicted life.

"He did not tell his bishop," Spong continued. "The price was simply too high. The Church has always been willing to receive the gifts of its gay priests, but it has seldom been willing to acknowledge with honesty their presence or to affirm their being. The Church that Ray knew would rather participate in a cruel denial. That denial goes on today. The Church's word to homosexual people is forthright: You cannot be who you are. You must, therefore, pretend to be who you are not. That is the price of survival in this institution."

As the bishop spoke, Barry felt the weight of his fears lift. Spong was making a statement to his diocese not just about the tragedy of one man's hidden life and horrible, lonely death, but about the cost of duplicity. Did this mean there was still hope for his ordination?

"Ordination to the priesthood is only open to those gay and lesbian people who are willing to be dishonest and hide," the bishop continued, casting his eye around the full sanctuary. "If one is honest, then ordination is forbidden, lest the wrath of the disturbed hierarchy descends in rage. Included in that disturbed hierarchy are both gay bishops and bishops who have quietly and secretly ordained 'practicing' homosexual persons. . . .

"My grief for Ray Roberts is on two levels. First I grieve for the human being who was my friend and one of my clergy, whose creative energies were terminated before he had entered the fiftieth year of his life. Secondly, I grieve over the realization that the prejudice and fear in which I, too, have shared killed Ray Roberts long before the moment of his death."

The bishop's eyes sought out Barry and found him staring in wonder and hope. He continued to build his remarks, citing religious prejudices, Christian imperatives for compassion, and scientific revelations that are slowly changing society's understanding of a people that have existed in every culture throughout history. He carefully constructed what sounded like an oral justification for an action he was about to take, preparing his defense ahead of time, a warning shot, as it were, across the Church's bow. Barry felt both his hands being squeezed by friends. His emotions couldn't have been more confusing.

"We commit Ray Roberts to the care and keeping of the God we worship; a God to whom there are supposedly no outcasts and a God to whom none are judged to be unloved. We Christians assert that we see the human face of God in a Christ who reigns with outstretched arms of welcome from a cross to which the cruelty of humanity has nailed him. From that painful throne this Christ issues an invitation. 'Come to me all who travail and are heavy laden. I will give you rest.' It is a scandalous outrage that the Church that claims to be the body of Christ cannot make good the inclusiveness of this invitation. May God grant to Ray Roberts the divine gift of life and peace and may God call this Church of ours out of our blatant hypocrisy and into the honesty of both truth and integrity. Amen." A resounding amen answered his own, grabbed it up, and carried it to the rafters and the heavens beyond. The bishop had not made any promises. But he seemed like a man ready to make them and to do battle. Seeming was good enough for Barry. Hymns of hope swelled in him as the heart of the diocese reclaimed his moral footing.

So difficult, though, harder than hard was it for Barry to carry that coffin out of the church and through the oak doors for burial. If his future as a priest was now ensured by Bishop Spong's resounding courage, then Barry's hope would spring from the soil of this grave. It was not an altogether pleasant thought.

" 'How long, O Lord? Will you forget me forever? How long will you hide your face from me? How long? Must I endure grief in my soul and sorrow in my heart all the day? How long will my enemy be exalted over me?' " Barry recited the ancient psalm as he bore Ray's body out of the church for the last time.

Chapter 22

Holy persons draw to themselves all that is earthly . . .
The earth is at the same time mother,
She is mother of all that is natural,
mother of all that is human.
She is the mother of all,
for contained in her
are the seeds of all.

—*Hildegard of Bingen*

Within six weeks of Bishop Spong's passionate oration at Ray Robert's funeral, a delegation of clergy and lay leaders in the Diocese of
Newark went to New York City to meet with the presiding bishop.
They went expressly to press for Barry's ordination on June 2, 1990,
but also to learn what the mind of the Church might be concerning
the ordination of gay and lesbian candidates. This was a group of
very faithful, thoughtful people who gave, and still give, much time
and prayer to the Church they love. If God had led them to accept

gay and lesbian people, why were they being condemned by the national Church? Why was their bishop being excoriated by his peers? Why, if they proceeded with Barry's ordination, had it been loaded with the language of schism, destruction, and non-collegiality? Could they not find a way, the presiding bishop and this delegation from Newark, to proceed without appearing to split the Church?

The presiding bishop had a tough job holding together the two very passionate camps that had taken sides in the sexuality wars. A good, gentle man, whose inner quiet and faith has the power to renew everyone whom his life touches, Ed Browning prayed for, worked for, pleaded for peace in his Church. And he was humble enough to accept that there was nothing he could do to ensure Barry's ordination without trampling over the canons of the Episcopal Church, something Ed Browning would never do no matter how strongly he felt personally about the cause of justice. This issue would have to work itself out in the democratic processes of the General Convention and House of Bishops. In the meantime he prayed for guidance and for the unity of the church.

The delegation did not get a yes nor did they get a no. They returned from their meeting in New York more uncertain than ever about a seeming turn in the spirit of their Church.

"We have to get out of here," Barry told me the morning of June 1, 1990. Tomorrow Bishop Spong would ordain Barry's class of deacons. Without Barry.

"I can't be here this weekend," Barry went on. "I think if I'm here I'll just explode. I'm so angry." It was written all over his body.

"Call your dad," I suggested, "and see if we can go to the cottage. They should have it open by now." A small, clapboard-sided fishing retreat, it was his family's getaway on Penns Creek in central Pennsylvania.

"It's open, but I'm sure they'll be out there this weekend." Barry's rage was turning inward, becoming the sort of depression where all acts of volition become nearly impossible.

"Well, then, where do you want to go?" It didn't matter to me. He needed to leave; I would go with him. Anywhere.

"Let's go to the beach!" His stormy eyes flashed a brief, bright sunrise just long enough for me to hold, enjoy, and watch it set again. We had no money for a room at the beach, let alone eating out in expensive surfside restaurants.

"I'd love to go to the beach, honey." I took his hand now. "There's nowhere in the world I'd rather be with you."

"I know." The longing to live by the sea cleared the overcast of his heart. He put his arms around my neck. "I'll call Dad and Alice. Maybe they're not using the cottage this weekend."

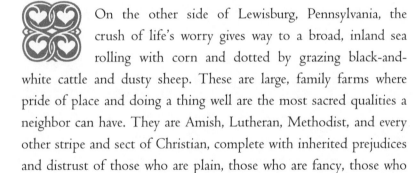 On the other side of Lewisburg, Pennsylvania, the crush of life's worry gives way to a broad, inland sea rolling with corn and dotted by grazing black-and-white cattle and dusty sheep. These are large, family farms where pride of place and doing a thing well are the most sacred qualities a neighbor can have. They are Amish, Lutheran, Methodist, and every other stripe and sect of Christian, complete with inherited prejudices and distrust of those who are plain, those who are fancy, those who are different. The earth and the care of the earth bind them together in the unromantic labor of scratching a living out of the soil.

Just west of Mifflinburg we dropped off the state two-lane onto a narrow, unlined county road, roller-coaster riding through fields of newly planted corn, past white-trimmed red barns and green-trimmed white houses, past Jack's Stud Service, and Sampsell's Barber Shop and Ammunition. It was too early for the weatherbeaten, gray fruit-and-vegetable wagons along the road: Cucumbers four for a dollar, tomatoes ten for a dollar, cantaloupes two for a dollar, and a jar for your money. Honor goes a long way here. God, the air seemed so fresh!

And then we were running right under Penns Creek Mountain, a proud, straight-backed Appalachian mama in the heart of Bald Eagle State Forest, a spitting image of my hometown East River Mountain in West Virginia. I can almost see the outcropping where, loosed from the valley below, I would survey the domain of my childhood and be free of my other names: *sissy, pansy, faggot.* Barry pulled off the side of the road, although it wasn't really necessary. No one was likely to pass this way in anything faster than a tractor.

"Look at that!" He wasn't pointing at anything, just hunkering over the steering wheel and looking out. Two hills over, the cows picked so slowly through their field they seemed painted in the high, morning light. "I tell you I could just sit right here all day and look at that." And he could, too. I watched him watching his beloved valley, his taut facial muscles visibly easing, his shoulders relaxing. "Oh, to be able to breathe like this! To live like this, right next to these silos, even. That would be a life." For the first time in months he was happy. I breathed deep myself, with a sense of relief.

"What, you gonna milk cows now?" I teased him.

"I know how to milk a cow! Do you?" He poked at me and noticed my eyes. "What's the matter?"

"Nothing," I hedged before going on. "You're happy. It makes me happy to see you like this. That's all." He reached over the seat and drew me into a kiss and snuggle.

"Yee-haw!" An old Dodge screamed by, honking and waving, scaring the bejesus out of us. When his heart popped back down from his throat, Barry started laughing.

"You think they saw us?"

"Of course they saw us!"

"I mean, do you think they saw us kissing?" He was getting himself worked up.

"Hell, no!"

"How can you be so sure?"

"We'd aheard something besides 'yee-haw'! Maybe a gun." We collected our scattered wits and pushed on to the cottage.

It's nothing fancy: an old twenty-by-thirty frame fishing cabin that has been prettied up over the years, in between floods. It sits at the end of a long, sloping farm looking south across Penns Creek, so close to the mountain it's nearly noon before the sun breaks through the willow, oak, and black-walnut canopy.

"Hey, there! Welcome to the cabin!" Marlin Stopfel waved at us through the smoky haze of a trash fire.

"Hey, Dad!"

"Hi, Marlin," I greeted him. Hugs all around.

"Alice is inside fixin' lunch," Marlin said. "Just thought I'd clear up some trash and brush before we take off."

"Hi, there!" Alice called from the screened-in front porch. Alice Hoover was widowed a little before Carolyn Stopfel died. She, her husband, Bill, Marlin, and Carolyn had all raised their children in the same church, Alice even serving as one of the advisors to Barry's youth group many years before. About a year after Carolyn's death, their pastor suggested that Marlin get together with Alice for fellowship and support, since she was going through the same pains of loss and adjustment to single life. Three years later, feeling no need to rush in, they married quietly in the church that had seen them through every day of their lives for over fifty years.

"It's nothin' much," Alice apologized as we climbed the steps. "Just some store-bought barbecue. Beans and slaw."

"Sounds great to me," I said, hugging her.

"Oh, and I made your cake, Will."

"Not your coconut cake?"

"Yes," she smiled delicately, pleased I remembered. "But I only brought half, it's so big. Hope you don't mind?"

"Oh, Alice, that's gracious plenty. Thanks!"

The first time Barry took me to Hummelstown to meet his dad

and Alice and his brother, Butch, Alice had laid out a spread of rich, home cooking and hospitality.

"Can you believe this?" Barry whispered in my ear while Alice bustled platters and bowls onto the table.

"It looks great! I'm gonna die. Right here."

"You might! So be careful," he said, reminding me of my ultra-sensitive digestive system. "Don't make yourself sick," he was still whispering. "We're all nervous and I know you. You'll eat more than you want, just to be nice."

As Alice passed plates around the table she anxiously described each dish to me, worried I would turn my citified nose up at her Pennsylvania country cooking.

"Those are pickled eggs. You might not like those."

"I love them!" It was true.

"I like my sweet potatoes sweet. Hope they're not too sweet for you."

"Too sweet for me? Hardly!"

Ham and turkey and filling and gravy and eggs and salads and peas passed around and around the table. About ten minutes after Barry and Butch and Marlin finished eating, I shoved back from the table and groaned with the rest of them.

"Well," Alice chuckled, "you sure can eat. It's nice." Barry stared at me like I had lost my mind. But I know a home-cooked meal for a new in-law, straight or gay, is really a test of character, especially in small towns, where riches from the larder are the great gifts of hospitality. It had been an easy test; I hadn't eaten food like that in years.

"You'll be sorry!" Barry mouthed at me. He knew what was coming but didn't give me fair warning.

"Dessert?" Alice trilled as she brought out a mile-high cake, white frosted and slathered in fresh coconut. We were all struggling unsuccessfully to keep from sliding out of our chairs (it's just common politeness not to collapse at the table). The Stopfel men begged off, swearing they would have some later.

"Will?" Alice looked to me, offering the final exam.

"I'd love a piece!"

I was about to burst but was not about to fail now. Fussing that her husband and his sons didn't know what was good, Alice set a towering slab down in front of me. Barry and Butch laughed so hard they nearly choked. Marlin just sat back, lit a cigarette, and watched. If I had spotted this wonderful cake before dinner, I would have refused that third round of butter rolls. It would have left a little more room for my *second* slice.

I passed the test. I was part of the family.

It is a family where intimacy grows slowly. While some of that hesitancy comes out of a natural respect for other people's privacy, mostly they just didn't know how to talk about our kind of life. They didn't know other gay people; gay people weren't talked about with their friends or at church. So we left a lot of words unspoken during lunch at the cottage. That was fine. Their love for us was obvious in their quiet respect rooted deep in the soil of their Christian faith; I will take that over words any day. We had heard a lot of sweet words and sermons over the past few weeks. Being fed and nurtured at the cabin was a welcome change.

"It's a terrible tragedy," Marlin told him between bites of barbecue, expressing in few words the whole of his feelings for his son.

"I'm praying for you every day, Barry," Alice told her stepson. Even though we didn't talk much about our personal lives, Alice knew Barry's heart was broken. But the language of faith and hospitality are universal. She baked us her best cake.

After they headed back home, we knew we needed something besides coconut cake to eat, so we rambled over Jacks Mountain to Walnut Acres and stocked up on grains, organic vegetables, and maple syrup for tomorrow morning's pancakes. As long as we were there, we decided to drop into Penn's Creek Pottery.

Barry guided the car down a gravel track and pulled up beneath a hulking, four-story mill that had been converted into a potter's workshop and store. We had gone there many times, had never bought anything, and probably wouldn't this time either. Beautiful as it was, even a mug was beyond our budget. But we loved to look.

"Howdy," a mountain of a man covered in gray, clay-coated coveralls drawled behind the wheel where he was throwing a pot. "Y'all just help yourselves. Look around."

"Thanks," we answered in our deepest, manliest voices and moved quickly in opposite directions. We had some trouble getting through the heavy, counterweighted barn door on our way in and, I guess subconsciously, didn't want to seem too much like pansies. Sure, this guy threw pots. But he was big, and this was Pennsylvania.

"Can I help you with anything?"

I nearly jumped out of my skin. He was right behind me.

"You always sneak up on your customers?" I covered my fright.

"Yeah," he chuckled, tilting his head to one side, an incongruous, gentle pose for a burly man so light on his feet. "That way they drop things and have to pay for 'em." Barry caught the humor first and started laughing.

"You've been in here before, haven't you?" he asked.

"Yes, we have," Barry answered. They looked at each other over an array of brilliant blue and purple and brown glazed pots. "But we've never been able to buy anything," he admitted, answering the unasked question.

"Well, that's all right," the potter smiled, "you keep coming back! I'm Bill Lynch."

"You're the potter." I blurted out the obvious, breaking my death grip on a forty-dollar bowl we couldn't afford to break. "These are beautiful! I love your work."

"So do I," Barry echoed genuinely. "The weight, the colors. They're so rich."

"Well, why don't ya buy one, then?" Bill Lynch twinkled a smile at us, hands on his hips. This guy was definitely punching all my

Southern do-the-right-thing buttons. He engaged us in conversation, making this a personal, rather than a business, transaction; made us laugh, upping the ante; and went for the jugular once he knew we were hooked on his product.

"You're a good salesman." I laughed.

"Well, not all that good." He sighed and ambled back to his wheel. "I get to thinking if I was all that good at selling it, this place'd be finished," he said, sweeping his arm around the great, timbered workroom. "Some things would finally get fixed down at the house. You know," he laughed easily, "we might even have a car that ran most of the time." He didn't seem real bothered about the car, or anything, for that matter, and went on. "We do all right, considering. Anyway, those are just things."

And so he drew Barry and me into a conversation about money and values and ethics. Soon we were telling parts of our histories to each other. He had met his wife in the Peace Corps in Africa. She was a teacher, so we talked about education in America, and politics, and National Public Radio. Man, can first impressions miss the boat!

An hour later, a tall, graceful woman banged her way hips-first through the door.

"This is my wife. Sharon, meet Barry and Will."

"Hello!" She was easily cheerful, but eyed the unfinished pot on the wheel and silently counted the drying rack behind him. He had been talking all afternoon.

"Honey, Will went to school in Chattanooga."

"Chattanooga? UTC?"

"No, I was in prep school there."

"Baylor or McCallie?"

"McCallie."

"Oh, well," she rolled her eyes, "*I* never dated a McCallie boy!" the clear inference being she never met one she liked either. But common geography is thicker than prejudice. We rattled on about ridges, lakes, and battlefields of our youth.

"Why don't y'all come to dinner tonight?" Sharon asked. We hedged. But being from the South she saw through the politeness of our refusal. "Come. We're having some friends over I think you'd like to meet."

"Well . . ." I started an excuse.

"We'd love to," Barry jumped right in, ever impatient with my two-stepping. "What can we bring?"

For nearly six hours we talked with their two not quite teenage kids, Ben and Emily; friends from Ghana, where Bill and Sharon met in the Peace Corps, and two neighbors. We covered international monetary policy toward so-called developing nations, the mean-spirited turn politics was taking in this country, and, inevitably, the failure of Christian churches to provide leadership on issues of hunger, housing, and homosexuality. Coming out to them just flowed right out of the conversation (like they couldn't tell!). Barry explained why we were at the cottage this weekend.

"You're not being *ordained?* And that's tomorrow?" Sharon was appalled. "Why? What happened?"

"It's kind of a long story."

"I want to hear it," Ben declared.

"Me, too!" Emily echoed her older brother. Having been raised without the dulling influence of television, Ben and Emily were as lively, thoughtful, and opinionated as their parents. I envied their upbringing. They were nearly as comfortable with the subject of homosexuality as they were with politics and macroeconomics. I found myself grinning at Bill and Sharon: hippies in the sixties, parents in the nineties. What a gift!

"I was out in my ordination process," Barry began slowly. "I have to admit, I wasn't planning on being as out as I was. The Episcopal Church is not exactly straightforward about queers in the clergy."

Ben laughed. His mother shot him a look. "What?" He shrugged.
"I just never heard anybody call himself a . . . you know . . ."

"A queer?" I prompted him. "It's okay. You can say it. We like
the word."

"Right. I never heard anybody call himself a queer before. It's
funny." His adolescent honesty cleared the last taboo on politically
correct language for the evening. Everybody laughed with him and
settled back to listen.

Once Barry finished, with hardly an interruption, eight people
stared back at him. "But why did this happen?" Emily asked, still
trying to grasp the complexities of the story.

"Because he told the truth," Ben answered for Barry. "And since
he told the truth he's being kicked out. Right?" With one sentence
he reduced our experience to its essence.

Everyone sat in the silence for a long time, allowing the pain to
soak down to the earth. Slowly Tina Okyere, a strong, Christian
woman from Ghana who had struggled against her people's cultural
genocide at the hands of Christian missionaries, asked, "How do the
other people feel? I mean, the other people being ordained. How
could they go ahead and be ordained if you're not? Especially the
other gay woman." She knew the value of community. Her experience in Ghana was that people with the same struggle stand together. It was the only way to triumph over oppression.

Barry shrugged. How can we ever know the reasons people do
what they do? He looked around at our new friends, his heart full.
The microscopic scrutiny of his ministry, his powerlessness in the
face of church politics he didn't understand, and the relentless on
again-off again emotional roller-coaster ride from February through
June had worn him to the bone. This weekend his faith was on the
verge of collapsing.

But here, deep into the night in an old farm kitchen beneath a
mill set by the side of Penns Creek, strangers gave him a drink of

living water—they fed, listened to, and comforted a man they had never met before. Through the hospitality of strangers with compassion enough to revitalize our own, we were powerless no more.

"Barry," Tina stood and approached him, "we have just met, but I feel you are a brother. May I embrace you?" So saying, she gathered him up into her powerful arms, arms that had brought irrigation to her people, carried their children to health, and taught them to read. She held him close.

After a minute they broke. "Thank you," he said, smiling.

"Thank *you*," Tina Okyere bowed. "It is an honor to give and receive strength from a courageous man."

When we woke the next morning the sun was glittering on Penns Creek.

"Come on!" I called. "We're gonna be burning up on the trail!"

"No, we're not, silly," Barry insisted. "We're going to be in the woods!"

We got over Penns Creek Mountain and headed off on Bull Hollow Trail, hiking between Little and Thick mountains, brushing through thick stands of mountain laurel just opening their pink-lined white faces, catching a peek now and then of Jacks Mountain rising another thousand feet out of pine and oak forests. Jacks Mountain would wait another day; Barry had climbed enough mountains for one spring, had negotiated enough "Jacks." We were looking for a spring of fresh water when Barry whispered, "Oh my God! Look over there!"

I froze, hoping for white-tailed deer or bear.

"Oh my God," I whispered back at him, aware there was nothing else to say. Set below us was a fragrant, humid valley of ancient, old-growth pine and hardwood trees, their trunks so big around that the two of us wrapping our arms around them, reaching for each other, could barely touch each other's fingertips; so tall their tops disappeared beyond the shorter, younger oak and hickory surrounding them. As we walked, the spongy, damp floor intoxicated us with its scent of pine and earth and a constant, mysterious sweetness from some unknown forest flowers. Soon, we were too overwhelmed to speak even the one word we had been saying over and over for the last half hour: *Look!*

"You know what's happening right now?" Barry asked.

"I do. God is revealing herself," I said. "We should take off our boots, you know."

Barry reached for my hand. "I love you," he said. "I love how you keep me in touch with what's really going on." He kissed my hand, nestled it between us, and grew quiet.

"What's wrong?"

"I just remembered that right about now Jack Spong is laying hands on those people and ordaining them as deacons in the Church."

"And you see, my precious lover, who's laying her hands on you, on us, in this holiest of holies, this temple of tall timbers."

On the banks of a small run coursing through the cathedral of trees we took off our boots and socks, filled our thermos, and soaked our feet in the biting water. On rocks covered in moss as thick as an eiderdown comforter Barry stretched out.

"Listen," he whispered, his ear pressed deep.

Putting my head down next to his I felt, more than heard, an arrhythmic burbling up from the hollows of the earth. "It's the earth spirits singing," I whispered.

"Or the water spirits." Barry grinned. Too long we had sojourned among concrete and steel, living as immigrants in a country whose rhythms no longer delighted, no longer nurtured with their incessant, mechanical repetition.

Water was running every which way under our heads, tapping stones of every size and shape together, floating them up, then dropping them down, rushing up from untapped wells and down from melting snowdrifts. Eyes closed, we listened to all the rivers of the world chattering beneath us, racing one another to the sea, to the sun, to the clouds, and back again. We listened, rocked by the water beneath us, until we slept.

Chapter 23

Sometimes I feel discouraged,
And think my work's in vain,
But then the Holy Spirit
Revives my soul again.
There is a balm in Gilead,
To make the wounded whole;
There is a balm in Gilead,
To heal the sin-sick soul.

—AFRICAN-AMERICAN SPIRITUAL

Up to the last minute Bishop Spong was working on how he might ordain Barry to the diaconate. Priests, bishops, and church administrators from all over the country were consulted. Barry was not. He had no idea what was being said to whom and by whom, didn't know the diocese's spin to the press, didn't know what to say to all the reporters who called for the two weeks this little tempest played itself out in the press. (Who leaked the story? Nobody knows.)

Taking a cue from Robert Williams's unsuccessful foray in the media spotlight, Barry simply refused to speak to the press. His life was being decided by others who didn't see a need to consult with him about their decisions. Angry over his powerlessness, terrified that his speaking out might encourage a media circus, Barry had taken me to the cabin.

When we got back from Penns Creek the phone machine was overloaded with messages. Bishop Walter Righter, assisting Bishop Spong, preached at the diaconal ordination service and spoke at length about the one person not there, canonizing his absence, as it were. The diocese was abuzz with his sermon.

"I have watched painfully the agonizing that has been done by Barry Stopfel, by his rector, by the bishop [Spong], and by the various committees. For the sake of the Church, in the hope that the inclusive nature of this Church may mature and grow, in deference to a request by the presiding bishop, but in the knowledge that the presiding bishop will speak in support of the ordination of gay and lesbian persons, Barry Stopfel has decided not to present himself for ordination and the bishop has decided not to ordain him."

No one in the halls of power ever asked us why all this came to pass as it did; many of them knew full well that a closeted lesbian was seated in the sanctuary, listening to Bishop Righter's words, waiting to be ordained that day. But secrecy is the key here. Deception, or the ability to manipulate the system to achieve one's goals, is considered a hallmark of character in many corporate institutions, the mark of a survivor, a winner, a player. Religious institutions have embraced only the larger culture's perverse form of social Darwinism by encouraging people to believe the race is to the swift. But the institutional myth, with its costly, nearly narcotic hold over the human mind, is that everybody is *in* the race. We are not.

Some run in the race for a while, as Barry did, gaining real insight into the lives of those men and women who daily come through his door. Some eventually stop, take a look at the ground beneath them, seeing the life which is a gift rather than a goal, and self-consciously step out of the race for frayed ends of insignificant grandeur. Of these, some choose to pass water bottles to the runners and bandage the bites from other nipping dogs.

Barry knew there was no game to be played for his ordination, no race to be run. Once he had left the race by refusing to compromise himself, his faith took over his fear. He never saw the priesthood as a glittering prize to be won. He felt an urging, a drawing toward a kind of work that grew out of his whole life. Faithfulness to the call within, not the prize, was what God was asking of him.

So the runners were calling the race, setting the course, declaring the victor. All fine. The more gentle folk journeyed a different route.

"Dear Bishop Spong," the priest's letter began,

> This last week Louie Crew told me of his decision to undertake a eucharistic fast until such time as all the sacraments of the Church are available to all persons without regard to sexual orientation. This morning, at the altar in St. Thomas' Church, I felt compelled to join him in that fast. . . . I will continue to faithfully administer the sacraments at St. Thomas' without regard to race, gender, nationality, sexual orientation or any other barrier that the Church might adopt out of fear or prejudice. Please pray for me that I may have the strength to carry on without the nourishment of the Eucharist. I remain your faithful presbyter, Norman J. Mol.

Louie Crew, that indefatigable founder of the gay/lesbian advocacy organization in the Episcopal Church, Integrity, board member of Oasis, and champion of gay rights in the Episcopal Church, protested Barry's nonordination with a small, personal sacrifice that was mushrooming through the entire Diocese of Newark. Others, mostly laypeople, joined the silent witness to injustice, and made certain their bishop knew about it.

"Dear Bishop Spong," Tim Croneberger wrote, "Hypocrisy is

something that has always confused me. The ability to believe one thing and say another; or in some cases, to gain recognition for one set of beliefs, and then prove through your actions that those same beliefs are not your own; I think that is the true essence of hypocrisy." Tim, Jack Croneberger's gay son, felt compelled to cover his letter with a disclaimer that the letter was written to his bishop, not his father's boss, and that the thoughts and opinions were his own, not his father's. Jack Spong had been a close, influential friend to Tim as a young man. The betrayal Tim experienced was deep and visceral.

"Unlike so many others you have already ordained," his letter continued, "Barry Stopfel has chosen *not* to live the life of a hypocrite. As a servant of God, he has chosen to be open about his sexuality. Undeniably, those who preach from the closet are scarcely heard, and to punish those who have opened their doors is unforgivable. Today, in the Episcopal Church, the dreaded disease of hypocrisy runs rampant, and you, Bishop Spong, are an infectious carrier. Signed, Timothy J. Croneberger."

Jack knew how bad his decision looked to his friends; Tim's gut response to him was the price he felt he had to pay in order to secure a future for gay and lesbian people in the Church. Barry knew full well the pain Jack was going through. It is a terribly lonely place to stand, out on the ramparts of social and religious change. No matter how one gets there, whether by our own or another's volition, the right and wrong of our actions must be weighed by our faith in God and tested in the crucible of our communities of accountability.

Dear Barry: On behalf of the Newark Clergy Association I write to express our solidarity with you during this time of trial. That you were not ordained on June 2 was a great disappointment to us. . . . We are mindful of your pain and frustration, and we grieve that the church is being deprived of the full expression of your ministry. We affirm your ministry and look forward to the day when we can celebrate your ordination with you. . . . Thank you for calling us into this ministry of reconciliation, and for the integrity with which you and Will have lived and ministered during this difficult time. God bless you both, The Rev. Elizabeth Wigg Maxwell.

The support of his community encouraged Barry for many days and nights. But the community anger toward his bishop worried him. Without the same support Barry was getting, would our great advocate in the Episcopal Church be able to withstand the attacks of his adversaries?

 Jack Croneberger was hopping mad. He had worked very hard and very well to bring a conservative, upper-middle-class, suburban congregation along in support of a gay man for ordination. Yes, he understood the reasonings behind his bishop's decision, but he still had to deal with the intolerant few who took the bishop's action as an affirmation of their own opinions. Jack believed Barry needed to know that this congregation, and the entire Diocese of Newark, stood with him on his journey toward ordination and so planned and publicized a Service of Affirmation for the Ministry of Barry Stopfel.

A half an hour before the service was to begin, the stone and timber suburban church was jammed with folks milling about, sharing stories about Barry, keeping up a cheerful din until, with a triumphant processional, the organist blasted them to their seats.

As we entered the sanctuary and stepped down the aisle with the other participants that late June night in 1990, I took Barry's arm. It was a jubilant, noisy, happy crowd, and wave after wave of their strength and faith washed over us. We have never done a Blessing of Union for our relationship, but that warm night, as we processed through the church, we never felt more united in our loving, or more supported for it. I could hardly hold back my tears as people clapped us forward, reaching out to touch Barry or me, slap him on the back, grinning in delight just to be part of a moment in time where the celebration was not for a victory, but for love. Barry was terribly uncomfortable being the center of attention like that. Me, I liked watching him blush.

Usually jovial and easygoing, preferring to speak in a freewheeling, improvisational style, the Reverend Jack Croneberger carefully set a prepared text on the lectern and braced himself against the sides of the pulpit, as if the words he was about to speak might carry him away if he didn't hang on tight.

"This is called 'Speaking the Truth About Doing the Truth.'" He began his remarks for the evening as he began all his sermons, gently pulling people along with him through humorous anecdotes. Swiftly he grounded himself in a text from the Psalms using the great Anglican authority of Scripture, Tradition, and Reason. We were rapt: a man who rarely challenged his congregation to think deeper than a Robert Fulghum story was about to share with us the base, source, and power of his faith. I understood then that he was hanging on to the pulpit not to keep from flying, but to draw courage from the symbol of his teaching office.

"My task this evening is to place on the table a piece of life that we have come to call homosexuality, in order that we might openly look at it, and—if Brian McNaught is right, that ignorance is the parent of fear, and fear the parent of hatred—we might just take another step toward that kinder, gentler world I keep hearing about. Or maybe get a better glimpse of the peaceable kingdom."

With great humor and scholarly support he smartly dispatched those Hebrew Scripture passages commonly used to bludgeon homosexuals.

"Can the Sodom and Gomorrah story really make a convincing case against homosexuality, while at the same time approve the offering of virgin daughters to satisfy an angry mob for what, today, we might call gang rape?

"Or the Leviticus account of the Holiness Code. Yes, male homosexual behavior is condemned, but the code also disqualifies those who are blind, or lame, or hunchback, or dwarves. The code demands execution for cursing, and prohibits the eating of lobster or New England clam chowder or pork chops. On what basis do we determine the parts of the Holiness Code which are from God and for all time, and the parts that might no longer be useful?" He had taken his congregation smartly through the few texts by way of twentieth-century reason. We were all with him, but in our case, he was preaching to the choir.

"In the New Testament Jesus says nothing about homosexuality, not a reference in all four Gospels, and nothing in Acts. That leaves the epistles from Paul and others, and especially the ones to the Romans and Corinthians." I felt, more than heard, Barry groan. Jack rolled on.

"There's no mystery here; Paul is definitely opposed to homosexual behavior. But this is the same Paul who apparently never married, didn't relate very well to women in general, and clearly saw women as subservient. You know, the keep your head covered, be quiet, ask your husband when you get home stuff." The congregation's chuckling grew with each culture-bound allusion.

"This is the same Paul who was somewhat anti-Semitic and urged men and women not to marry unless it was absolutely necessary. On what basis do we believe that the Church has rightly transcended most of Paul's teaching about sex, marriage, and women, but by golly, Paul must have been absolutely right about homosexuality?" The whole house agreed with him in a shout of laughter, no mean feat in an Episcopal Church. And then he capped it off.

"In the context of all Scripture, there is a cry for justice and equality, for the goodness of all of God's creation and the invitation to come before our God just as we are . . . having been made worthy, not by our acts, but by the saving act of Jesus Christ." The truth of our religion settled over us, preparing our jubilant hearts to hear the truth we are called to live by.

Jack explained how, in the 1970s, he had armed himself with erroneous teachings about homosexuality (there was plenty to draw from back then). "I went off to General Convention as a delegate, voted to affirm the legal rights of homosexuals, to study homosexuality (that's always safe), but not to recommend ordination. That's simply where I was in 1979."

Suddenly his rhythm changed. He began speaking in parenthesis, halting before prepositions, and dropping his voice. I knew he was getting into unfamiliar territory.

"And then one day in 1984 the world seemed to become one sharp stick that poked me right in the eye. Our son, Tim, then eighteen, quietly decided he wasn't needed anymore, left a suicide note in his room, and set out to carry out those plans. As life sometimes has it, the son came home and we three, father, mother, and son, cried and talked and hugged and cried again, and went for help." He had never told this story in public before tonight. I held on to Barry, knowing what was coming.

"In the midst of all of that, Tim found the courage to tell his parents that he is gay. And for him, at the time, the suicide attempt was really the only visible way he could see to resolve the conflict of his own sexuality. We loved him the day before he told us," Jack's voice began to falter, "we loved him the night he told us. And," he stopped, cleared his throat, and took a deep breath, "we loved him the day after he told us. And every day since." If Jack wasn't crying, he was the only one who wasn't. "You see," he ended his story about his son, "there's *plenty of room* to be inclusive, and *no time* to be exclusive." The Cronebergers had been given another chance; thousands of other families weren't so fortunate.

"Oh, it was marvelous!" Shirley Redfield beamed up at me after the service. We were standing in the gymnasium, crowded with folks bellying up to a feast of cookies. I, of course, was eating one of Bea and Marie's confections.

"It's the best sermon I ever heard Jack Croneberger give!" Shirley said, taking my arm and bending me closer to her so she could whisper above the celebration. "I never knew that about Tim! A beautiful story."

It was a cathartic coming out for Jack and his family. Coming out does that. Coming out isn't just something gay people have to do. Coming out is the task of showing ourselves as honestly to the world as we can so that we might get on with the business of living and transformation.

Lives were changed that night. People who had never thought about homosexuality and people who thought negatively about it found themselves embracing the call of Christ and loving one another as he loved us.

"Dear Barry," a colleague at Cathedral House wrote the next day,

What can we say? After Tuesday night, probably of the seven candidates for ordination you are the one who is most assured of your calling, for you have been stunningly affirmed. I was especially delighted by the elderly women who were sitting just in front of us. You are certainly a very important person in their lives. . . .

Despite the absence of Episcopal hands on your head, it seems to me that your people regard you as a fully endowed minister of the gospel. So, my friend, just go about the business of doing the work that is yours and mine. I rejoice in our companionship along the way. Denise Haines

Denise was right: Now Barry just had to be about the task of ministry. Hands or no hands.

Chapter 24

I am grateful to you for your willingness to be the symbol, first of the church's homophobia and second, of the church's hope. It is not an easy witness that you have been forced to make but you have done it with both dignity and integrity. May God bless you and the ministry to which you are so clearly called.

—*The Right Reverend John S. Spong,*
LETTER TO BARRY STOPFEL, SEPTEMBER 25, 1990

In September of 1990, the House of Bishops met for their annual meeting in the humid Potomac River basin of Washington, D.C. The air pulled at the spirits of this august assembly of men and women for whom the Church itself had become their ministry—a rigorous calling for which a high level of skill in the arts of diplomatic persuasion and human compassion are necessary.

Long before the first day of the meeting, both sides of the move to disassociate the House from Jack Spong's ordination of Robert Williams were intensely lobbying for votes, both working late to do good for the Church. Good can be difficult and heart wrenching to discern—particularly for men and women who believe that the most acceptable service of God is doing good for others—for there is no good which does not come at a price. Each bishop struggled to answer the question of cost, both to themselves and to the Church at large. For many, it was just as difficult to cross over and listen to the opposing side as it is for the rest of us.

The vote for Jack Spong's disassociation was called for and taken as soon as the opposition had a majority. With a margin of four bishops against him, Jack Spong asked the presiding bishop for permission to address the House immediately after the vote was taken.

As a "disassociated" member he spoke eloquently about the history, theology, and practice of the Episcopal Church concerning nearly every social issue it had debated throughout its history.

"I wonder," Bishop Spong said, well into his lengthy address, "if this House can embrace the fact that other bishops besides Episcopal Synod bishops have a conscience that cannot be compromised?" He was referring to an informal association of Episcopal bishops, vehemently opposed to the ordination of gay and lesbian people, who still refused to ordain women, thereby breaking canon law since 1976.

"The way the church treats its gay and lesbian members," he continued his address, "so deeply violates my conscience that it strains the very fabric of my life by tearing it between my loyalty to Jesus Christ, who made a habit of embracing the outcast, and my loyalty to a Church that historically has rejected blacks, women, and gays, in succession . . .

"The Episcopal Synod members say the canons opening the ordination process to women are permissive, not binding. But many of the bishops of the Synod have argued that the 1979 resolution on human sexuality, which *was* recommendatory and not prescriptive, was, in fact, binding. Permissive canons and binding resolutions? My sisters and brothers, only great fear and prejudice would enable us to talk that way without laughing at ourselves."

Church canons become binding law in the Episcopal Church once they are passed by both the House of Bishops and the House of Deputies at the triennial General Convention. Once canon law, a bishop ignores them at the threat of heresy and dismissal from office. Resolutions may be passed by either the House of Bishops or the entire General Convention, and serve as channel markers on the Church's voyage through many and varied issues in its life. They are nonbinding. A resolution is a statement of the majority's opinion on a particular issue at a particular moment in time and are always accompanied by statements of conscience in opposition to the majority. This structure has allowed the Church to debate and record its progress, for decades, if necessary, until it can come to a clear, single mind about an issue, like the ordination of women. If the day came when resolutions of General Convention were de facto canon law, then the whole constitutional process in the Episcopal Church would be controverted, wagged by the proverbial tail. As Jack drew to the close of his address, his remarks grew personal. He put a human face on Barry, the layman whose ministry the House of Bishops had just subverted.

"We, in the Diocese of Newark, have been shocked and amazed at the response of hatred and condemnation that has marked some parts of the Church. But I have also been blessed. The great gift that many of you have given to me is the clear realization, and experience, of the hostility and prejudice that are the daily bread of gay and lesbian people in both our homophobic society and our homophobic Church. I have felt their pain as never before by bearing your homophobia. It has been a rare privilege for which I will be eternally grateful. I will never be the same. Our goal in Newark is to do ministry in Christ's name to those who are victims of human prejudice. We resent being the victims of your hypocrisy."

Many were moved by Jack Spong's righteous rage, some even admitting as much. That evening, six men approached him individually, each of them apologizing, explaining that if they had heard him speak before the vote was called, they would never have voted against him. Two of those bishops, both married, came out to him as gay men. One voted in his favor. The one who voted against him had tears in his eyes and said he couldn't afford to be "soft" on the issue; being publicly opposed to gay issues was his only defense against exposure. Two men, among too many, living lies to themselves, their families, their Church, their God. Every day a broken promise to someone. It exacts a horrible toll.

Overnight the vote against him turned into a majority behind him. He had won, no matter what the record stated. Jack Spong returned to Newark in triumph, committed to proceeding with Barry's ordination, the only such ordination ever openly debated on the floor of the House of Bishops in the Episcopal Church.

Dear Barry,

"As you are aware, the House of Bishops decided by an 80 to 76 vote, with two abstentions [one being Spong's], to affirm as a body the action taken by the presiding bishop and his Council of Advice last February. That action was to disassociate themselves from the decision of the bishop and Standing Committee in the Diocese of Newark to ordain an openly gay male [Robert Williams]. . . .

"I am grateful to you for your patience during this long process. . . . However, I am now aware of the ordination and reception of at least four other gay/lesbian persons in the United States, by bishops who knew that these persons were non-celibate. It is intolerable to me that the Diocese of Newark be held to a standard that other dioceses and other bishops do not hold."

Barry raced home from church and gave me the bishop's letter of affirmation. I was speed reading my way through it.

" 'Intolerable' is an awfully pleasant word to use, don't you think?"

Barry laughed. "Yes, it's an interesting choice, given the hell they've put him through. Finish the letter!" he said, shoving it back under my face.

"For this reason," I read outloud, "I will no longer prevent your diaconal ordination."

I jumped up and down, hugging him. "Finish it!" He shoved me down in a chair.

> There are those who believe that I am forbidden by the House of Bishops' action to proceed with your ordination. So as not to complicate your ordination with the presence of those negative pressures, I will not be the ordaining bishop. But neither will I forbid another bishop who is willing to stand beside you and me in this fight, from proceeding immediately to make you a Deacon. . . . As the last price that this deeply prejudiced church will exact from me on this issue, I will stand aside in order that your ordained ministry may be established in this church.

"Who? Who? Who?" I gasped at Barry.

"Walter Righter, of course!" Barry was grinning for the first time in months. "Walter Righter is going to ordain me a deacon." His delight bubbled up, knowing as he did that his gentle mentor, companion, and friend through these months of torture would be laying hands on him and investing him as an ordained clergyman.

"When?" My own joy had reduced me to one-syllable sentences, a novelty.

"Next Sunday night!"

"Why so fast?" I was thunderstruck. What kind of celebration could we pull together in ten days?

"I think the bishop wants to avoid any press, if that's possible— lots of people already know this is happening. By acting quickly he doesn't give his enemies a chance to mount a counteroffensive in the news media. Anyway, he'll be in Belvidere, I think, for a confirmation service. It'll throw people off our trail."

"But, honey," I wailed, "it's your ordination! Your family should be here, all of them. It should be a *huge* celebration! We won't have time to do it right."

"All that doesn't matter." On top of everything else he had to deal with, he had to comfort me. "We'll have a big party when I become a priest."

Barry took my face in his hands, the way he does when he is being very serious with me. "The people who need to be here will be here. I believe that, and I know you believe that. Anyway, I've already told Bea and Marie Branfuhr, so we know there'll be a ton of food at the reception."

I dropped my eyes and then confessed my real hurt. "It's just that I won't get to do anything special for you."

"Oh, Will." He gathered me in his arms, rocked me, and for the first time in ages we wept for joy.

Chapter 25

Jesus calls us; o'er the tumult
of our life's wild, restless sea,
day by day his clear voice soundeth,
saying, "Christian, follow me!"

—*Cecil Frances Alexander*

"I need a hug."

"Barry," I pulled my cake out of the oven, balancing it in one hand while I fought with terminally snarled wire racks, "I'm a little busy." *Company coming for dinner after the ordination and he needs a hug. Honestly!*

"I still need a hug." He sneaked up and tickled me, hard. "And you're going to give me one. Now!" No fool, he waited until my Southern rum-soaked cake was safely on the rack.

For the last ten days we found ourselves often holding each other—really, I guess, holding *on to* each other—as preparation for the ordination swept us along. In bed each night for months now, the shadows of doubt, both physical and spiritual, closed around us, isolating us farther from each other. Eventually we couldn't even ask each other for little things, like a back rub. We weren't doing a very good job of keeping the public issues about our life separate from our private life. But for the past ten days Barry's new hope released a new joy in our life together. I was as happy with him as I was *for* him. I set that cake down and hugged him right back. (To the victor go the spoils.)

 In late September the sharp, evening air of Tenafly is warmed by pungent mountains of rotting leaves. Standing over one of the fuming piles, for the first time in ages Barry contemplated the riches he had been given. For reasons he still couldn't fathom, he knew God had put a hand on his shoulder and led him into a vocation of service. He could have taught, counseled, healed, any number of things, but no: God had unambiguously prodded him into serving within the Christian community of church.

How strange, he thought as he looked down the hill at his storybook church, with its gabled roof and jewellike windows. I never, ever thought the journey would be like this. Be careful what you wish for, he imagined his dear friend and compatriot, Mark Polo, whispering in his ear. Sure enough, he had gotten what he wished for, but at such a cost.

He thought of the many people who believed in his ministry, counting noses within his circle at Atonement. It was humbling. In his distraction over events, Barry had nearly forgotten about these, the ones who stood by him, with him, feeding him, pouring forth a bounty of affirmation. Understandable, considering.

Yes, Barry confessed, knowing God was listening, he had become infected with hate over and over again for the past many months. But he had tried to live through it with faith, had never once spoken demeaning words about his enemies' viewpoint, never once trafficked in inflammatory rhetoric (except with his family and closest friends!). Instead he had kept silent, letting the Church call itself names, letting it accuse itself where it needed to be accused, choosing not to return hate for hate.

It is grueling work. Barry carried within him the same internal impulse to get even as most of us do. To live by faith meant that he had to trust that something, someone, God would take care of any justice which needed meting out. And when God was not quickly forthcoming, for God inevitably moves in a rhythm counter to our own, Barry had to work hard to temper his anger and the impulse for revenge. One of the more difficult aspects of living one's faith is the hourly discipline of the soul to make more space for God. As that space increases in our hearts, people of faith in all times and all places have found that God fills it with the courage and strength to obey Jesus' great commandment: Love.

Eventually the impulse to reconcile overcame the impulse to get even. How? Why? It's a mystery, and is still a mystery to Barry. But that is the nature of God. Only after we have journeyed down the road in front of us can we look back and know that we were guided by the Deity. It is only *after* we have walked awhile that we can look back and see the healing and reconciliation with others that has happened in our wake. It is only *after* we live the hour by faith that we can see the guidance of God in our lives. It's not an easy way to live. Faith runs contrary to our urge for certainty, to our longing to know the end before we begin the journey. And it takes a toll.

Few, save myself and a handful of close friends, knew the extent of that toll. Lee Hancock, Mark Rubinsky, Ann Evans, and Mark Polo loved him well, kept the faith when his was waning. For what hands does God have on this earth if not our hands? What heart if not our heart? We believe that is the good news Jesus talked about: God is with us. We healed Barry with our loving, absorbing his hurt time and again. "The hate stops here," we told him with all the faith we had; "the rage goes no further."

It was humbling, in the richest sense of the word, to remember these gifts he had been given.

Always count your blessings, Barry! His mother's voice visited him across the years. *God is in the gifts. Count them, son.*

I am, Mom, I am, he thought. And, so strengthened with the love of these gentle warriors, he walked into his church as a layman for the last time in his life.

 "There's press here," I told Barry. It was a quarter to eight and we were pacing around his small office. Bea and Marie had brought by a small, "special" basket for Barry, but sugar would have tipped our anxiety over to hysteria.

"I know," he said, peeking through the blinds to the churchyard. "Someone with a vested interest in embarrassing Jack Spong made sure the papers and television station knew exactly where and when this was happening."

"We didn't want this to be a dirty little secret, remember?"

"Right." He drank some water and splashed a bit on his face. "We didn't want a circus either."

I held him tight while, outside, police directed traffic and kept the media as far away from the guests as they could.

"So," I asked, "after tonight, do I have to call you Father Stopfel or Deacon Barry?"

"How about lover?" He kissed me.

"Barry, you ready?" Walter Righter and Jack Croneberger popped in on cue. "Sorry," Walter said, and they popped back out.

"No, come in, come in." Barry laughed. "I guess I'm as ready as I'll ever be." Walter came in, hugged Barry, and started to lead him to his ordination.

"You need one more thing, honey." I handed him a small box with a huge bow. He loves my bows. "I think you should have it for tonight." Tearing through the wrapping in short order, he pulled a four-inch-tall, hand-carved, veined-rosewood cross from the box.

"It's beautiful!" he whispered, turning the bonelike carving over in his hands. "It feels old; hammered and beaten, worn smooth for a long time. Yet," his eyes flashed with tears, "unbreakable." He hugged me again.

"It's beautiful," Walter said, gently holding it in his big hands. "Where did you find it?"

"I made it." Barry's mouth dropped open and Walter and Jack stared. I went on quickly. "I've been working on it for a long time. We've had a long time to wait. And you never knew? It's changed a lot, taken on a lot in the last year and a half. But I just kept at it. I knew you'd wear it someday." I took the leather strap from his hands and placed it over his head. "You wear it, and every time you wear it you remember that, eventually, death is swallowed up in victory."

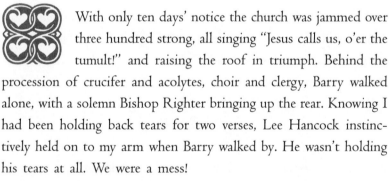 With only ten days' notice the church was jammed over three hundred strong, all singing "Jesus calls us, o'er the tumult!" and raising the roof in triumph. Behind the procession of crucifer and acolytes, choir and clergy, Barry walked alone, with a solemn Bishop Righter bringing up the rear. Knowing I had been holding back tears for two verses, Lee Hancock instinctively held on to my arm when Barry walked by. He wasn't holding his tears at all. We were a mess!

What a crazy quilt this congregation was. There were many who had supported Barry from the beginning, many more who never imagined attending the ordination of a gay deacon, but who were seeing life in a new way because they had fallen in love with Barry and he with them.

Barry bounced with joy and thankfulness into the church. God was doing an outrageous thing with him. Truly, given all the opportunity for human failure, with God all things are possible. And so he wept.

But there was little time for tears. The service of ordination moves swiftly. Over thirty people from Barry's parish, diocese, and extended family, speaking in one voice, presented Barry for ordination to Bishop Righter.

"Walter Righter, bishop in the Church of God, on behalf of the clergy and people of the Diocese of Newark, we present to you Barry Stopfel to be ordained a deacon in Christ's holy and catholic Church."

Following the sacred rite, the bishop asked, "Has Barry been selected in accordance with the canons of this Church, and do you believe Barry's manner of life to be suitable to the exercise of this ministry?"

In one voice we proclaimed our faith in Barry's call to a ministry he'd been doing for three years, a ministry he had been called to when still a boy.

"We believe that Barry has satisfied the requirements of the Church, and we believe Barry to be qualified for this ministry!" I saw Barry's shoulders shudder under the power of this affirmation. Thank God we couldn't look into each other's eyes.

Walter surveyed the hall of faces. He had come to the part of the service he had every reason to dread.

"Therefore, if any of you know any impediment or crime because of which we should not proceed, come forward now and make it known."

"I object! I rise to question!" a man bellowed deep from the back of the church. Every head turned. He shot his eyes around the church, making certain no one would stop him, and marched forward, where Barry was kneeling before the bishop, his back to the congregation, his head bowed.

Austin Menzies had flourished for two years under Barry's aus-
pices, finding Barry a worthy match for his own piercing intellect.
Menzies enjoyed a good argument, sometimes at the expense of everyone else in the room, but Barry was quite easy with him, recognizing in him the same longing for God that everyone in his classes
shared. After two years of these frank, nurturing explorations in faith
and ethics, after two years of finding his life made richer by a deeper
involvement in the whole life of the congregation, Menzies quit the
church outright when he learned that Barry was gay. Barry had not
changed; he had been gay from the first debate Menzies drew him
into. The only thing that had changed was what Menzies knew
about him. Unfortunately the information created such an irrecon-
cilable dissonance within Menzies's religious rationale that he felt he
had no choice but to leave.

"I protest this ordination!" Menzies shouted as he strode down
the aisle, his late sixties/early seventies' body trembling. "Barry
Stopfel is a self-admitted homosexual," he declared and paused, as if
that were enough information. When Walter Righter did not move,
Menzies looked down at his sheet of written notes, drew himself up,
and went on.

"Homosexuals are sexual perverts and their sexual activity involves
genital contact between men which is a perverted use of the physical
difference between men and women, which differences were God
created for procreation. Homosexuality has been condemned by all
Christian churches for over nineteen hundred years. In the Genesis
Sodom and Gomorrah stories. In the Leviticus codes and in many
other sections of the Bible. Priests are role models for all Christians
and particularly the young." It seemed impossible, but his voice was
actually rising in volume.

"Ordination of this person will encourage children to believe
there is nothing *perverse* or *immoral* about homosexuality, that *two men*
showing their mutual affection by making *genital contact* is *perfectly*

normal!" He shook his tattered paper at Walter, and, still getting no response, stormed down the aisle, grabbed his sister on the way, and exited the hushed and airless house of God.

After a moment of absolute quiet, Walter spread his arms to enfold the congregation. He stood in the vacuum of silence, looking over at me to see if I was all right, checking through the congregation to the back aisle, giving us all the time we needed to breathe again, to remember where we were and why we had come.

Finally, he settled his arms at his side and spoke with simple authority and deep compassion. "Barry has been subjected to every test and every screening process in this diocese on his journey to this day. He has not only passed these tests, he has shown brilliantly through them the true marks of a priest. There is no doubt in either Bishop Spong's mind or in my mind that his calling to the priesthood is genuine. Therefore," he opened his missal and let his resounding bass voice roll through the sanctuary, "I will proceed with this ordination.

"Is it your will that Barry be ordained a deacon?" Walter continued the liturgy of ordination.

"It is!" we shouted the Prayer Book response and stamped our feet and shouted and cheered and generally behaved most unepiscopalian. I gave up holding back the flood of tears as Lee and Mark embraced me. This house we were worshiping in was repurified by a magnificent din of love.

Walter embraced Barry, then turned him around to see the congregation's response. Barry didn't want to look; he was afraid he would lose his grip. But Walter Righter is a wise man. Seeing the smiling, laughing faces of those who had encircled him with love for so many years, Barry was overcome with the knowledge that his life was not entirely his own, nor would it ever be. He came from, lived in, and would forever be a part of a community of people whose faith makes them a family.

Walter laid his hands on Barry's head, quieting the tumult. "Will you uphold Barry in this ministry?"

"We will!" we shouted.

"In peace let us pray to the Lord. The Lord be with you."

"And also with you." With expectant spirits, we knelt, ready to experience God's Spirit surrounding us.

"O God of unchangeable power and eternal light," Walter began the ancient prayer, calling heaven down on Barry and all of his family. "Let the whole world see and know that things which were cast down are being raised up, and things which had grown old are being made new . . ." Walter's rhythmic voice poured the ancient prayer, now alive with meaning, into our hearts, reawakening in us the dream of God.

Then, just before the Examination and Consecration of the Ordinand, our generously spirited friend, Michael Kelly, sat at the piano and played until our hearts and minds and spirits were centered again in the solemnity of the calling Barry was about to accept.

Michael began with one hand, playing the joyful, unadorned melody line of "Tis a Gift to Be Simple," one of Barry's favorite hymns. Into his cheerful plainsong Michael added layers of intonation and depth, slowly introducing another theme beneath the delightful melody. Shifting his song, Michael reminded us that we were about to witness a sacred moment and began to ask us in earnest, "Shall We Gather at the River?"

Anchoring himself to a long, swelling crescendo, Michael's whole body leaned into the piano as the song lifted him up in its powerful affirmation of life.

> Yes, we'll gather at the river!
> The beautiful, the beautiful river.
> Gather with the saints at the river,
> That flows from the throne of God!

Quietly he finished, repeating the last stanza of the great hymn as simply as he had begun. We were hushed, gathered together in the solemn spirit of this moment.

Bishop Righter asked Barry to kneel again before him and began the ancient Examination.

"Barry, every Christian is called to follow Jesus Christ. At all times, your life and teaching are to show Christ's people that in serving the helpless they are serving Christ himself."

Barry's mind wandered a moment. All those people who had fought him and Jack Spong had been ordained with the same commandment. Had they forgotten? Did power corrupt that absolutely? Could it happen to him?

"Barry," Walter held Barry's eyes, bringing him back to the moment, "do you believe that you are truly called by God and his Church to the life and work of a deacon?"

How long had this seed been planted in the soil of Barry's life? Since he could remember. In the past forty years his faith had been expressed in many different ways, yet never had it strayed from the teachings he learned in the backseat of his mother's Oldsmobile. Christians are called to love. When we do, the promise says, our simple acts of tender mercy will eventually tilt the earth on its axis and slowly, one loving kindness at a time, the world will be changed. As he took a deep breath Barry felt the full power of his confessional faith fill his body in an instant: Christ has died, as we die daily; Christ is risen, as only love will call us to new life; Christ will come again, Barry's undying hope that the commonwealth of God might live among all people on earth. Barry looked up into Walter's eyes and answered his bishop's question. "I believe I am so called."

Walter asked us to stand for the Prayer of Ordination. In a moment the slamming of kneelers and shuffle of feet stilled to quiet. Walter lifted his hands and placed them on Barry's head. "Therefore, O God, through Jesus Christ your Son, give your Holy Spirit to

Barry; fill him with grace and power, and make him a deacon in your Church." In the succession of apostles begun the day Jesus first placed his hands on his friends' heads and told them to go, do what he had taught them to do, Barry was now ordained a deacon in the Episcopal Church. We had reached the beautiful river.

 The press were, well, the press. It was easy to see how Robert Williams had been drawn into saying things he hadn't thought through. But Barry answered his own questions, sidestepping the reporters' traps. With no sensation, no name calling, no escalation of the debate by the press of questions, the reporters grew bored. We had simply refused to lie about who we are, and now wanted to be about the task God seemed to have in mind for us. This wasn't news.

The issues we might have reflected on, had we been asked, are complex. For instance: How has the way of Jesus, a way for people on the fringes of the dominant culture, been controverted by the dominant culture? How has the way of love and inclusion become distorted into a way of hate and exclusion? How has the command to forgive been twisted into a call for crucifixion? Complex issues that weigh heavily on the souls of those who work for transformation within the institution of Christianity.

"Well," Curtis Hart, Barry's mentor at the Hospital Chaplaincy, bounded up to him at the reception, "the lunatics are running the asylum now!"

We weren't even through the door when we saw it.

"Oh my God," we said in unison. A twenty-foot-long table bisected the gymnasium, bowing under a mountain range of cookies. Bea and Marie Branfuhr dashed over.

"Isn't it magnificent?" Bea asked. "People just kept bringing so much!"

Barry stared in awe at the spectacle. "Bea, this is going to live in myth as The Great Cookie Ordination! It's fantastic! Thank you." He laughed, hugging them both.

It was a heavenly banquet, a living image of God's abundant love poured out, indiscriminate and overflowing. Sweetness and generosity and hospitality from and for the family of God.

"Oh, we're so thrilled to see this day!" Marie patted his face. "God bless you, Barry." They rushed off again, dodging sugar-charged children apoplectic with delight. There were going to be sweet dreams tonight.

 The long waiting was over. Barry had kept his own counsel while, for months, the national Church debated his ordination. He believed God was calling him to be a minister to the people he was serving at Atonement, not simply a gay "poster minister." The people at Atonement had called his priesthood out of him, and to them he had to give his full mind, body, and spirit.

However, there were some gay and lesbian colleagues who thought his decision to keep his own counsel lacked courage. One of the closeted lesbian priests in the diocese had even referred to him as a "wimp." But there is tremendous power in silence. Sometimes we are called into the vulnerability of silence in order that evil might be absorbed and transformed into life. Barry had grown up knowing that in loving God and following God there is the danger of a cross—the danger that his life would be upset, loaded with the burdens of others as well as his own, and that he would be thrown into deadly combat with strong powers of evil. But he believed that Jesus the Christ had paid a price for him, affirmed him, and called him to share in a ministry, along with all the other men and women called to be a part of a holy people of God, that transforms our weaknesses into a life and resource for others.

Is that not the vocation of all baptized Christians? Are we not all called to be role models for all people of faith, proclaiming in the name of Jesus the Christ that evil and injustice will never have the last word? No, they never will as long as Christians dare to be courageous in our loving.

Chapter 26

There's a strange way in which we're united to those most opposed to us. Their resistance and rigidity somehow come out of their own suffering. Some use a traditional theology of sin, cross, and atonement against us.

Our witness for transformation leads us, too, into our own suffering, our own experience of The Cross. It's sad we can't have more ways of cutting through the opposition and finding new ways of meeting.

—*The Reverend Dr. Carter Heyward*
IN THE VOICE, OCTOBER 1991

Barry was ordained a deacon in the Episcopal Church on Saturday, September 30, 1990, delayed out of deference to a personal request of Jack Spong from the presiding bishop, the Most Reverend Edmund L. Browning, who hoped the delay would keep the dialogue open "for the good of the Church." The very day Barry should have been ordained, the Right Reverend Ronald Haines of Washington, D.C., publicly ordained to the diaconate our good friend and classmate the Reverend Elizabeth Carl, who lives in an open, committed relationship with her lesbian lover. Did no one from Episcopalians United, the Prayer Book Society, or the so-called Episcopal Synod think Bishop Haines's action significant enough to call the press? No one was breathing down his back. Or had these people so thoroughly demonized Bishop Spong that he, not the ordination of gays and lesbians, had become the issue?

I had told Walter Righter, after my first meeting with Jack Spong, that I thought Jack was paranoid. Walter laughed and disagreed, of course. Walter has traveled a few years more than I. It's easy to misunderstand another person's fears—easy, that is, until one is willing to travel with them, see the road from their vantage point, hear the terrors that scream through their nights. Each of us wears the blinders of our own particularities: We are straight, gay, bisexual, transgendered, transsexual, nonsexual, single, divorced, happily married, miserably married, conveniently married, widowed, separated, monogamous or not; we are a species of multiple races and mixed ethnic backgrounds, with their various influences marked in our lives or not; we live within the boundaries of our class, some striving to change, some fearful it will be changed out from under them; we walk the earth with our various capabilities vulnerably exposed to any and all who might cruelly mock them. Today we live on an earth far different from that of our parents, and stranger still than that of our grandparents; many more and different eyes are close upon us. Unfortunately, as a species, our ability to see and talk with one another has outpaced our ability to look into one another's hearts and hear what we are saying. Our cunning has outpaced our compassion.

Usually the ordination to the priesthood happens six months after one's ordination to the diaconate. *Usually.* That would have meant Barry should have been ordained a priest in March 1991. But these were unusual times.

Soon after Bishop Walter Righter ordained Barry as a deacon, the presiding bishop asked Bishop Spong, Bishop Spong asked Barry, and Barry asked me if his ordination to the priesthood could be delayed until the Church met at General Convention in Phoenix, July 1991, ultimately delaying Barry's ordination for a year.

"Absolutely not!" I shouted my predictable, knee-jerk reaction. "Who knows what could happen in a year?" I took a deep breath, then asked, "Of course, we don't have any choice, do we?"

"No, not really," Barry explained. At General Convention there would be a move to pass an amendment to the canons expressly forbidding the ordination of "practicing homosexuals."

Bishop Spong was fairly certain that the majority built after his disassociation in the House of Bishops would hold for a year, ensuring that such a restrictive canon would not pass. But Spong, and those who agreed with him, had a year of hard work to hold the center together.

Bishop William Frey, resigned Bishop of Colorado and dean of the Trinity School of Ministry in Pennsylvania, introduced the dreaded amendment to the canons at General Convention in Phoenix, Arizona, July 1991. The proposed resolution became known as the Frey Amendment (an appropriate homonym), although, due to the vagaries of Church legislative process, it was actually offered by Bishop John Howe of Central Florida. It stated in part that "It is expected that all Members of the Clergy of this Church, having subscribed to the Declaration required by Article VIII of the Constitution, shall be under the obligation to abstain from sexual relations outside of Holy Matrimony."

This covered a lot of territory for twentieth-century humanity. Although Frey claimed it was not aimed at eliminating gay and lesbian people from the Church, that he himself felt "great compassion for them," it was generally held by both the House of Bishops and the House of Deputies to be a punitive measure and was defeated. Holy Matrimony is not an option for homosexuals.

A compromise was proposed, which, in true Episcopal fashion, tried to hold together the two opposing sides and prevent a split in the Church. First the compromise statement affirmed the Church's historical teaching on marriage; then it acknowledged the "discontinuity" between the Church's teaching and the experience of some of its members; it confessed the inability of Church leaders to reach a definitive conclusion; and, finally, called for continued study(!). It easily passed both Houses.

"It's a positive sign because it affirms traditional sexual morality," crowed Bishop Clarence Pope of Forth Worth, president of the Episcopal Synod of America, who was still breaking canon law by not ordaining women. "That's the only real positive, that it affirms traditional belief," he added. "It doesn't stop the problem of continuing ordination of practicing homosexuals. It has no teeth in it."

Well, thank God! In July 1991 the Episcopal Church said to the world that they were not in the business of eating their wounded. It was a moment when the Church turned away from politics of exclusion and turned toward the Holy Spirit of inclusion.

Bishop Frederick Borsch of Los Angeles remarked that "You saw a House with different minds on the issue strike out with integrity. In the long run the debates have helped people see that here's a Church that wants to love with mind along with heart, to really, in a thoughtful and prayerful way, look at the great issues of our time, such as sexuality." Borsch understood that everyone would never be of one mind, but that there is room in the commonwealth of God for all of God's creation. Our task is to believe in a bigger, more powerful God than we have ever yet dared to believe in.

Oh, it was a hot General Convention in Phoenix. Retired Bishop Gerald McAllister of Oklahoma initiated a resolution to censure two bishops who ordained homosexuals in the past year. Only two? Through private conversations we knew that at least twelve bishops ordained gay and lesbian people in the same year, 1990, that Walter Righter ordained Barry. But only two bishops ordained honest queers honestly: the Right Reverend Walter Righter and the Right

Reverend Ronald Haines. So they were finally going after Elizabeth Carl's bishop in Washington, D.C., as well as Barry's ordaining bishop. A friend once told us that the House of Bishops reminds him of a dog let out for the hunt: Once it gets the smell of blood up its nose, there is no calling it off. Fortunately the resolution to censure was a miserable and humiliating failure for McAllister. The House of Bishops was beginning to understand that sniping and attacking one another was not the way to collegiality.

 The stress of waiting for the convention to end was too much, so Barry and I took our new black Labrador retriever puppy, Spirit, to Penns Creek. And she is quite a spirit. Having never been in water before, she jumped out of the truck and ran right for the creek, stopped, tactfully walked in, and swam like she had been doing it all her life. Why, if we can accept that a dog has a genetic predisposition to swim, can we not accept that a gay man or a lesbian woman has a genetic predisposition to love someone of the same sex? I suppose Galileo and his friends faced the same opprobrium when they affirmed Copernicus' observations that the earth does indeed orbit the sun. Understanding takes time.

Genetic predisposition notwithstanding, our morality as sexual creatures, whether we are gay, straight, bi, active, or inactive, is about finding genuine, nonabusive ways of relating to one another, not about what we do with our genitals. A sexual morality for Christians is one where we live richly connected with the whole world and express that compassion in thousands of loving acts.

"Barry? Jack Spong." The bishop caught up to us at Penns Creek. "I'm in Phoenix and the news is good." He could hardly contain his delight.

"As of this date there is no canon preventing my ordaining you a priest in this church. I, for one, am looking forward to the day."

"What's he saying?" I whispered seventy times seven times, each one acknowledged with a violent wave of Barry's hand for me to shut up and go away. The bishop was talking, telling him the whole story of the debate, vote, and outcome on human sexuality and his ordination.

Finally I heard Barry say, "Why, September fourteenth sounds great to me, Jack! I'll check with Jack Croneberger. . . . Oh, you have? Well, great then. September fourteenth it is!"

Though it was late in the afternoon, we hiked into the sanctuary of our old-growth forest, and introduced our Spirit to its. She liked the running waters best.

Chapter 27

Heroes take journeys, confront dragons, and discover the treasure of their true selves. Although they may feel very alone during the quest, at its end their reward is a sense of community: with themselves, with other people, and with the earth. Every time we confront death-in-life we confront a dragon, and every time we choose life over nonlife and move deeper into the ongoing discovery of who we are, we vanquish the dragon; we bring new life to ourselves and to our culture. We change the world.

—*Carol S. Pearson*, THE HERO WITHIN[9]

It was early morning, dark and sticky hot, when the phone blasted me awake on September 14, 1991, Barry's ordination day. I thought it must be Gerard, an old friend of Barry's, calling from Berlin. He was forever screwing up the time difference.

"Hello?" Nothing. Normal transatlantic delay. "Gerard?" Then I heard it. Heavy Breather.

"Oh, it's you," I said with all the ice I could muster at 5:30 A.M. In the past two weeks we had gotten so many of these we started giving them names: Sleepy, because he (she? I doubt it) never spoke; Pervert, because it was the only word he spoke before hanging up; and Heavy Breather.

"It's kind of early for you, isn't it?" I asked the guy on the phone. Heavy breathing.

"Are you in love with me? Is that it? You really in love with me, Heavy Breather? Want to talk about what kind of courage it takes to love your fellow man instead of hate him?" *Click.*

"Why did you talk to him?" Barry was ashen in the bed next to me.

"I'm not sure," I said and rolled over to him.

"Will," Barry was shaken, "don't encourage these people. Don't affirm their perversion."

"Maybe I'm feeling generous," I joked with him. "Today you become a priest!" I tickled him, hard.

"Stop poking me!" He kicked me away. I knew he was still worrying about the calls. Ever since the newspapers started carrying the story of his upcoming ordination, we had been getting several of these semi-harassing calls a day.

"Look," I said and pulled him close to me in the bed, "you're a shy, introverted kind of guy. And you've had the most intimate details of your life exposed to the public and examined in the press. If he calls again, I'll try to draw him out. Like you drew out the Morrissey boy last week. Maybe Heavy Breather's life will change, too.

"Yeah," Barry smiled, remembering a lesson that twelve-year-old Christopher had taught him. "But at church it's safer."

 Christopher Morrissey was one of those startlingly beautiful children who either drown in the vanity of praise or rise above it and lead. Christopher was bright, musically gifted, and an easygoing kid who cared about his friends.

He was a leader. When it came time for him to join the church, his parents enrolled him in confirmation class, considered by generations of preadolescent boys to be a kind of parental-imposed purgatory. Christopher hated it. His parents made him go (true), none of his other friends had to go (false), it was a waste of time (matter of opinion), and he didn't care about joining the church (not quite true).

On this Sunday, Barry steered the class to discuss what they felt made them worthwhile as people. He sat spellbound as the kids took over the conversation and talked about their looks, their athletic abilities, what they did outside of school, how much money they (their parents) had, where (and if) they went on vacation, their clothes, and friends. After talking around the issue for twenty minutes, they decided that none of these things really made them worthy people—they were nice things to have but they were extras. When they couldn't quite put their finger on what made them *essentially* worthwhile as people, they looked to Barry.

"Tell me something," Barry began. "When you look in the mirror, what do you see?"

"Myself. My reflection." The answers came quickly from an exceptionally bright group of kids.

"Your image, right?"

"Right," the MTV generation chimed in, eager for Barry to hurry this idea along and get to the next point.

"What do we know about images from the Bible?"

"God created man in his image," one of the boys said.

"And women too!" more than one of the girls corrected.

"Right!" Barry said, laughing with them. "So when God looks at us, what does God see?"

"God sees his image. God sees himself," they put the answer together quickly. As the implication of this thought sank in, their eyes lit up and their heads cocked to one side.

"You are the image of God," Barry spoke into their splendid

silence. "Just as you are. God looks at you, at us, and sees God's self. There's nothing you have to do; in fact, there's nothing you *can* do to prove your worth. God has given you all the worth you'll ever need: You are made in the image of God."

Out of the silence, a still, small, self-possessed voice asked, "So what about if we hate things? Does that mean God hates them, too?"

"Tell me what you mean, Christopher," Barry urged. Christopher was comfortable enough with Barry to say just what was on his mind.

"Well," his brilliant, cheery face lit up as he looked at the other boys, "I hate coming to confirmation class." Snickers, mostly from the boys, and a few gasps from some of the girls in the room. All the kids loved Barry, he was *their* priest, he let them talk things out, he listened to them—they would never hurt his feelings. Christopher must have something clever up his sleeve. He amplified his thought.

"If God sees himself when he looks at me, does that mean God hates confirmation class, too?"

Did Jesus really say it's a sin to dance? Barry remembered asking Reverend Aungst at Christopher's age. Twelve *is* hard on adults.

"Tell me something, Christopher," Barry began. "When you look in the mirror, doesn't your right hand look like it's on your left side?"

"Sure," Christopher jumped right in. Bright kid. "That's because the image is reversed. So you can write backwards and see it forwards."

"Right," Barry said. "So what does God see when God looks at us?"

"A reversed image?"

"Well, without beating the image to death," Barry laughed, "maybe a not-quite-perfect image. Tell me, are you God?"

"No," Christopher answered, perturbed this wasn't going quite the way he planned but drawn into the argument all the same.

"Of course not," Barry agreed with him and pressed his point.

"When God looks at *all* that God creates, God sees God's self. Not just one of us, but all of us together."

Young Christopher Morrissey's whole body twitched with dissatisfaction at this answer.

"God created everything with its own worth," Barry went on, "because that's who God is. Each one of you has worth, because that's who *you* are as the image of God. God looks at you and finds worth. When you look at things, you need to find the worth in them for yourselves because you too are in the image of God. Christopher," Barry asked him quietly as the weight of all this sank in, "is there anything worthwhile about being here? Anything worthwhile about being in this confirmation class in this church?"

Christopher unself-consciously rubbed his blinding white-blond hair, put his elbows on his feet and his head in his hands, and thought. None of his mates snickered or snorted or teased. They, too, wanted to know the answer.

"Well," Christopher replied after a good minute, "this is the only place where I don't get put down."

The flood of Barry's childhood surged through his heart at Christopher's uncluttered honesty. It was the sum and total of Barry's theology, his hope for a Church he was called to serve. Church is the place where we don't get put down.

 It had dawned late-summer hot that Saturday, September 14, morning and just got hotter. Hundreds of people spilled out of cars, vans, and buses from New York, New Jersey, Massachusetts, Pennsylvania—all here to celebrate Barry's ordination as a priest.

There were dozens of folks we didn't know—students from several seminaries on both the East and West coasts, representatives from most of the Protestant denominations, a vanload of sackcloth-cassocked friars—all of them celebrating, all hopeful that the new spirit blowing through the Episcopal Church today would signal a turn in both church and secular life. And of course there were friends from every walk of Barry's life—from his childhood in Hummelstown through seminary in New York City. And our family—Marlin and Alice Stopfel, his brother, Butch, and Aunt Polly; Lee Hancock, Mark Rubinsky, Hannah and Sarah; Mark Polo and Ann Evans.

We were avoiding the crowded, overhot church as long as possible, tugging at our damp clothes, watching the very snappy Tenafly policemen direct traffic and neatly herd the media into legal parking areas, all the while keeping an eye out for possible troublemakers. My own fear was high and bitter in my mouth. Since we didn't know who half these people were, and since too many had already declared it open season on homosexuals, a few right here in this church, I made Barry stay inside.

Not my brother, not my sister,
But it's me, Oh Lord,
Standin' in the need of prayer!

Marc McGinnis threw his deep, rich, African-American voice out over the throng and called us together for worship. And how we sang! More than 450 people wedged themselves into the church and sang about freedom, liberation, and joy. We were singing with Miriam and Moses after the Israelites crossed the Red Sea; singing and dancing the joy of David, stark raving nude as the Ark of the Covenant came into Jerusalem. (We kept our clothes on.) A joyful din! Today we were crossing out of bondage into freedom. God had brought all of us home.

Pressing the joy a notch higher, Margaret Wright, dressed in a traffic-stopping red suit, took the floor and, with Michael Kelly once again at the piano, packed the chancel with her golden, big-band-era voice in Kander and Ebb's wildly exuberant call to life, "Yes!" As she gave to me at my ordination, Margaret gave to Barry at his—she sang heaven down upon the gathered people of God. By the time she rang out the closing crescendo—*Say yes! Yes! Yes!*—Margaret opened the roof over our heads with her joyful, evangelical message and brought us closer to the presence.

The circle of love is never broken. Fifty people from every walk of Barry's life stood before Bishop Spong and presented Barry for ordination as a priest.

"John, Bishop in the Church of God," the official service of ordination began, "on behalf of the clergy and people of the Diocese of Newark, we present to you Barry L. Stopfel, to be ordained a priest in Christ's holy catholic Church."

Anita Berhle and Paul Swartz, Judith Witmer, Kirk and Jean Seibert, Richard Matrisian, who flew in from Seattle to surprise him—Barry's lifelong friends gave witness to his life of faith. Bishop Walter Righter, Ann Evans, Mark Polo, Lee Hancock and Mark Rubinsky—our family and dozens of friends stood to commit Barry to Bishop Spong for ordination. The Diocesan Commission on Ministry, the Standing Committee, the vestry of The Church of the Atonement—all the people who had tested Barry, and been tested themselves in the process—all stood with full hearts and certain faith before Bishop Spong.

And Barry, standing before his God and his bishop, was overwhelmed with the circle of love and Spirit around him. He prayed he wouldn't fall down.

Jack Spong was beaming. He had gone through hell and back for this celebration, this act of honesty in the Episcopal Church. He had withstood prejudice, personal attacks, and ostracism, experiencing at length, as he had told the House of Bishops, the daily fare of gay men and lesbian women in this country. He was ready to celebrate and easily filled the church with his deeply resonant voice.

"Dear friends in Christ, you know the importance of this ministry, and the weight of your responsibility in presenting Barry Stopfel for ordination to the sacred priesthood." Just one year ago Walter Righter had said these same words and we all held our breath. This time I was ready. Bishop Spong hurried on.

"Therefore if any of you know any impediment or crime because of which we should not proceed, come forward now, and make it known."

"I rise to the question!" It was Austin Menzies. (Déjà vu all over again.)

I stepped into the aisle before Menzies could come close to Barry, spread my arms, and started singing an old, lilting plainsong:

Love is flowing like a river,
Flowing out from you and me;
Flowing out into the desert,
Setting all the captives free.

As Menzies reread the same words he had read one year earlier, people joined me in the familiar song. We had heard him before; we didn't need to hear him again.

Furious, the protestor shouted to be heard above the gentle chant now sweeping through the sanctuary. He wasn't. I stood with my body planted between this man's rage and Barry, arms stretched out, my eyes full of tears, and sang with the hundreds until the bitter man stormed away.

The congregation wasn't finished. Once more they brought the verse around, and, as if calling out in prayer to the man who had just left, sang after him their forgiveness. I turned to Bishop Spong, nodded, and retook my place with my family.

"That was a beautiful song," Alice whispered in my ear. "Are you all right?" I nodded I was. Alice shook her head as folks do who know right from wrong. Sometimes, she seemed to be saying, people are just too awful.

But Barry stood, strong, flushed, and peaceful—like a man just given his life.

Suspecting there would be such an interruption, Bishop Spong was prepared with his statement of defense. But Austin Menzies would not hear these words.

"The Reverend Barry Stopfel, deacon," Spong began, "has been judged by the decision-making processes of this Diocese of Newark, operating under the canons of the Episcopal Church, to be a worthy candidate for ordination to the priesthood. . . .

"Because of the debate that has raged in our Church over the issue of homosexuality, Barry Stopfel has become a unique symbol of the Church's struggle." Spong then outlined the all too familiar three-year history of this ordination, and explained the resolutions just ratified at General Convention.

"The General Convention in Phoenix refused to amend the canons to prohibit the ordination of qualified gay and lesbian people." Jack Spong started when the congregation erupted into a roaring standing ovation. His head shot up from his notes, and quickly saw that his words had unleashed an uncontrollable joy. He beamed again.

"The General Convention refused to pass any resolution that places hurdles in the path of qualified gay and lesbian persons that are not in the path of any other aspirant for Holy Orders." Every sentence greeted by cheers.

"The General Convention refused to censure those bishops who have honestly admitted to ordaining homosexual persons." A roar went up when Jack turned and asked Walter Righter to stand. Today, these were two of our heroes.

When we had quieted down sufficiently, Bishop Spong continued. "The General Convention refused to amend the canons to guarantee that the ordination process is open to all baptized members, because it was asserted that the canons *already say* that the process is open to *every* man and woman. That language was judged to be itself *totally inclusive*, making further canons unnecessary."

Bishop Spong cast a solemn look around the crowded sanctuary. Some here had written him painful, hurtful letters; some had been supportive of their bishop; others of us had vacillated. All of us had labored long and painfully to comprehend the Episcopal Church's struggle for integrity.

"In this public debate," Spong continued gently, quietly, "my deepest privilege as a Christian has been to experience firsthand the hostile negativity that is the daily bread of gay and lesbian people." He stopped, his voice caught in his chest. Taking a deep breath he went on.

"In a new and powerful way I now know what it means to take up the cross and follow the path of the Christ. I thank God that I have been able to respond to this vocation. I thank so many of you here today for walking with me in that way of the cross, the way that has led to this day of life and resurrection for the whole Church." He paused just to catch a breath, but we stood and filled the moment with our ovation. Jack Spong had summoned the courage to put his body where his faith is. Having experienced firsthand the hate and violence that is the regular fare of gay and lesbian people, he would never again be the same. Jack dropped his eyes and then his head as our praise washed over him.

Jack Spong is a man proud of his many accomplishments. But pride lives in creative tension with his humility, flip sides of the same coin, yin and yang. He might have stopped us from lauding him, might have stretched out his palms, shaken his head, saying, "No, no." Instead he humbled himself that day, and stood before us with bowed head, and received our thanks and our love. When, finally, we had finished, he spoke directly to Barry.

"More than anyone else in the Anglican communion, Barry, you have been the symbol of the Church's struggle on this issue. I salute you for your courage and your patience and I announce that this ordination service will proceed."

The walls of Jericho gave way beneath our stomping feet and roaring voices. We shouted and danced the victory.

"Is it your will that Barry be ordained a priest?" Jack Spong shouted above us, continuing the liturgy.

"It is!" we shouted in turn.

"Will you uphold Barry in his ministry?"

"We will!" We were quiet then, but just barely.

"In peace let us pray to the Lord." Having settled down (somewhat), we entered into the service that would inexorably move us to Barry's ordination as a priest.

In four-inch pumps, black chiffon culottes, and a golden-red Pentecost stole with phoenix ascending and an image of Mother God over her left breast, Ann Keeler Evans walked to the center of the sanctuary. Fully embodying the message of the book spread open before her, Ann read from Carol Pearson's *The Hero Within*. Curtis Watkins canted the Hebrew Scripture lesson, singing "Go Down Moses and Miriam"—a traditional hymn rewritten with new images of God's inclusive power. When Curtis left the center of the sanctuary, a slim woman with a head full of wild, blond-brown-gray curls, a wide smile, and eyes as deep as mountain springs stood and climbed up to the pulpit.

For the next twenty minutes, in her silver, Southern voice, the Reverend Dr. Carter Heyward, professor of theology at Episcopal Divinity School in Cambridge, Massachusetts, charged the congregation, and specifically Barry, to live our lives in a spirituality of compassion.

"I believe that the hardest part of compassion (which reflects the passion and suffering of God) is to be *open to forgiving those who cannot receive this forgiveness because they are not repentant.* They do not see, or believe, that they have done anything wrong, anything to hurt, wound, or violate us. . . ." Her voice rose and fell with the ease of a born storyteller's.

"I want to suggest that this is where we gay and lesbian Christians find ourselves today, insofar as the Spirit of God is working through us:

"*We do not deny* our ongoing need for repentance and forgiveness for such sins as our own greed, our duplicity, our racism, and the harm that we do to others through our internalized homophobia and misogyny.

"At the same time *we are ready to forgive* those brothers and sisters, in this church and elsewhere, who exclude and patronize us and others. *We are ready to forgive* those brothers and sisters who wound and violate us and others. *We are ready to forgive* them because they *do not know* what they are doing. *They do not know* that, through their fear, their confusion, and their barely veiled hatred that they are breaking our body, the Body of Christ, which is, in fact, their *own* body. . . .

"Is this not what Jesus meant when he asked God to forgive his brothers and sisters, *for they know not what they do?*" Quietly she finished her sermon. "I believe this yearning to forgive is at the very heart of God. And it is *always* the basis of a sacred reformation, a truly liberating revolution."

So Barry had lived to this day—a reluctant hero (*least likely to succeed,* his high school counselor had said), awkward under the lens of public scrutiny (*Never draw attention to yourself:* the humble, Brethren way), unwilling to exchange hurt for hurt (*Don't ever judge another; you don't know what they've been through*—his mother's abiding lesson).

There was no doubt in Barry's mind that he was exactly where God wanted him to be. With an open heart he knelt before Bishop Spong to be ordained a priest while we in the congregation sang the ancient prayer for the presence of the Holy Spirit, *Veni Sancte Spiritus.*

Bishop Spong drew close to Barry, stretched out his arms, placed his hands on Barry's head, and prayed the prayer of consecration.

"Therefore, Father, through Jesus Christ your Son, give your Holy

Spirit to Barry; fill him with grace and power, and make him a priest in your Church. . . ."

Throughout the church I heard the muffled sounds of tears held in check, a painful, joyous underscore to the bishop's prayer. And then the bishop was calling me up front to join him and Barry.

"My brothers and sisters in Christ, I present to you the newest priest in the Episcopal Church, the Reverend Barry Stopfel, and his life partner, the Reverend Will Leckie. The peace of the Lord be always with you."

"And also with you!" The crowd shouted the ancient response and cheered and clapped and, at last, wept openly. Barry and I hugged and for the next ten minutes were passed from the arms of one friend to another.

Barry wanted to sing "How Great Thou Art" for the closing hymn. It was his dad's favorite, but Barry was afraid that, following the very Anglican Eucharist, it might sound trite.

"Don't you worry about a thing, honey," Marc McGinnis assured him a week before the service. "By the time I'm done this organ will sound like Radio City Music Hall!" With 450 voices behind him and five verses to work it, Marc gradually pulled every last stop on that organ until the trumpets were sounding and the bells were ringing. The great evangelical affirmation of faith, first learned from his mother and father, carried Barry through the church and into his life as a priest.

Then sings my soul, my savior God to Thee.
How great Thou art! How great Thou art!

 "So," Mark Polo had his hands on his hips. "What do you think?"

"Oh my God," Barry whispered.

"Oh, Mark!" I cried. "It's perfect sissy magic!"

He and our friends Howard Kauffman and Denise Morrissey, Christopher's mom, had transformed the cavernous gymnasium into a nomadic sultan's palace. Hundreds of yards of red and white fabric swaddled the walls, cascaded in great swags from the four corners of the enormous hall, and converged in the middle to one, enormous draping pouf.

"You like it?" Mark asked.

Barry could hardly catch his breath. "This is unbelievable!"

"I'm so glad," Denise purred. What was not to like? It was an outrageous, fantastic gift. "We were up most of the night. Mark's very particular about things, you know."

"Well, it had to be done right. Right?" Mark ribbed her. "Besides, we've got a famous priest, three famous bishops, and a house full of homosexuals. My reputation's at stake here. If you're going to make history, I always say, do it in style!"

"Barry, there's somebody here who wants to see you." Denise dragged him away, smiling like a cat two courses after the canary.

"Congratulations, Barry." It was Christopher Morrissey. He reached up to hug him.

"Thank you, Christopher." Barry knelt and hugged him back. "Thank you so much for being here."

"I just wanted you to know," he said in his quiet, sturdy voice, "my mom didn't make me come. I wanted to be here."

With his heart in his throat, Barry could only offer his thanks with a hug.

 The endless day of celebrating and celebrity was past. The church had long been cleaned up, the thousand yards of fabric transformed into tablecloths. The spoils from our own dinner party for fifty that night were history (thank God!). A week later and the press no longer called: We were yesterday's news, which was even more of a relief than the fact that Sleepy,

Pervert, and Heavy Breather had stopped calling. We settled comfortably, if a bit anticlimactically, into our jobs as pastors and counselors, with each day growing more full than the last. Nights were spent recovering: cooking, talking, and reading to each other.

"Listen to this," Barry interrupted my pulp novel. "It's something I wrote in *The Voice* about my ordination." Not really into the endless plot twists of my underwater global-terrorist novel that nightly lulled my mind away from the cares of hospice work, I set it down and listened.

He shared a poem written by a seventh-grader named Moogi Ayanna Mogengege:

If there were such a place where there were
only peace and love
And there were no such
things as hate and war,
I'd definitely find some
way to get there.

"How's that for a glimpse of the realm of God?"
I asked Barry to read it again.
"Yes," I said with my feet up and my eyes closed. "Children have the keys to paradise."

Chapter 28

Hung up between two criminals at his death, Jesus was no polished white icon on a marble altar. He was a beaten, powerless trouble-maker in an occupied territory whose life appeared to be a failure. . . . And yet he was God. . . .

God is not revealed in our power over others. God is revealed in our powerlessness, our hopelessness, our defeat, our pain. . . .

We know God and the Christ on the crosses of our human struggles: as husbands and wives, sons and daughters, lovers and partners struggling for meaning in our family lives. . . .

As professional people struggling to make right Christian choices in the midst of a business environment morally adrift. . . .

As people of all stripes together struggling against hatred and injustice. . . .

Hung up next to Jesus the guilty one cries, "Remember me!"

And the promise calls from the cross, "I am with you."

—*Barry Stopfel*, SERMON, NOVEMBER 1992

A year later, December 1992, the vestry at The Church of the Atonement decided that they could no longer afford to keep Barry as a full-time associate. Knowing that an openly gay priest would have a difficult time finding another job, they dutifully debated their ethical responsibilities toward Barry and determined that they had been accepting and supportive, had seen to it that he "got what he wanted," and now it was time for him to move on.

As much as we had been through with these people, as far as we'd traveled together, Barry and I misjudged exactly how far they had come with us. In the euphoria of gaining Barry's ordination, we believed we had been fully accepted as two *gay* men, and that the "deep, dark pool" of human sexuality (as Harold Barrett referred to it years before at Grace Church) had been enlightened. We couldn't have been more wrong.

The week before Christmas, on Barry's "good-bye" Sunday, we made Jack Croneberger an honorary gay man. Now, this is an honor rarely bestowed but always given out of great affection and gratitude. Gay church folklore has it that Bishop Paul Moore, retired from the Diocese of New York, was once made an honorary lesbian in appreciation for his ceaseless efforts at social and religious justice. It is a symbol of gay and lesbian people's affection for those who have traveled the road and endured the hardships with us. A sense of humor and self-possession are requisites for such an honor. Jack Croneberger had more than earned it.

David Norgard, then executive director of Oasis, the Diocese of Newark's ministry to gay and lesbian people, wrote a heartfelt letter which Mark Polo read during the reception:

> Jack, you have so fought for the acceptance of lesbian and gay people that you have not hesitated to identify yourself totally with us. Such is foolishness to the world but it is also a mark of true Christian discipleship as we are all called by our Lord to be at one with each other. . . .

"As you know, Jack, the rights and privileges one obtains as a gay man are still few. Yet with champions like you on our side, I trust there will come a day when sexuality will bring neither special favor nor scorn in either church or society. Thank you for all that you have done and we look forward to what we will be together."

Among the several symbolic gifts of his office we gave Jack at the reception was a condom. In explaining this symbol we acknowledged that, as a father of a gay man and an advocate for all gay people, we were grateful that he had consistently cared for us enough to be concerned that we should also be safe in our sexual relationships.

The sudden hush of a whoops-in-progress was new to us; we didn't recognize it. Jack froze. The room froze. Apparently we could not have done anything more offensive. We were displaying a symbol of *human sexual activity* right there in the *social hall* of the church! The symbol was too much for this suburban congregation.

The "condom caper" turned into an out-of-control purge of heretofore unvoiced fears about human sexuality *(any* sexuality). For a large number of parishioners it was the last straw in a pile of events that refused to let them do something they longed to do: forget that Barry Stopfel was a gay, sexually active man. Jack accused Barry of deliberately setting out to humiliate him and lash out at his congregation, a church that had "come a long way" in being supportive. Jack's castigation culminated by suggesting that "several people" were concerned Barry was planning to do something equally vile at the Christmas Eve services.

Lash out? Humiliate? Vile? The turn of Jack's affection crushed Barry. Jack Croneberger transformed an error of judgment into the definition of Barry's humanity. This is not an uncommon human reaction; we can all plead guilty to oversimplifying our world in times of trouble. Somehow they had both erred.

We didn't realize that, while embracing the concept of homosexuality, many in the church were unwilling to embrace its reality (symbolized, in this instance, by a prophylactic). For four years the church, along with Jack and Barry, had been so focused on keeping Barry's sexuality a nonissue that they had not created opportunities to talk to one another and learn about the sacred in the sexual. Barry and Jack had created a straw house which could collapse under the weight of a single condom.

Barry complied with the church's wishes that Christmas season. We worshiped at St. Paul's Episcopal Church in Paterson, New Jersey, where, in an inner-city parish, among people whose struggle for survival didn't afford them time to ponder the teapot tempests of doctrine, purity, and condoms, we joined hands with prostitutes and lawyers, homeless men and teachers, drug addicts and their lesbian priest, and sang about the hope born in the world through the illegitimate child of a young Palestinian Jew named Mary.

For the six months he had been on notice, Barry had been pursuing a call to parish ministry while trying to discern what other options for ministry might open up for him. Boston appealed to us: its human scale, and especially its proximity to Martha's Vineyard, where we had spent some wonderful weeks with Lee and Mark and Hannah and Sarah. Barry had done his undergraduate work at Boston University and I had spent a summer in the area many years before. So when a Boston church showed interest, we were elated, ready to strike out in a city for which we both had fond feelings.

But Bishop Johnson, then bishop of the Diocese of Massachusetts, informed the parish that he wouldn't license Barry to perform the sacraments in his diocese. Apparently Bishop Johnson felt Barry's "lifestyle as a practicing homosexual" would be an unwholesome example, not only to the children and people within the parish, but in the diocese as a whole. Three years later Bishop Johnson committed suicide rather than face public charges of sexual impropriety brought against him by several women in the diocese with whom he purportedly had had "relations." A horrible price to pay for him and those who loved him, another tragedy of the Church's continuing disintegration of our spirituality and our sexuality.

Without Barry knowing it, Bishop Spong recommended him to Saint George's Church in Maplewood, New Jersey. The search committee sent an "away team" to meet Barry and hear him preach at Atonement in November 1992. Afterward, Ulysses Dietz, Nancy Richardson, and Peter Sittler, a computer systems consultant who was opposed to calling a gay or lesbian person to Saint George's, took Barry to lunch for a preliminary interview.

Even though Barry had led an adult education forum at Saint George's during his last year of seminary in 1988 and felt it was the kind of place where he would like to do ministry, he didn't believe anything would come of this interview. "Big steeple" churches, like Saint George's, do not call queers to their pulpits. So, freed from the anxiety of presenting himself well, lunch was fairly relaxed and comfortable.

During coffee Nancy asked Barry, "Who is God for you?"

"Many things," he replied, then thought awhile, framing his response to this gargantuan question to fit the confines of a luncheon meeting. "God is my breath, the very essence of my life. God is the one I turn to for help and guidance. God is the one who makes it possible for me to love and be loved. God is the one who knit me together in my mother's womb, the creator of everything that is. Everything. There is nothing that is not God, yet God is more than what we can see, more than what we can know about her or him. Who's God for you?" Barry asked the three of them in return.

The three-hour lunch passed amiably as they explored their several spiritual journeys, the nature of their faith, what church community means, and their role in the world as Christians. It was a long, easy afternoon's discussion, filled with companionable quiet and regard as one or the other revealed a deeply felt personal truth.

"I don't think I'll hear from them again," Barry told me when he finally got home around four-thirty that afternoon. I took the lengthy meeting as a good sign. He felt differently.

"It was a great conversation. These people were fantastic: intensely spiritual, seriously committed to social justice in the church and in their own lives, vulnerable, accessible, and," he added the whipped cream to the cake, "they have a great sense of humor."

"So what's the problem, honey?" Everything he said added up to a great interview.

"Well," Barry rubbed the back of his head, "even though it was a great conversation, I don't think it was an interview. They were very interested in me, what I believe," he sat down at the kitchen table and stirred the tea I gave him, "but we never talked about the business of running a church. I've never been a rector, and Saint George's is a pretty big operation. It's hard to explain, but I didn't feel they were seriously interviewing me for a job."

They were. Impressed with his preaching, intrigued by his spirituality, and calmed by his personal manner, Ulysses, Nancy, and Peter, whose fears had given way to faith, decided the entire search committee needed to meet this man. In February 1993 Barry was called to a final, intense interview at the church and I was to join them at an informal luncheon in a parishioner's home.

"I don't believe we're still in New Jersey," I said as we roamed hilly streets lined with ancient oaks, maples, and sycamores. Here and there a few giant elms still stood, their fragile symmetry majestic in the February bareness. The homes were old, stately, rambling affairs of stone, timber, and brick set back from the road and separated from one another by a forest of trees and rhododendron. I imagined Barry and I sitting on any one of a number of broad, deep porches during spring and summer evenings watching kids race by on their bikes or listening to them play kick the can.

"Do kids still play kick the can?" I asked Barry.

"No," he said, remembering a similar childhood. "They play soccer."

We turned down Ridgewood Road and wound our way between the old Erie Lackawanna Railroad and South Mountain, from where General George Washington watched the battle for Springfield more than two hundred years ago. The interview was upon us.

"Oh my God. That's a *big* church," I whispered as I looked up at the massive stone structure rising sixty feet to a steeply pitched roof. "No steeple, though. But look at all those stained-glass windows. And the education wing!" It was an old, Tudor-style building of stucco and timber with a deep, covered porch set beneath tiered gardens that begged one to come in and enjoy. It was beautiful, old, and well cared for. Every fiber within me twitched with covetousness. My left leg jumped so badly I disengaged the clutch and set the hand brake.

"I wish we hadn't seen this." I was still whispering.

"I wish we hadn't, either," Barry whispered back. "But we've got to remember this is just geography and architecture. If we're called here," he took my hand in his, "we're called to a church, not a building. It's the people that make this place beautiful for me. You haven't met them yet. You'll see what I mean at lunch."

I reached across and hugged him. "Thanks for reminding me."

Barry hopped out of the truck and walked into his final interview.

For the next couple of hours I wrestled with my clotheshorse demons at the Short Hills Mall, reliving early years in New York and shopping at Saks, Bloomingdale's, and Barneys. Now Brooks Brothers was looking pretty good. That shook me up so badly I treated myself to a sack of Mrs. Fields cookies and left before I did any serious damage.

Gail Austin, senior warden of the church, welcomed Barry warmly and made sure he had a cup of tea. Seated in a circle in the large upstairs lounge filled with childproof crate furniture, the search committee introduced themselves in a curious way: first their names, years at Saint George's, and then why they came to this church.

"I grew up Episcopalian . . . I'm an ex-Catholic . . . I wasn't anything at all . . ." Then the revelations went deeper.

"It's a community I feel safe in . . . I can ask a lot of questions here without being judged . . . My children are welcome here, as rambunctious as they are . . . It's the place where I begin to make sense out of the crazy lifestyle I lead . . . We care about each other, not just Sunday caring, but everyday caring . . . My partner and I are welcomed here . . . My inner, spiritual life is unapologetically cared for here . . . We don't accept easy, pat answers to life's difficult questions . . ."

The search committee, chaired by a very gregarious Cathy Wolf, had delved deeply into their hearts for the past eighteen months. They had risked a high level of vulnerability with each other, meeting their differences of opinion about the future of the church in prayer, sometimes gentle, sometimes heated conversation, and always with respect for each other's inherent worth. The ease with which they shared their feelings showed that they had been diligent at the gentle art of compassion and the hard work of consensus building.

They were most intrigued by Barry's journey from marketing executive to the priesthood. Why had he changed careers and how did that inform who he was as a man of faith?

An old fear crept over him: Were there hidden traps in their seductive openness? Barry shook himself, prayed our mantra (deep breath, love yourself, and tell the truth), and began talking about his childhood.

He shared stories about his Brethren upbringing and early charismatic experiences in a small-town church, preaching his witness as a child, and his run-in with Reverend Aungst over the church youth dance. As he tried to share with them how he came to make this enormous, midlife change, he told his humiliating story about the homeless woman and his truffles.

"Though I wasn't aware of it at that moment," Barry told the rapt committee, "what happened for me was an epiphany. God came to me in the broken body of a woman I didn't see until I kicked her in the head." He stopped, took a deep breath, loved himself again, and went on with as much truth as he knew at that moment.

"I don't remember the dinner party at all. Late into the night I wandered the streets of New York asking myself over and over, *What am I doing with my life?* I knew God was asking the same question of me." Barry fell silent with the memory.

"How did you know it was God?" someone in the circle asked gently.

Barry looked up from his hands into the woman's eyes and smiled. "Lessons learned in my childhood, from my mother, from my church. I knew it was God because I know that God is always for the weak, the outcast, the one without voice." His voice caught and he stopped. He looked up at the timbered ceiling. No one said a word. They waited.

"I believe God speaks to us," Barry finally continued, "through the better nature of ourselves. We *know* God is speaking to us at certain moments because they're always filled with a terrible conviction of our sin. Or our apathy. I'd lost my way in the world of business. Me. This wasn't a general conviction of business." The room full of professional men and women laughed. "In my heart I knew I had to choose another path, another work for my life. I knew my professional life had to be in the ministry. I had to be about the business of leaving the world a better place than I found it. And I had to do that through the Church."

Now the conversation opened up and delved into the nuts and bolts of running a church: how Barry would rebuild an education program, increase membership, and secure the financial well-being of the parish; i.e.: Could he walk on water?

"All of these are really issues of faith," Barry explained. "We must constantly ask ourselves and our communities two questions: What do we believe God is calling us to do? And what gifts do we have among us to get the job done? When we do that we're modeling healthy leadership.

"Churches aren't run by a rector any more than they're run by the wardens and vestry," Barry went on. "Churches are run by God. If we're diligent about our lives of faith—prayer, meditation, worship, and service—then we can hope we're doing the will of God. As a priest, it's my job to make sure our inner lives of faith are well grounded in the Gospel's mandate to love one another as well as we love ourselves. Learning to love ourselves is no small task. But as we do, the details of ministry will take care of themselves.

"Relatively little of your time has been spent reading dossiers and interviewing candidates," Barry reminded them. "You've been about the hard, slow work of building your faith and your relationships. Now, in the last weeks of your task, the details of the call are working themselves out. Out of our faithfulness God moves in the world. I believe my task, as a priest, is to call a community to its faithfulness. When our faith is sure, the tasks will get done."

For what would prove to be the longest and most difficult section of the morning's interview, Diane Sammons, a tall, beautiful single mother of two young children, cross-examined Barry about his counseling methods and sexual ethics. She posed the questions without prejudice: a tough lawyer doing her job. Still, Barry felt he was on trial. He was.

"How would you counsel a young person who was confused about their sexual orientation?" was Diane's first question. Barry spoke about his belief that sex is a gift from God, an integral piece of every holy relationship.

"What spiritual leaders need to be teaching," Barry explained, "is responsible human sexuality. It's not my job to steer a young person (or old person, for that matter) toward a specific sexual orientation. I believe my job as a priest is to guide each individual with whom I work into a spirituality that is whole and healthy, whatever their orientation." Diane pressed him to elaborate further.

"I am a priest," Barry said, "not a therapist. When someone comes to me with issues that are beyond what I can handle, I refer them to other professionals who are equipped with other skills. Part of being an adolescent is to be confused about sexuality, life, friend-ships, attractions, likes, dislikes, parents, acne, hair, makeup, muscle size and tone." Every parent in the room grimaced with understand-ing.

"I try," Barry continued, "to calm whatever confusion is presented to me by agreeing that much of life is confusing. Then I work with people to try and illumine their own spiritual center, their faith, so that they no longer feel powerless about the terrific changes taking place. But," he told Diane and everyone, "I refer people to others when it's necessary."

After about her seventh penetrating question, Barry cried out: "You *must* be a lawyer!"

"I am." For just a second Diane smiled and tilted her head to one side. In that briefest smile and gesture Barry saw Diane's genuine concern show through her well-honed professional demeanor.

"These are important issues we have to be very clear about," he reassured them all. "But they need to be asked of every candidate, not just the gay ones." For a moment he thought about how to frame his next thought.

"The overwhelming majority of sexual abuse among the clergy is done by straight men. The Church has not done a very good job of integrating people's sexual and spiritual lives into a healthy, life-giving whole. By teaching that the body is separate from the spirit, the Church has thrown kerosene on the fires of human sexuality for centuries. In essence, the Church has left us as confused about ourselves as we were when we entered puberty. The Church has never outgrown its own adolescent attitudes toward sex, and *that* is the great sin that is finally, painfully coming to light."

Every question was asked in the context of Barry's faith. What did he *believe* about this or that issue? He would answer, or start to answer, and suddenly find himself involved in a conversation with several people on the question. This was not a roomful of sheep looking for a shepherd. These were men and women of already great faith looking for someone to guide their own spiritual journeying.

 When I returned for the luncheon, Ulysses Dietz and Gary Berger welcomed me into their comfortable home filled with family heirlooms. Even though I kept reminding myself that we were here to explore our lives of faith and love with the search committee and the vestry of Saint George's, I couldn't help longing for a similarly commodious, tasteful home.

I was braced for the highest-stakes coffee hour of my life but was caught off guard by everyone's easy familiarity and good humor. Obviously, these people were good friends and welcoming of strangers.

Gail Austin introduced me to Patti Savoulidis, a member of the vestry, as Barry's partner.

"Oh," she chirped in her bright, English accent, "how nice to meet Barry's partner." Emphasis on *partner*. Uh-oh. This was news. She didn't know the candidate they were interviewing was gay.

"I saw you drop Barry off at the church in a pickup truck this morning. Is it yours?"

"It's Barry's and mine, yes," I answered, unsure of the ground we were standing on.

"Interesting," she mused. "So typically *American.* Very macho." I saw the wheels turn in her eyes as she tried to reconcile our mode of transportation with our sexuality. Exactly what is a *gay* car?

"Yes," I laughed, "we think so."

She laughed, too, and deftly shifted the conversation. "Don't you just *love* the color of this living room?" I smiled that she could read my gay beads so easily, and agreed with her and chatted about the antiques, the window treatments, and soft colorings of the house.

Since lunch was to be with both the search committee and vestry, Ulysses and Gary made sure to give us plenty of time to relax and chat before it was served. I didn't know if they were loosening us up or fattening us for the kill. I had to remind myself that these people were seriously interviewing a *gay couple*, for Pete's sake; the stakes were equally high for them. We all needed time to get our bearings straight (as it were).

After a standing, plate-in-hand meal (I was too nervous to sit, eat, swallow, and talk at the same time), it was time to gather around the living room for the carefully orchestrated "informal conversation."

"Hey," I protested when I saw Ulysses position two chairs before the inquisitive throng. "I thought this was supposed to be *informal?* This looks more like a tribunal!" I laughed on the outside, but my insides were doing a dance of death.

"My dear," Sue Mangasarian, a matriarch of the church and member of the vestry, coughed back her great big laugh, "it's just so we can all *see* you. It may be our last chance to get a good look at you." Her eyes shone with a mischievousness that comes to people of a certain age who've earned the right to say just what they want.

Gail Austin asked Barry the first of the "heavy" questions. "How many people left Atonement because of your presence there?" We had not talked about the "loss management" of calling a gay rector at all. But it was a topic that had to come up if they were seriously going to consider Barry for the job.

"We lost four families because of my presence there." He knew exactly. "Three had been on the fringes for some time and many on the vestry felt they were just looking for a reason."

"And the fourth?" Gail prompted.

Barry rubbed his beard a moment, remembering. "It was an older man, widowed. He left before he knew I was gay. He was just angry at what I taught. When he later learned about my sexuality, he accused the rector of forcing him to leave the church by hiring a gay priest. We all knew better, but he made a lot of noise." People smiled and nodded, knowing just what sort of person he was. Every church has at least one.

For the next twenty minutes we talked about the implications of calling a gay person to their pulpit. By their questions Barry and I could tell that the vestry and search committee weren't even thinking about, let alone focusing on "loss management." The call to their pulpit was an issue of faith: Is this the person God is calling us to guide our spiritual growth into the next century? We talked together frankly about both their concerns and ours.

"Is Saint George's the kind of place that would be welcoming to me and Will? Not just accepting, but nurturing for us as well?" Barry asked. There was a long pause while everyone mulled over the implications of his question. Could they care for us as strongly as Barry, and to some extent I, as clergy spouse, would be called to care for them?

"I think Barry's asking—" I turned to him. "Sorry to do this to you, dear but . . ." I looked back at everyone smiling at my inter-ruption. "We sometimes slip into the bad habit of explaining what the other really means." Patti laughed out loud and everyone else smiled. They knew all too well that longtime partners often inter-pret one another, and that it *is* a bad habit.

"What Barry's asking," I continued, "is that, as strangers, we've never been more welcomed anywhere than we have here today." I had to catch my breath and hold back the surge of emotion that swept over me. Barry finished for me.

"Is Saint George's like you?" he asked. "Is it the kind of place where we could thrive, where our relationship could thrive? Are you truly representative of the congregation?"

Everyone jumped into this conversation, not that any of them were shy about getting their oar in, and talked about various people and their possible reactions to a gay rector. They were proud of the breadth of tolerance in the congregation, something many of the people in that room had taught and nurtured for years. It was thrilling to sit back and listen to them talk about their long commitment to an inclusive community of faith and how its creation was, for them, an act of social justice. Yes, they told us, they were representative of the church.

I noticed that Bill Lorentz, an aggressive state prosecutor whom Barry and I had met years earlier at a diocesan gay function, and Ulysses Dietz sat in the back of the room and rarely spoke. They seemed to be chafing at the bit, eager to dive in and ask the good questions, show off Barry as the kind of priest the church needed. But they sat meekly, and watched and listened. No mean feat for Bill. He and Ulysses reined in their strength and held fast to their belief that this room of people would discern God's Spirit without feeling any pressure from the gays.

At one point when the conversation hovered around his life as a gay priest, Barry interrupted.

"I'm not a gay priest," he corrected them. "I'm a priest who's in a committed relationship with a man."

"Oh, right," I interjected before I could stop myself. "He's not gay. His lover is."

Nancy threw her head back and roared. I guess she never heard that old chestnut before. Everyone laughed, their love for the silly and the sacred mixed effortlessly.

"What I mean is," Barry went on, "my sexuality is as much a part of who I am in my relationships with others as yours is for you. Gay or straight, we are all sexual beings." He caught Patti's twinkling eyes. She had more on her plate than most in the room—three small children and a critically ill husband—yet the love and compassion in her eyes encouraged Barry every minute of that afternoon to delve deeper into himself and share with them the inner truths about who he is.

"As a priest," Barry said, "I look and listen for the *whole* of who someone is, not just some particular aspect presented at a given time. If any of us were judged for any single moment, any single action in our lives, we'd all be in deep fat. But we're not. And that's the grace of God at work in all of our relationships. To the degree we're able to embrace and love ourselves, all of ourselves, we learn to love others. And in loving others we learn to love God. Then we find out that God loves us. Just as we are."

"How do you two care for each other?" someone asked. "You've been under a lot of public scrutiny. How have you handled that?" I saw Barry swallow hard. Me, I nearly wept. In the past four years no one except our closest friends had ever cared to know what this had cost us.

"We walk a lot," Barry began. "We spend as much time as we can walking the beach, or taking our dog, Spirit, on walks in the mountains."

"What?" Patti Savoulidis interrupted in her sharp, English accent. "What's your dog named?"

"Spirit," Barry repeated.

"What a fabulous name for a priest's dog!"

"We like to be outdoors," Barry steered the conversation back to the point. "When we go for a hike or a walk, we talk quietly or walk in silence—meet each other again. When we go to the woods, go into something wilder, something older, it's easier for us to experience God's presence. It's one of the ways we take care of each other."

"Where do you go to the mountains?" Roland Spiotta, a very fit, distinguished-looking gentleman asked from across the room.

"Barry's folks have a place in central Pennsylvania," I told him. "We can drive up into the mountains and hike trails all day and never see another soul."

"I see," Patti said. "That's why you have that big, macho, four-wheel-drive truck?" Her eyes positively shone. "I wondered what that was about."

"Yes, it's great in the mountains," Barry told them. "My brother helped us get it. He thought we should have something we really wanted."

"But what about when you can't get away?" Gail Austin asked. "What about day to day?"

Barry looked at me and put his hand on my arm. "You have to understand," he said, "that we're both men of faith. When Will cooks for me, and he's a terrific cook, he's giving me more than just a meal. When I rub his shoulders I'm caring for more than just his body. We can read, or just sit quietly together not really needing to talk, and we're caring for each other." Barry thought a moment and went on. "It's being together, seeing each other as a reminder of all the gifts God has given us. That's what nourishes us. We know we love and are loved by God because we love each other. And isn't that what the Eucharist reminds us every week?"

I spoke into the thoughtful quiet that had settled over the room. "My faith is not dependent upon doing religious gymnastics. Just like you, we worship and pray a very small percentage of our time. But every minute of every day in everything we do, we are always people of faith."

"Tell them your favorite Bible verse," Barry nudged me.

"You tell them," I nudged him back. "You're the priest."

"Yes," Barry teased, "but you're the Southerner!"

I quoted from the sixth chapter of Micah: *What does the Lord require of you, but to do justice, love mercifully, and walk humbly with your God?*

"Would you like to see the rectory?" Cathy Patton, a member of the search committee and a librarian in town, asked.

I answered, "No."

"Yes," said Barry.

"Well," she laughed, "you're obviously two different people. Why not, Will?"

I wanted to tell her I didn't want to see what we weren't going to get. As good a priest as Barry is and as good a meeting as we had just had, I didn't believe they would call Barry to their pulpit, let alone two gay men to live in their rectory. But all I said was "We don't need to take the time now."

"So why don't I take Barry, since he wants to go," Cathy smiled back at me, "and you can sit in the car."

No, I didn't want to see the sprawling, center-hall Colonial, but my gay genes couldn't resist.

As soon as we walked in I got dizzy. The living room was forty feet long with a panel beamed ceiling, massive fireplace, and three sets of French doors opening down onto a high, screened-in back porch. Summer evenings were calling.

But the kitchen really clawed at my heart. Oh, how I longed to cook in that kitchen. Originally a butler's pantry, kitchen, and break-fast room, it had been opened up to one large room, preserving two walk-in pantries and three old-fashioned, floor-to-ceiling hutches. There were acres of cabinets and yards of counter space. I saw din-ner parties for fifty and receptions for hundreds. However, the dozen variously patterned floral wallpapers would have to go!

"Lot of flowers, don't you think, Cathy?" I asked.

"Oh, yes." She winked at me. "But we have a refurbishing bud-get."

As we descended the winding, split-landing stairway, papered in disorienting brown, geometric circles within squares, and carpeted in something shrimp, Cathy asked, "Quite a house, isn't it?" I thought how beautiful it would look in simple off-whites and taupes—particularly at Christmas with garland on the balusters, candles in the windows, a giant tree in front of the French doors, and a fire blazing away.

"Yes, it is," I said, willing the picture of someone else's future out of my mind.

 We left Saint George's feeling like we had fallen in love.

"If they can get past the queer thing," Barry said as we crept back to Leonia through a snowstorm, "they'll call us."

"That's a big, big if, honey," I said, and tried to keep my eyes on the freezing road.

We mused together over our pessimism about church communities and gay people. It is so hard for any of us to walk the theological concepts we talk (I had just spent most of my day coveting other people's oxen and asses!). Our experience so far was that most church people didn't like to talk about queer clergy to their friends in the grocery store checkout line (Shirley Redfield being one of the great exceptions in our life). Generally, though, institutions do not risk their futures to live by their faith.

"Barry," I said as we pulled up in front of our three-room, one quarter of a row house wedged butt up against three other Depression-era, two-toned, aluminum-sided row houses of sea-mist green and white. "Do you think it's possible you could be called to a rectory?"

"No." He laughed out loud. "But *you* could be!"

"I wonder . . ." I took his hand. Barry was shaking.

He took a chill, it turned into a fever, and he spent seven days in bed with the flu.

Chapter 29

And Mary said,

"My soul magnifies the Lord,

and my spirit rejoices in God my Savior,

for he has regarded the low estate of his handmaiden.

For behold, henceforth all generations will call me blessed;

for he who is mighty has done great things for me,

and holy is his name,

And his mercy is on those who fear him

from generation to generation.

He has shown strength with his arm,

he has scattered the proud in the imagination of their hearts,

he has put down the mighty from their thrones,

and exalted those of low degree;

he has filled the hungry with good things,

and the rich he has sent empty away.

He has helped his servant Israel,

in remembrance of his mercy,

as he spoke to our fathers,

to Abraham and to his posterity for ever."

—Luke 1:46–55

I leaned at the kitchen window and watched the snow storm through the gray Saturday afternoon light. Beautiful, but this was late March 1993, and Barry and I were ready for crocus and daffodils. Even Spirit refused to plow her way through the two-day drifts, declining her morning constitutional. Instead, she curled up under the kitchen table and dozed with one eye on my smoked ham hocks cooling from the pea soup. She knows I am a little careless when chopping meat. Smart dog. But smart enough to know I drop things on purpose? Probably.

Barry was reading, preparing for an adult education forum the next day. Since his termination at Atonement he jobbed out to various churches around the diocese whenever he could, keeping fairly busy. However, as it did for millions of other Americans, the uncertainty of part-time work ate at his soul. Daring to hope before all rationale to the contrary, he prayed constantly, keeping his heart open to the possibility that God just might part the waters of history.

Seductive as the thought was, Barry kept reminding himself that a priesthood at Saint George's was not the prize. Just like every other Christian throughout history, Barry was called to be faithful—his eyes on the road before him, not the prize. So, to help him focus his faith, doubts, fears, and questions, the night before he prepared an altar in the study.

On his altar Barry placed a candle, which burned through the night and the following day. Next to the fire he put his father's pocket-sized New Testament. This leather-bound gift was given to Marlin by his church his last Sunday before he was shipped out to World War II. He carried it with him through every flight, every battle. It was in his breast pocket when he was shot down over the Battle of the Bulge, still with him as he was shuttled from field hospital to field hospital and finally home to his young wife and baby boy to recover as best he could from his catastrophic burns.

Next, Barry placed a dish of earth from our garden and a bowl given to him at his ordination by Edie Lauderdale, one of his great friends at Atonement. In the bottom of the delicate, porcelain bowl is a feathery blue marking resembling a bird in flight or, perhaps, the victorious phoenix. This he filled with water. Next to these he put a talisman of feathers, pine cones, and twigs gathered on weekends many years before in Pennsylvania with his old friends Alan and Holly. Next to the New Testament he carefully leaned a small, fading sepia tint of his mother, whose faithfulness encouraged him still, twenty-three years after her death. Last, he placed a red crystal heart I had given him on Valentine's Day.

These were holy pieces of his life, whose reminders and power he needed close to him on this wintry day potent with hope. Hope is hard work for everybody, especially for people who have hoped in the face of historical and cultural traditions. But all people who hope find it is a calling at which we labor because we all dare to believe the impossible. God's fools, I suppose.

A great part of Barry was still a doubter, for one cannot hope without doubting. We fell in love with the people at Saint George's, as we felt they had with us. But Barry knows how hard it is for any of us to act on our hearts' passions, particularly when they run contrary to all that we have known. So, on his altar, he gathered around him his past, present, and future, images of the sacred in his life. He sat in their company along with his doubts and his faith that night and all the next day, and continued to pray.

We jumped every time the phone rang, even though we assumed the search committee wouldn't meet in this storm. Ann Evans, Lee Hancock, Mark Polo, Sue and Mary Ann—our family had all called to say they were thinking of us, praying for Barry. They didn't want to keep the line tied up so, "Just relax," they each counseled Barry, and "Let us know as soon as you hear anything. We're praying for you." The phone rang. Again.

I jumped, again. Barry calmly picked it up. I guess my Zen cook-ing meditation hadn't been as centering as his altar.

Barry was in the study with the phone to his ear, listening. I went to the door and leaned in, listening. Spirit, who had figured out by now that *something* was up with the phone (smart dog), leaned against me and watched Barry.

"Well," Barry spoke into the phone, "I'm very happy to hear from you." He stopped talking and listened some more. I wasn't sure what this conversation was about and held my breath.

"Praise God," Barry said into the phone. I had never heard him use that expression before and now was really confused.

"Praise God," Barry said again. What was going on? He wouldn't turn around from his desk and give me any kind of sign.

"Praise God." He said it again! This was *very* unusual behavior from my fairly reserved, Episcopal lover. I started to shake. Had the impossible just happened?

"Oh, yes," Barry laughed a long, satisfying laugh, "I'm delighted to accept the call to be your rector. And Gail," Barry took a deep breath, collecting himself, "please, thank everyone for me for their faithfulness." He listened again.

"Yes," he said to her, "it *is* a remarkable thing God's doing here. . . . I'll be praying for you all, too."

He hung up and turned to me, laughing and clapping his hands. I was in a puddle of tears on the floor with Spirit licking my face.

All of a sudden there wasn't enough air in the apartment. We bundled up and then plowed out the back door. With the snow all the way up to her noble chin, Spirit chose to walk behind us, hop-ping from one footprint to another.

The wind tore at our faces. We threw our arms up and howled back at the wind. Snow poured into our mouths. Tears froze on our faces.

"I can't believe it!" Barry called over the snow.

"Believe it, Barry!" I hugged him as hard as I could through our down coats. "Believe it today, and tomorrow, and every day of your life. God and Saint George's are calling you to a new life of faith—for yourself and for Saint George's." I hugged him again. "Believe it!" I shouted above the storm. Against all odds the people of Saint George's Church had the courage to love us into their community, their heart, and their spirit.

We howled some more and tripped over curbs hidden beneath hills of snow and, where we fell, made giant, laughing angels in the snow. Spirit pounced and rolled between us, turning herself into a black Abominable Snow Beast. Our lives would never be the same. And neither would Saint George's.

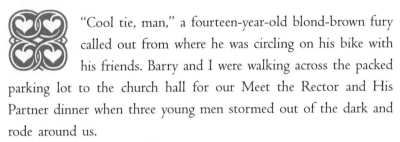 "Cool tie, man," a fourteen-year-old blond-brown fury called out from where he was circling on his bike with his friends. Barry and I were walking across the packed parking lot to the church hall for our Meet the Rector and His Partner dinner when three young men stormed out of the dark and rode around us.

"Thanks," I called back to them, unable to distinguish one from the other in the scant light spilling from the church hall.

"Are you coming to the dinner?" Barry asked.

"Maybe." "I don't know." "Yeah," they all answered at once, circling, circling, circling.

"Church dinners are rough," Barry said from behind me. Our defenses were up: orbiting teenagers meant trouble. We had lived too long in New York City. "I don't blame you for not wanting to go," Barry said and then laughed. "I'd rather be riding with you guys, too."

"Yeah, me too." I laughed a little too boisterously. "But there are a lot of folks in there who want to meet their new priest. I'm part of the package so I gotta go, too. See you in there?"

They shrugged and grunted in that alien language peculiar to adolescents, never once taking their eyes off us as they swept in close and circled away. They were checking us out. Having a gay priest had to be an awesome experience for these guys. After all, adolescence is the stage when we define ourselves by what we are not (*I'm not a queer!*) and "faggot," the lowest of low epithets, is routinely hurled at those we dislike. They needed to see what kind of faggots we were before they decided whether or not to sit through a church dinner with their parents, surely one of the most painful of teenage tortures.

When we walked into the hall Barry was cool and comfortable. I was as nervous as I'd ever been in my life.

"Will!" Sue Mangasarian bounded out of the kitchen, where she led an army of helpers for tonight's dinner. "Meet my husband, Dick."

"Very nice to meetcha," a slightly stooped but sturdy graying man with thick glasses drawled and grabbed my hand in a death grip. "My wife tells me you're quite a cook. You'd better watch out," his mouth crinkled into a deep grin, "she'll have you helping tonight."

"Dick!" Sue shushed her husband. "I just want him to meet some people." And with that she took me away from Barry (*Oh, God, now what? I'm on my own!*) and dragged me through the crowd to the kitchen.

"I want you to see what we're cooking and tell me if you like it." Sue Mangasarian's gracious instincts surrounded me in the warmth of her kitchen, where she figured, rightly, I would be more relaxed with a small group of people. She introduced me to everyone on duty and for a good ten minutes talked about the rigors of cooking for large crowds, checked and rechecked the roasting chickens, and kept her eye on the clock. It was clear she relished this job.

"You know," Sue hooked her arm through mine, "every year the kids bake pumpkin pies from scratch at Thanksgiving to raise money. Maybe you could help them this year."

"Sue!" Dick called from the door, a threshold he was obviously not invited to cross. "Leave him alone. And isn't it time for dinner?" He wrested me from his wife and brought me back out to the hall. "Didn't I warn you?" He laughed, enjoying how well he knew this woman he had loved for fifty years.

After dessert, coffee, and tea were served, Cathy Wolf, who chaired the search committee, told a bit of the story of how they'd come to call Barry to be their rector. After a day of silent prayer and meditation, they had all chosen Barry on private ballots. Each one was, to a greater or lesser degree, frightened by their depth of feeling for Barry. They had no history to call on, no precedent to assure them that a gay priest could successfully model a spiritual future for their community. Yet on that stormy March Saturday they each had stories about how they felt, heard, and experienced the Spirit of God moving them to be courageous, to go where their hearts were being drawn.

Gail Austin, one of the two wardens of the church, stood after Cathy introduced us, and asked Barry and me to say a few words.

"You go first," Barry whispered and gave me a little push.

As I looked around at all the people, I was overwhelmed by the grace that had come to Barry and me through their love. I thought about my dad and how he would have been so happy for us, so proud of this church for their courage. I wished he had lived to see this day. So I told my new church family a story about him.

"I was born and raised in southern West Virginia," I began, "the son of two parents with larger-than-life personalities. My mom flew with the WASPS during World War II and ran her home and five children with an almost militarylike ordinance. My father was a big man, powerful, a former college football player. He was a man who worked men in the coal fields of southern West Virginia, a man who loved the sea and boats and the furies of the earth, a man who was never more alive than when taming the chaotic elements of the earth.

"As a boy I frequently heard, 'Your father is a man's man.' He was admired for his strength and fierce devotion to his friends. A third-generation Scot from a clan who had dwelt close to the border with England, fierceness came naturally.

"I was deeply devoted to him, in awe of him, as were my brother and sisters. His being permeated my life, even though he was rarely present, and then only on the weekends.

"Since age fifteen, when I went off to school, my father called me every Saturday morning of my life, a habit which continued after I moved to New York City. It was often a strained experience for both of us—he wasn't much of a conversationalist. 'Oh, I'm fine,' he always answered my regular question. 'Mom's fine, the dog's fine. How're you?'

"I would relate the successes, failures, and discoveries in my school and work, and the excitement of big-city life. He'd spent a lot of time in New York as a young man and loved hearing about his old stomping grounds, even though I was stomping on very different ground.

"Mostly there was silence between us. We were two very different men. But we respected each other.

"When I moved in with my first partner, I left it up to Dad to handle however he wanted. I wasn't being malicious, we just didn't have much practice at talking about this sort of thing. How does one come out to one's parents anyway?

"Regular as rain, Dad phoned my first Saturday morning in my new home with my new love. The usual checking in, the usual chatter about nothing at all, but wanting to hear each other's voice, making sure we were still 'fine.' And then the earth spun away beneath me.

" 'Has anyone told you today that they love you, son?' Dad asked, and waited for an answer.

"I'd never lied to my father. But what was I to do? How could I confess to this nearly mythic being in my life, this 'man's man,' that I was also a man's man, albeit with a different bent?

"I took a deep breath, loved myself, and told the truth.

" 'Yes, Dad, they have.' Yes, I kept the gender neutral. I was free-falling through a personal chaos, feeling death, my death, rushing up at me, crushing the air out of my lungs.

"How could I tell my father I was gay? What would he say? Even worse, what would he think? I was sure he loved me, although he never said those words. If I said right out who I was, would I destroy the silent bond between us? My heart stopped as I heard my father speak across the thousand miles between us.

" 'Well,' he said, 'that's good. I love you too, son.' "

It was absolutely still around the dinner tables in the church hall. The memory of that day flooded my eyes and throat. My voice caught. I looked down at Barry, unsure of the water I had gotten myself into. He smiled up at me and ever so slightly nodded his encouragement. *Go on*, his eyes said. *Tell them the story.*

"You see," I started, then choked, cleared my throat, and went on. "It was the first time my father ever said that to me." I stopped again. The memory overwhelmed me, but I would not, *could* not cry! I swallowed, smiled, and shook my head in apology for this embarrassing moment. The apology was not needed. In their eyes I saw a compassionate, eager willingness to listen and to know about me. I saw then why I was telling this story.

"All of my life I wanted my dad to love me in the ways I needed him to love me. But he didn't. He couldn't, and that used to hurt me. You see," I said, looking around at my new family, "love doesn't always come in the size and color we want it to. It's not always available in the shape we want.

"We can't make the lover over in our own image; I couldn't make my dad love me the way I wanted him to. Love comes to us in its own way, on its own terms. But it does come. Maybe not in the color and size we think we want, but it comes."

I stopped and looked down at my feet, then up at a high window. I couldn't look at Barry again; I could feel him holding on tight to his own feelings. I looked out at our new family.

"Love has come to us," I went on, "in a way we never dreamed of. You," I lifted my hands and gestured to the room full of people, "came to us. And for the future we have together, we're going to see and feel and know love in ways none of us has ever dreamed. Thank you for your tremendous heart."

I sat down, a dozen thoughts flying through my mind—my inner critic in full whine about how I should have tied the story up better, made a stronger point, been less personal. *Go* should *on yourself*, I reminded myself and leaned back to listen to my partner introduce himself to his new parish.

"What a wonderful meal," Barry began. "Sue, everybody . . ." He started applauding. Quickly the parish hall echoed with cheers and whistles.

"One of my favorite proverbs," Barry went on as the applause died down, "is a Celtic one which says, 'The one who bids me eat, bids me live.' So I am very grateful for the blessing of life which you have so generously given me and Will tonight."

He stopped a moment and collected his thoughts. "Like all of you, I have wonderful childhood memories of parish dinners— Martha Crook's meatloaf, Mary Olson's spaghetti sauce, and Kathryn Brehm's homemade peanut-butter-filled chocolate eggs at Easter. We learned in our interviews that this is a parish that loves to eat—"

"We do!" a woman (Sue Mangasarian?) shouted from the back, causing a roar of laughter to roll through the room.

"Then," Barry laughed, "I know we'll spend many evenings like this, getting to know each other over simple food offered with simple and loving hospitality. This is a gift you have in gracious abundance. Strangers will flock to your hospitality and be strangers no more.

"Now I know what I'm about to say is going to sound odd, but bear with me." Barry paused, looked around, and finally continued. "I feel a little bit like the virgin Mary tonight." There was a spattering of muffled laughter.

"So now you're probably asking yourselves, and rightly so, 'How is it you feel like the virgin Mary, Barry? I mean, aren't we going to be in *enough* trouble as it is?'" The spattering of laughter was now decidedly nervous. So was I. What was he talking about?

"Remember when the angel Gabriel came to Mary and told her she would have a son?" Barry asked his parishioners. "He told this unwed, teenaged woman that the power of the Holy Spirit would come over her body and she would give birth to the holy child of God. Gabriel even told her what to name him.

"Gabriel continues his terrifying visitation by telling Mary that her kinswoman Elizabeth, who is old and barren, is just about to have a son herself. That boy would become John the Baptist, of camel hair, locust, and wild honey fame.

"Mary, in one of the New Testament's great understatements, was 'greatly troubled.' Nonetheless, out of her terror of the unknown, she asks Gabriel, 'How can these things be?' And Gabriel, with unabashed angelic brevity, answers her, 'With God, nothing will prove impossible.'"

Barry stopped and looked into the eyes that were looking at him. Across the room he saw a table of ten gay and lesbian people beaming back at him.

"In the nearly one month since that fateful, stormy day which brought us together, I have asked myself over and over again, 'How can these things be?' How could this moment have happened, when so many thought it impossible?

"Each time I ask myself that question I think of Mary, for the good news we share together seems equally outrageous, equally impossible. We are carrying within us, we are *bearing* together something of the Holy Spirit. And as yet, we know not what it will be.

"But," Barry paused and cleared his voice of his own swelling emotions, "because it seems so impossible, I cling to Gabriel's words to Mary: 'With God, nothing will prove impossible.'

"We are not creating a future alone here. Our future is in God's hands. And it is God who makes the impossible possible." He stopped and picked up a book he had brought with him.

"I want to give the people of Saint George's something to commemorate this night and this call. It is Madeleine L'Engle's *The Glorious Impossible.* As a parting gift from The Church of the Atonement, I was given a copy of this book by the children in the church school.

"It is a book filled with wisdom, for it reminds us that possible things are easy to believe. But the glorious impossibles are hard to believe for it is they which bring joy to our hearts and hope to our lives. The birth of Jesus was a glorious impossible. And, like love, your love, it can only be rejoiced in.

"L'Engle writes, 'Jesus came to us for love, and he died for us for love, and he rose from the grave for love, and he ascended into Heaven for love, and the Comforter came to us to teach us to love. So, beloveds, let us love one another as Jesus has called us to do.' "[10]

He handed the richly illustrated book to Gail Austin and finished his brief talk.

"I give you this book with joy in my heart and hope abounding for the gloriously impossible journey God has set before us. Remember, with God all things are possible."

He sat. For a long moment the room was perfectly still. Their new rector had entered teaching, shining a light on their hope with his faith. Suddenly a hundred people stood as one and cheered. Way in the back I saw the three teenaged bikers laughing and clapping along with everyone else. I guess we checked out okay.

The great risk of faith had its critics. Not a surprise, but the echoes were hauntingly familiar.

"It is with much distress and disgust that I recently learned of your decision to hire Mr. Stopfel for the Rector position at Saint George's," a prominent, middle-aged lawyer wrote to the wardens and vestry. "I feel, as many of the people I grew up with feel, that your decision to hire a homosexual has placed a stake through our hearts and undercut the moral power and love we learned at Saint George's. It is a huge mistake that will tear the church apart. I urge you to reverse your decision. I can tell you that if you do not, I will never set foot in the church again." The man was raised in Maplewood, now lived a hundred miles away, and had not set foot in the church for years.

"You should know that all of us care very deeply about Saint George's," the wardens and vestry responded with kindness and hope. "Barry Stopfel is the right person for this church. We pray that your anger may cease and that your heart be calmed." This was their faith-filled response to the few objections from people outside the community. In May 1993, we moved into the rectory and began a new chapter of life at Saint George's.

The church was far from being torn apart. On her first Sunday at Saint George's, Martha Gardner, a steady, faithful worker for justice and community building in the Diocese of Newark, told the congregation, "I waited to come to Saint George's until after you called your new priest. When I learned that you had called Barry I was ecstatic, and so, here I am with my husband, Bill, and my children, Sarah and Matthew." The congregation smiled, as congregations do when newcomers introduce themselves.

"I don't know Barry personally," Martha explained, lest someone listening think her a "ringer" brought in by the new rector, "but I do know this: If this is a community that can call an openly gay man and his lover into their church, then this is where we believe our children will learn what it means to be a Christian in our world."

Dozens of people began streaming through the doors of Saint George's, mostly young families like Martha and Bill's, all of them sharing a similar hope for their children. "There's a feeling here," most spoke of, "a sense of God, the Spirit, that has been missing in our lives." "I feel welcomed here," others said. Saint George's was filling up with the glorious impossibles—faith, hope, and most of all, love.

 "It was good of you to welcome all the children," Lee Huggins, a parish member for more than forty years wrote after our first Epiphany open house at the rectory. A no-nonsense octogenarian who still took aerobics classes and managed the extensive church gardens, Lee had lived to see her church reborn and renewed. "It was a real, whole-parish affair, the sort of event that gels a disparate group, making individuals and couples alike feel part of a strong whole.

"I hear lots of good things, too, about the special children's services. You both have a way with the young which bodes well for the future of Saint George's."

Epiphany—the celebration that God has revealed God's self to the gentiles, to those not recognized as "chosen." God made visible in the love of a community of people. All people without regard for human distinctions. How can these things be?

How, indeed? a small faction of bishops were asking themselves.

Chapter 30

For I am sure that neither death, nor life,

nor angels, nor principalities,

nor things present, nor things to come,

nor powers, nor height, nor depth,

nor anything else in all creation,

will be able to separate us from the love of God

made visible in Christ Jesus our Lord.

—SAINT PAUL'S LETTER TO THE ROMANS 8:38–39

Barry stood talking to Walter Righter on the phone. Whenever he or his wife, Nancy, called, it was a welcome dose of warmth; their unflappable optimism and good humor always buoyed us up for our life in the fishbowl, as many priests and their spouses refer to the job of parish ministry. All of a sudden Barry's face and voice turned as cold as the January sleet of 1994, icing us in for another night.

"What's going on, honey?" I whispered, but was shushed when the phone book went flying across the kitchen.

"What in the hell do they think they're doing?"

"That's it, exactly," Walter chuckled over the phone. "Hell. That's what they're making. Hell."

Two days earlier a colleague phoned Barry to let him know that certain bishops in the church, urged by Jim Stanton and Bill Wantland, were going to bring a presentment against Walter for ordaining Barry to the diaconate. It was like a recurring nightmare for Barry: striving to be a man of faith, serving as a Christian minister, all the while being pummeled by doubts about his ability to remain faithful to his call in the midst of more public scrutiny.

Doubt and faith. Parallel streams of the soul's journey toward what is good, true, and of God. Barry cried with Saint Augustine and Saint Paul: *Lord, I believe! Save me from my unbelief!*

Surely these ten bishops, the number required to bring a request of presentment before the presiding bishop, would not succeed in getting the needed seventy-five bishops to proceed? Surely the presiding bishop would squash it? For the two days since he first heard of the action, Barry clung to this one hope. But on this freezing-cold January night, he learned that Presiding Bishop Browning was indeed allowing the ten to proceed.

"Perhaps it's for the best," Walter offered with customary grace. "Ed Browning believes this group needs to see how much support is or isn't out there for them. And he's right, Barry. Maybe the only way we resolve the issue of gays in the priesthood is to let the whole thing boil over now. They might get seventy-five to sign on to the presentment, but I don't think so."

Mixed equally with his doubt and ambivalence, Barry had an irrevocable sense of purpose about this event. He knew deep inside that the ten bishops would find the votes necessary to charge Walter with heresy. And he knew in the same instant the phone book went flying that he was also called to be a solid, faithful presence in the center of the storm. It was ordained to be, he thought; he was chosen to be here, now. So he threw the book. Like Jeremiah, perhaps, he didn't feel like being a hero, didn't know if his parish could stand the strain, didn't feel big enough to manage the certain public scrutiny of his life and ministry. But God doesn't choose big. God chooses faithful, however small and imperfect that faithful one feels at the time.

Faith and doubt are sisters. Could he be leading faithful Christians into the chasm of heresy? Or was God hardening hearts again, like Pharaoh's heart was hardened against the Israelites? Was there death ahead, or a promised land? Barry was torn every day, for how is one ever sure, before God reveals God's self, what is truth? Episcopalians discern truth through Scripture, Tradition, and Reason. But these three guides were at odds with one another.

From January to August of 1995, we waited for God to reveal how she would move in our life, the life of Saint George's, and the life of the Episcopal Church nationwide.

Barry had been at Saint George's not eighteen months. The honeymoon was not even over. Was the new bond between them strong enough to withstand the close scrutiny of a heresy trial? Plus he had all the complications of uncharted territory to navigate as an out gay rector. It all seemed overwhelming. Was there ever a priest in the Church who had been under the microscope for so long?

Would he shine light, or throw shadows on faith? Would he remain faithful to the Gospel of Jesus? Would his faith sustain him? Would I leave him because I never bargained for any of this, and he knew how deeply I resented the terrible cost of his ordination to our relationship?

"I didn't think it showed!" I kidded him one night in our season of waiting. He was not in a laughing mood.

"This is serious, Will," he said, sitting me down in the kitchen. "Our whole relationship has been overshadowed by my struggles with the Episcopal Church. It's taken a toll on you." He took my hand across the table and went on.

"Ordained ministry is never easy on anybody's relationship, and it's been particularly hard on ours. You've always been there for me, but I haven't always been there when you needed me. Our life, our loving, our times together have all paid too high a price. You yourself complain how distant I am a lot of the time."

"Honey," I said, grasping our hands with my free one, "nobody ever said it'd be easy. You've done a lot of good for a lot of people. But," my eyes started tearing up, "you're right. Sometimes I wish there was more time for us."

Sometimes Barry wished he could just chuck the whole call to ministry and return to being a well-adjusted, responsible, professional gay man in New York City—read the *New York Times* over brunch in the Village, go to the theatre, see the ballet again. He never reveled in slaying dragons and knew that God would be God with or without him or the Episcopal Church. Besides, there were plenty of places that needed help in our world, would welcome our help. Was he hiding his light under a bushel by working in a mainstream denomination? His waking nightmare was that God would call him up one day and say, "Barry, you've been very brave and you've helped change many lives for the better in the Episcopal Church. You've been faithful and compassionate in response to my people, who disagreed with you and even wanted you dead.

"But," God continues, for there is always a "but," a conviction, when God speaks, "what about your gay and lesbian brothers and sisters who are hungry, broken, and unattended? Have you forgotten about them?"

Even with his innate, stubborn will to prevail, the doubting questions continued to hound Barry as we headed into the fray. On a hot August afternoon in 1995, Jack and Christine Spong paid a special pastoral call on Barry at the rectory. In the course of the afternoon Barry confessed his doubts about staying in a Church that didn't seem to want him. Barry's bishop gently reminded him of the many people before him, women and blacks, who had struggled for full inclusion in the Church. Yes, some had left, but others had stayed, and through their steady, faithful witness, changed the Church for the good. They prayed for God's will to be done.

But Barry's questions would not be set aside for long and, by the time I got home, he was furious with doubt.

"Am I so stupid that I *want* to live in the belly of the beast? Why do I remain in an institution that doesn't want me? Do I stay because I can't tell the difference between priestly sacrifice and downright masochism anymore? Do I not know the difference between martyr, prophet, and fool? Is there a point where enough is enough?"

We sat together in the vortex of his emotions and doubts, holding on like fools to the belief that this would one day make sense. Finally, out of the silence, Barry knew the answer to his questions.

"I know, I know," Barry said to me. "It's the same thing the prophet Jeremiah went through. Remember when he got fed up with being mocked because he spoke in God's name?" Sure I did, and nodded.

"Every time he wanted to quit proclaiming the name of God it burned within him and would not stay down. He grew weary of trying to hold back the Spirit of God within him. I am weary like Jeremiah, but have no choice but to be in the midst of this right now. I know I have to do this. But I am so tired!"

Barry knew that God had used his silent witness five years earlier to help move the Episcopal Church to a public proclamation of the faith and principles they espoused. Now, with Walter's presentment and possible heresy trial looming, Barry believed God was calling him out of yet another closet: his silence. All of us, gay and straight together, have so many closets of fear to come out of every day of our lives. Opening the door and claiming in public what we believe is an act of faith. And faith grows in community.

By August of 1995 our season of waiting came to its conclusion: The ten presenting bishops secured the seventy-five bishops necessary to bring the Presentment of Heresy against Walter Righter. We were stunned that such a thing should happen to our friend. And the cost? Both the spiritual and financial toll would be tremendous on Walter and Nancy, for the Episcopal Church paid to try him, but not to defend him.

BISHOP NOW FACES THE HERETICS BRAND. ORDINATION OF GAY MAN AS EPISCOPAL DEACON BRINGS RARE CHARGE. A CEREMONY IN NEWARK FIVE YEARS AGO ECHOES THROUGH EPISCOPALIANISM. A CHURCH'S DISAGREEMENTS ON HOMOSEXUALITY FIND A FOCUS, the *New York Times* heralded the news.

Once again our privacy was gone. Barry began to wonder just what kind of call God had in mind for him. Had he asked to go on this particular type of public, spiritual journey? During that hot August he read back through his journal entries from ten years earlier, just before entering Union Theological Seminary.

"I realize that what I am called to do, just as I was called as a young man, is to create hope in people, create gentleness around them . . . by sharing my faith and my deep love of God. In every prayer I ask to be drawn closer to God."

God's moves are mysterious. Ten years later he knew that being drawn closer to God is not always an easy thing to experience.

"I love the Gospels," Barry wrote in 1985. "I pray to God that I will be given the opportunity to witness . . . I want to use the gifts God has given me to create hopefulness in other people. I will continue to listen for God's guidance."

In the unforgiving glare of public scrutiny about to wash over him and us in 1996, Barry pondered the future to which these journal entries pointed. Hope, love, gentleness, the Gospels—would these four armaments make him a strong enough, gentle enough warrior for the witness he was being called to make?

 Shortly after the first *New York Times* article broke, the *Times* ran a feature story about Barry and Saint George's Church in the Sunday "New Jersey" section: THE PASTOR'S TALE. A MAPLEWOOD PARISH RALLIES ROUND ITS MINISTER, EXHIBIT A IN THE FIRST HERESY TRIAL OF AN EPISCOPAL BISHOP SINCE 1924. Being "Exhibit A" was oddly amusing—was he the blunt object of destruction and downfall, a crime, an impediment? But as the story spread across the nation in newspapers, radio, and television, the scrutiny got hotter and the stakes got higher.

Barry sat in his office with Dan and Gail Austin, who was now senior warden of Saint George's. Both people of deep faith and strong commitment to their family, church, and community, they are also graced with a delightfully twisted sense of humor.

Dan and Gail had been great friends to both Barry and me, encouraging Barry through the normal problems of being a rector, feeding us, laughing with us, lending an ear when we had to talk through the difficulties of being a very visible "clergy couple." Dan and Gail raised their two sons in this church to become gifted, faith-filled, compassionate young men. They believed in the great vision of an inclusive community of faith when they helped call Barry to be their rector, and believed it now when that call was being closely examined.

"Will it all fall apart?" Barry asked them. "Will the vision of hope and justice be destroyed by the fearfulness of the few? Will Saint George's," Barry asked, expressing his deepest worry, "succumb to the fears expressed in this action against Walter? Will it die because of this?"

They sat in silence. There was no crystal ball in which to foresee the future, and no false encouragement that all would be well. Only silence.

The story goes that when the prophet Elijah encountered God on Mount Horeb, a great and strong wind rent the mountains and broke the rocks before the Lord; but the Lord was not in the wind. Then there was an earthquake; but the Lord was not in the earthquake. After the earthquake a fire; but the Lord was not in the fire. It was only after the fire and all the calamities of nature had passed by that Elijah heard God in the silence.

Barry and Dan and Gail sat with their questions storming around them. There was nothing to do but be faithful to the course God had set them on. They listened in the silence for the still, small voice of God.

 Saint George's Church was a strong, faithful, and growing parish, solidly supportive of their new rector. But institutions filled with diverse people who listen to one another are sensitive creatures. A unilateral decision about how to invite the press into their community life could not be made by a few while maintaining a welcome, safe place for all. So the church discerned together how visible it wanted to be through the time of trial.

When Barry broke the news to the leadership during a vestry retreat, they were stunned, angry, and hopeful all at once. "How could the national Church have become so wrongheaded?" they asked. Then immediately asked, "What opportunity for witnessing to Christ's Gospel is here? Can our hope for the future of the Church become the world's hope as well?" And then they prayed.

"Let's take the roof off the church," Bill Albinger said, expressing the feelings of the whole vestry. "Let them in! Let the world see and know what God is doing at Saint George's." And with that affirmation, the doors and the people of Saint George's were opened to any and all press with no restrictions. "Let the world see and know how Christians can love," Bill said. And the cameras and the reporters came and saw, and went away and told others of what they had seen.

 On Epiphany Sunday, January 1996, our home was flooded with well over a hundred hungry men, women, and children for our annual Epiphany brunch. Also one reporter, Mary Rourke. Finishing an article for the Sunday *Los Angeles Times Magazine*, Mary braved the frigid Northeast during one of the decade's worst snowstorms in order to meet Barry and me and the parish that had caused such a stir in the media.

"Mary," I took her by the arm and elbowed our way to the dining table, "I want you to be *sure* and get a slice of the Epiphany cake."

"Why?" she asked with professional caution. Her eyes darted around the dining and living rooms, taking in everyone and everything.

"Mary," I teased her, "you attended seminary. You know the tradition. If you get the slice with the coin in it, you'll have a year of good fortune and happiness."

"Yes, I know," she said, catching a four-year-old who had stumbled into her with sticky fingers. "But there's a hitch, isn't there?"

"Of course." I laughed. "Whoever gets the year of good fortune and happiness bakes the cake for next year's celebration! You want to come back, don't you?"

Mary joined the party and was welcomed like a new member of the family. She wasn't going anywhere soon; the storm outside was howling. But inside by the fire, playing with Spirit, talking to parishioners, Mary discovered firsthand what many reporters had already learned: The people that make up the place called Saint George's Church are alive with a great faith.

"For several parents in the parish," Mary wrote in February 1996 in the *Los Angeles Times Magazine*, "Stopfel and Leckie embody the diversity of modern life. They want their children to be exposed to it. 'I told my kids about a gay couple in the congregation,' [Gail] Austin says. 'They said, "Noooooo." Their image of a gay couple was very different, based on the things they'd heard other kids say at school. Hopefully, this will teach them to be more tolerant.' "[11]

Late in the afternoon Mary thanked us for our hospitality and for the warmth of the whole church. At one point in the morning worship service, she told Barry, she had been moved to tears. Barry smiled and explained it was a fairly common experience for many during their first visit to Saint George's. The reasons? They are never more explicit than "There's a spirit here."

"Why is it so hard for the Church to be like this?" Mary asked.

"I don't know, Mary," Barry answered and shook his head. "I don't know."

 It is a discipline of the spirit to be in waiting—waiting to see, to learn, to know what we were being called to do next. We waited from August 1995 to February 1996, seven months to learn what the court was going to do. Not so long for God, perhaps, but long enough for us.

We read the presenters' opinions and charges in the Episcopal Church press. Once again Barry was told it didn't really concern him, so don't take it personally. He did. To be called a deviant sinner in public, compared with adulterers, prostitutes, and embezzlers is hard on one's faith. And he still had the ministry of a parish to maintain.

Finally, after two dioceses refused to host the Court for the Trial of a Bishop, the Cathedral in Wilmington, Delaware, agreed to host it on February 27, 1996. Saint George's Church prepared for a prayer vigil.

"This is outrageous! This is sick!" I was shouting very nearly at the top of my very big voice.

"Calm down, honey," Barry tried to shush me.

"I will not calm down! This is the grossest sort of hypocrisy!" I paced around the living room, dodging Spirit, who thought we were playing a game.

"They're starting the trial with a *Eucharist?*" I could not believe the agenda. "They're subjecting Walter and Nancy to this cruel torture and want to bless that with a *Eucharist?* Jesus is weeping!"

"He may be," Barry agreed, ever the conciliator, "but the Eucharist isn't about people. It's about the body of God."

"What body?" I cried. "They're trying to cut off Walter and you and every queer and everyone who cares for us from the body of God! And they're starting the trial with a *Eucharist?*" The apparent cynicism floored me. "I will *not* take the Eucharist, Barry. You do what you have to. You're a priest. But I will not participate in this shameful play-acting at being the Church. For Christ's sake! *Be* the Church, *then* take the Eucharist!"

"Why don't you call Nancy?" Barry suggested, knowing he would get nowhere with me. "See what she thinks about it, what she's going to do." Fifteen seconds later I was on the phone with Nancy Righter.

"I'm going to take the Eucharist, Will," Nancy said very calmly. "You've got to remember that Communion with God is not dependent on who's serving, or the times (or the trials!) we're living through. The Eucharist is there to remind me that I'm part of the body of God. And no one, I mean *no one* can separate me from that." She spoke out of the certainty of her faith. "So you'd better believe I'm going to be right up front when it's time!" She laughed now. "And you're going to be right there with me. We're going to stand up as people of faith and say that *our* God does not exclude anyone from his body. You got that?"

I did indeed. Who could separate us from the love of God? The great apostle Paul answered the ancient question nearly two millennia before: only ourselves.

Sure enough, on the morning of the trial when the call came to take and eat and remember that God is always with us, Walter and Nancy and Barry and I, along with everyone else, presenters and defenders alike, ate and confessed our humiliation in being an imperfect, broken body. We were in desperate need of a healing power we did not possess on our own. And the Eucharist reminded us all that God will be God, and we must follow.

Well, nearly all. Four of the men who signed the presentment against Walter Righter refused to attend the service because the Eucharist was being celebrated by the Very Reverend Peggy Patterson, dean of the Cathedral Church of Saint John. A woman.

"You don't strike me as someone who gets nervous easily," Ted Koppel said to Walter Righter on *Nightline.* It was the night before Walter's hearing on the Presentment of Heresy, February 26, 1996, and Barry and I were joined by old friends and new—gay men, lesbian women, straight women—all of us sprawled around a hotel room watching ABC's feature story about us and Walter.

I sat in front of the TV with my back to our friends, who had traveled long and far to be with us. Who traveled the last miles with Jesus? Who took him off the cross, where fear and betrayal had hung him up? Who announced his resurrection? The ones without power in a culture mad for power. The women. And tonight the gays and lesbians joined all the others. I turned away from these friends and wept, for I had no words to describe what this compassionate act of mercy felt like.

"Are you a little bit scared?" Koppel asked Bishop Righter near the end of the half hour. "I mean, to have devoted your life to the Church, and to now be confronting a heresy trial tomorrow morning must give you pause, at the very least."

There was the Walter Righter we loved and respected, straightforward, plain speaking, honest about his outrage for himself and the gay/lesbian community he felt was being scapegoated by this action. He enjoyed being on the fault line between the past and the future, believing it to be the place Christians are called to live, and found a lot of strength in the encouragement of friends.

"You expressed outrage a moment ago," Koppel pressed his point again. "Are you a little bit nervous?"

"No, not so much," Walter answered simply. "I'm a little tired of all this stuff and I'll be glad to have it past. Nervousness is not so much in my make up. I was probably more nervous," Walter said, scratching the back of his neck beneath his bishop's collar, "when I took a driver's test up in New Hampshire last year than I am now."

Ted Koppel, newsman, smiled.

 For the past several months Barry and I had grown accustomed to talking with reporters. The parishioners at Saint George's had grown pretty comfortable with them, too, inviting their questions and offering them their unvarnished opinions. "We just don't understand," Jerry Tuttle told one reporter during a Sunday coffee hour. "Barry's just a great guy. I guess I look at it simplistically: he's bald, and bearded, and gay. I don't care to be any of them. But he's a fine priest and that's all that matters."

But nothing prepared us for the bombardment on Tuesday, February 27, 1996, when Walter, Nancy, Barry, and I approached the Cathedral of Saint John in Wilmington, Delaware. We had all been willing to talk openly with the press and found that, in general, our openness and hospitality had stirred something in their own responses to this story. Something about this had captured their imagination, at least for a time, something beyond the "story." Their questions to the four of us inevitably came around to our faith. How did we manage the spotlight? How was Barry's church reacting? What did we believe God was doing? What were the implications for both the Church and society?

Taught to ask penetrating questions, the press, we were learning, had not yet been taught to listen to penetrating answers. Frequently one reporter or the other would prompt us for "Short answers!" Sound bites cannot address an issue as potentially transforming as the Church's renunciation of a historical bigotry. They had to listen to the long answers.

Walter believed that his accusers, a small yet vocal faction, had turned bitter and then angry as the Church consistently refused to pass a ban on ordaining noncelibate gay and lesbian people. For twelve years they had failed to legislate their idea of morality, and now were staging a desperate last stand in the Court for the Trial of a Bishop.

"Will they be successful?" a reporter shouted.

"Well," Walter drawled in his rich, bass voice, "it all depends on how the court interprets the difference between the resolutions and the canons of the Church. The presenters' believe that resolutions passed by General Convention are not recommendatory but canon law. Of course, that's never been the case, but we are in strange times." Another reporter called out another question but Walter wasn't finished with the last one.

"It *is* a canon law," Walter went on, oblivious to the reporters' growing uneasiness at the length of his answer, "that the priesthood is open to women. Yet four of these guys still refuse to ordain women or license them to serve in their dioceses." Walter laughed with the grace of a man who has lived long with human contradictions. "It seems irrational to me that the court will decide that canon laws are optional and resolutions are binding."

In the courtroom with Walter and Nancy it was disturbing to hear the lawyer for Bishop Righter's accusers objectify us, declaring that homosexuality is the expression of all that is evil. It seemed an image, language from another time long ago, with all the accompanying approbation either implied or spoken outright. Homosexuals were *de facto* sinners, a condition the Church has affirmed for centuries. To ignore this traditional teaching was to break with the core doctrine of the Church as it is contained in the Bible. But the lawyer's argument for the absolute authority of the scriptural record broke down as he tried to answer questions by the court about now accepted differences between the Bible and social attitudes concerning capital punishment, slavery, apartheid, or divorce.

Michael Rehill, chancellor of the Diocese of Newark and Walter's lead counsel, addressed the court in the afternoon. Throughout a long, detailed argument, Michael repeatedly told the court that he had "tried to find what our Lord said about homosexuality. And there is nothing. So how can there be a doctrine?" The doctrine of the Episcopal Church, Rehill argued, "is the fundamental tenants that must be believed in order to be a member of this Church." The core doctrine is found in our baptismal covenant: Christ has died, Christ is risen, Christ will come again. Based on this core doctrine, we all strive to walk in the path our Lord walked—loving ourselves, our neighbors, our God—but this striving is part of the discipline of faith, not the core doctrine of the Church.

"What Jesus is talking about is love and compassion," Rehill told the court. "He teaches us about loving and caring relationships.

And then I look at these relationships [of committed same-sex unions] and say, 'Is there something about these relationships that's inconsistent with the message Jesus brought to us?'" Of course not.

The following day the Associated Press showed Barry and me in an embrace. The love that dared to speak its name was pictured all over the world: an embrace at the Eucharist—the place where all distinctions are invisible to God and where all are made one with the Christ.

We left Wilmington knowing that we had another season of waiting before the decision would be reached. But we also knew that none of us in Wilmington would have the last word on this issue. God would have that word and we had to keep our ears open.

The hate mail increased for a while. But so did the members of Saint George's. All sorts of diverse families came and stayed, proving that, for many, the good news of God's inclusive love is a great reason to go back to church.

Ten weeks later, on May 15, 1996, we returned to Wilmington, Delaware, to hear the court's decision.

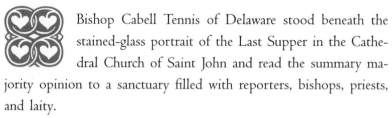 Bishop Cabell Tennis of Delaware stood beneath the stained-glass portrait of the Last Supper in the Cathedral Church of Saint John and read the summary majority opinion to a sanctuary filled with reporters, bishops, priests, and laity.

"The court finds that there is no core doctrine prohibiting the ordination of a noncelibate, homosexual person living in a faithful and committed sexual relationship with a person of the same sex, and therefore the court dismisses Count One."

Sometimes when what we have dared to believe possible jumps

up and says, "Here I am—what you dared to believe!" the air rushes out of our lungs; muscles, long tensed for battle, implode. Among the profoundest moments of disbelief in our lives are when we come face to face with a miracle. It takes our minds a few seconds to catch up with our hearts and shout the "Amen" of faith. And shout we did.

Essentially the court defined the core doctrine of the Episcopal Church very narrowly. Core doctrine is contained in theological statements about the nature and mission of Jesus Christ—God in Christ fulfills the Scripture; God became incarnate in Jesus Christ; Christ was crucified, Christ was buried, Christ rose again; Christ was exalted to God; God gave the gift of the Holy Spirit; there will be a day of judgment, therefore repent.

We had just heard the Episcopal Church affirm that no one is excluded from grace because of their ontological reality; no one is anathema to God. Cabell Tennis stood before the window of the Last Supper filled with morning light and proclaimed that the way of faith is open to *all*. The bush was burning, but it was not consumed.

The truth of the court's words resounded through the crowd, Christian and non-Christian alike: We may not claim more about God than what God has revealed to us. Deity is a mystery—people of God must walk in faith, and we must let one another have diverging opinions about the nature of that walk. The great heart of our Christian faith would guide us, a column of smoke by day, a pillar of fire by night. Standing in that granite cathedral, we saw heaven open around us and felt the very soul of God enfold us and breathe new life deep into our hearts.

The second count against Walter was then dismissed. Bishop Tennis read, "The court finds that there is no discipline of the Church prohibiting the ordination of a noncelibate person living in a committed relationship with a person of the same sex."

"I think what it's going to do," Barry told reporters after the decision, "is give us space for two things. One, to let the people of this Church continue to work on their understanding of human sexuality. And two, because the bishops haven't driven toward any firm doctrine or ruling, it lets gay and lesbian preachers like me continue to do good work. That's what's going to create change in the Church."

Bishop Andrew Fairfield of North Dakota was the lone, dissenting vote on the charges against Walter Righter.

Fairfield spoke at disturbing length about a "normative" sexual relationship being one that incorporated the complimentary opposites of male and female. He then declared that homosexuals are barred from the kingdom of God because we are either sodomites, whom he defined as active sexual partners, or "malakoi," which he claimed to mean the "softy," or passive partner in a homosexual relationship.

My gasp at this abusive, demeaning objectification from a churchman rang through the cathedral. Barry clamped his hand on my thigh out of fear I was about to jump up. I was.

Nancy Righter passed a note to us as Fairfield continued to pummel us with his opinion: *I'm sorry you have to listen to this. —N.*

I sat quietly then and prayed. What women and people of color had endured at the hands of the institutional Church we could endure as well. Maybe the abuse would stop now. Maybe.

"What we've closed here," Barry later explained to another horde of reporters, "is the idea that litigation is the right way to deal with this. One of the bishops said that we should not be taking each other to court, we should be taking each other to God in prayer. So," Barry finished his practical understanding of what had happened this day, "we've closed the avenue on something adversarial and now we can spend more time developing relationships and dialogue."

Bishop Spong preached a celebration at Saint George's four days later, May 19, 1996. He praised Walter, Barry, and the people of Saint George's at great length and then turned toward the future he saw for us.

"This Church of ours has done an audacious thing," Bishop Spong drew to his conclusion. "We will not now tremble at our own audacity. Rather we will step boldly into the future that we have helped to build, and we will remind the world once again that our calling as Jesus' disciples is the call to be faithful—nothing more. We are not called to be successful, just faithful. So we will turn now to the issues that will face us tomorrow, and seek in those issues the truth of God, come when it may and cost what it will." This witness of faith, the tireless Bishop Spong proclaimed, "is the witness that will ultimately revive the Christian Church and energize the Christian faith." And the people shouted, "Amen!"

Chapter 31

> I call heaven and earth to witness against you this day, that I have
> set before you life and death, blessing and curse; therefore choose
> life, that you and your descendants may live, loving the Lord your
> God, obeying God's voice, and cleaving unto God.
>
> —DEUTERONOMY 30:19–20

Our eleven-year-old goddaughter, Hannah, sat in the pew semi-listening to her mother preach at Saint George's. Some weeks before Walter Righter's trial, Lee Hancock spoke to the church about the sacrifices of discipleship now incumbent upon them as they journeyed with Walter Righter and their rector through the time of ecclesial trial. Hannah flipped through a newcomers brochure.

"In this church there will be no outcasts," she read the presiding bishop's words quoted on the cover. She thought that was pretty neat.

"The Episcopal Church says there will be no outcasts," she confronted her mother after the service. "How can they say that and then cast out Uncle Barry?" Of course she had mixed up the issues a little, but at eleven years of age Hannah already shared her mother's integrity and compassion for social outcasts.

Barry and I live our lives openly, honestly, with dignity and integrity. Ignoring the counsel of those who wished us to remain silent, we found our voices and declared to the mainstream of our culture, "No, you cannot make us over in a more comfortable image for yourselves. We are two men who love each other, deeply and passionately; we are two men who love others with as much compassion as has been given to us; we are two men who love God with all our heart, soul, and mind." Loving always costs us something of ourselves. Every day Barry and I, along with the hundreds of thousands of other out gay men and lesbian women, pay a price for our loving. As does everyone.

Most of us, certainly we, are very ordinary people who, each day, make a simple decision to trust in the integrity of love and seek for the divinity inherent in that loving. For do not all the law and all the prophets depend on the great commandment to love? To love honestly is to seek spiritual health. To love truthfully is to cast aside fear and believe in the Spirit of God as he or she is revealed in our loving. To love is an act of faith. For everyone.

Our society is in the midst of breathtaking change in its perception of homosexuality. Human sexuality studies in the Presbyterian, Methodist, and Episcopal churches have all favored a reappraisal of traditional patterns of sexual exclusion based on one's orientation. These, and other studies, have all affirmed that a sexual relationship, regardless of its orientation, must be nurtured when there is genuine equality and mutual respect among the partners. Slowly the Christian Church is reaffirming that relationships are made sacred, not by doctrinal decree, but by human beings, the image of God on earth.

The Reverend George Regas, rector of All Saint's Church in Pasadena, California, the largest Episcopal church on the West Coast, declared that he will perform church blessings for gays and lesbians, despite the opposition of many in the Church.

"The really serious problem for the people of the Book," Regas preached to his church one Sunday, "is not how to square homosexuality with certain biblical passages that appear to condemn it, but rather how to reconcile rejection, prejudice, hostility, and punishment of homosexuals with the unconditional love of Christ."

In Detroit, Michigan, the Reverend Ervin Brown, rector of Christ Episcopal Church, wrote, "In my twenty-five years of ordained ministry, I've blessed everything from fox hunts to rings, to animals, to fishing boats and houses. Why shouldn't I ask God's blessing on a couple who are acting on their love? And do it as faithfully, as lovingly as possible?

"It's not marriage," Reverend Brown continued. "Marriage is a specific, clearly defined legal and theological institution involving two people of the opposite sex. It's not a marriage, but rather asking God's blessing on a relationship of commitment and love. I wouldn't pronounce the Church's blessing on a heterosexual couple if they didn't intend a lifelong relationship of commitment and faithfulness. The same holds for same-sex couples."

Neither marriage nor one's sexuality sanctifies a relationship. People and God do. Adultery breaks the bonds of trust in any relationship where vows of sexual fidelity have been spoken. The longing for intimacy is at the core of what it means to be human, for intimacy is inextricably wedded to our honoring the dignity of every human being. The demands are the same for gay and nongay relationships, as are the hurts. Sexual orientation is morally neutral; our actions toward each other are not.

In our time, the terrifying and wonderful mysteries of human sexuality remain laden with emotion, folklore, irrational fears, adolescent information, and intolerance. The debate swirling around gay and lesbian people has become so inflammatory, in part, because we

282 Will Leckie and Barry Stopfel

are the last minority to be officially harassed by institutional religion. We are just now facing up to the terrible cost. Barry's ordination, along with Walter Righter's heresy trial in the Episcopal Church, is only a microcosm of humanity's ongoing struggle to be more human.

"To some extent," Thomas Moore writes in *Care of the Soul,* "care of the soul asks us to open our hearts wider than they have ever been before, softening the judging and moralism that may have characterized our attitudes and behavior for years. Moralism is one of the most effective shields against the soul, protecting us from intricacy. There is nothing more revealing, and maybe nothing more healing, than to reconsider our moralistic attitudes and find how much soul has been hidden behind its doors. . . . As we deal with the soul's complexity, morality can deepen and drop its simplicity, becoming at the same time both more demanding and more flexible."[12]

Moore poses the problem endemic in our society: Will we be bound by the muddied history of our religious institutions, or shall we make the leap of faith and live lives of the soul? They are not necessarily one and the same.

In its history the confessing Church has tolerated the Inquisition, the Holocaust, colonization and the destruction of indigenous peoples, slavery, misogyny, anti-Semitism, racism, and homophobia. With time we are slowly overcoming each of these great, historical oppressions. With time the liberation of love, what Jesus of Nazareth gave his life for, will break through the defenses we have built to shield us from those who think, believe, and act differently from ourselves. It is a slow, torturous process, for liberation is broader than mere civil justice.

Liberation swims in a stream racing from the beginning of the sacred stories in the Hebrew Scriptures, through the imperatives of Jesus of Nazareth, to the demands of survival in our own day. God is a God involved in history, who is at the same time far off and yet dwelling among the people. It is God who liberates, who lifts people out of oppression again and again, who parts the waters, and brings refreshment where there is none to be found. God is compassionate and just and longs for all the people of God to be free.

A God who desires that all of his or her creation be free is not limited to human constructs of rights and legalities, however necessary a component they are. God desires that our hearts be freed. It is this opening of our hearts, the softening of our judgments and moral edicts that are necessary if humanity is ever to discover a sane and compassionate path of coexistence in the midst of cultural and religious diversity.

One Episcopal bishop, when asked if he would ordain qualified gay and lesbian people to the priesthood, responded, "We baptize them, don't we?" Can we imagine Jesus proclaiming, "Come unto me all of you who labor and are heavy laden, except you gay and lesbian people?" The broader issue is not about justifying the place of gay and lesbian people in the Church, but whether the Church can justify fear, intolerance, and the resulting violence in the name of God.

Primate of the Church in the Province of South Africa and Nobel Peace prize winner, Archbishop Desmond Tutu spoke in favor of justice for lesbian and gay people at the 71st General Convention of the Episcopal Church in Indianapolis. "The ordination of homosexuals is an issue of justice," Archbishop Tutu told the capacity crowd, "just as the fight against racism was in my native South Africa." He sent a personal contribution to Walter Righter's defense fund and continues to speak and work on behalf of gay men and lesbian women.

There are many people the world over, gentle warriors all, urging us to more life. Scanning *Integrity News and Notes*, the quarterly news journal of the national advocacy group for lesbian and gay Episcopalians, we read a wide range of articles chronicling the battle for the soul of the Church.

A closeted gay bishop dies of AIDS.

The Queen's chaplain comes out in England.

The Episcopal Diocese of Rochester, New York, endorses same-sex unions at its diocesan convention.

The United Church of Christ reaffirms the ordination of gay and lesbian persons.

Some more conservative dioceses in the Episcopal Church decide to withhold their contributions to the national Church as retribution for what they see as the moral decay of national leadership with regard to gay and lesbian priests.

The American Baptists declare, "We do not accept the homosexual lifestyle, homosexual marriage, ordination of homosexual clergy or the establishment of gay churches or gay caucuses."

In Canada a gay priest is outed by his bishop and then defrocked.

South African Anglicans, urged by Archbishop Tutu, begin to look at human sexuality and the overwhelming prejudice and hostility toward homosexuals. They are questioning whether the Church will continue its moral condemnation or respond with God's love and compassion.

A prominent, retired Episcopal bishop, the Right Reverend Otis Charles, comes out as a gay man.

The Anglican Church of Canada, working with several corporations, develops a domestic-partner policy. It will begin to extend health benefits to same-sex partners of members who participate in the church health plan. How the policy will be followed is left up to individual dioceses.

In 1996 the Supreme Court struck down as unconstitutional Colorado's Amendment 2, which not only nullified existing civil rights protections for gays and lesbians but also barred the passage of new anti-discrimination laws.

At this writing, the courts in Hawaii are demanding that the state show compelling evidence why the legal rights of civil marriage should not be extended to a specific class of individuals, in this case gays and lesbians. (How many other people have been denied this civil right throughout history based on the color of their skin, the color of their partner's skin, or their country of origin?) Many in our nation seem intent on moralizing this most civil institution of marriage. Which is fine, but we are being dishonest if we moralize the committed relationships of some without moralizing them all. And if we choose to moralize, then we must be willing to raise the conversation to the level of the spiritual—we must be willing to explore the implications for good and the increase of love in our world in all of our wonderful and diverse relationships.

Thomas Moore writes:

> The great malady of the twentieth century, implicated in all of our troubles and affecting us individually and socially, is "loss of soul." When soul is neglected, it doesn't just go away; it appears symptomatically in obsessions, addictions, violence and loss of meaning. . . . We know intuitively that soul has to do with genuineness and depth, as when we say certain music has soul or a remarkable person is soulful. When you look closely at the image of soulfulness, you see that it is tied to life in all its particulars . . . and experiences that stay in the memory and touch the heart. Soul is revealed in attachment, love, and community.[13]

Attachment, love, and community are ways to spiritual health; they take courage to create and sustain. Spiritual health triumphs because of the ordinary courage of ordinary people in ordinary acts of love. The community at Saint George's Church cast aside their fear of the unknown, risked the institution's future, and trusted that the Spirit of God was calling them to a new life of love.

The debate over Barry's ordination is a part of the much larger question about who is in and who is out of power in our institutions as we head into the next millenium. This is not a unique struggle to Christians. In the sometime turbulent rapids of social change, we are all looking for guidance through the complexities of diversity, pluralism, the redefinition of family, our values, and the ambiguities that momentarily overwhelm our certainties. The hegemonies with which we have lived comfortably for centuries are being remade, and with them our attitudes, spirits, and hopes.

In the first century of the Common Era the Christian Church debated the integration of Jewish beliefs and the inclusion of gentiles in the new Jewish-Christian Church. Do Jewish dietary laws apply to all Christians? Do gentiles need to be circumcised? What are the marks of inclusion? Are we made righteous under the law or by faith? What weight does religious observance carry? Religious piety? Religious form? Are we made righteous in God's eyes by baptism alone?

Twenty centuries later the question is the same: Is God the God of all? Is any part of God's creation an aberration or an abomination? Is the love of God in Jesus, whom Christians call the Christ, limited or limitless?

"Love the Lord your God with all your heart, with all your soul, and with all your mind," Jesus of Nazareth, that despised member of a despised underclass, told his followers. "And love your neighbor as yourself." In his day, as surely as in ours, it is a call to revolution: a revolution of love.

One Sunday, Lily Cates, at ten years of age, asked Barry for a picture of himself. When he asked her why, she told him that she had to write a paper for school about a hero. They could choose Gandhi, Martin Luther King, Jr., Abraham Lincoln, or some other hero of their own choosing. She chose her priest and told her fifth-grade schoolmates how love had triumphed over hate, and how her church had helped make the world safer for all gay and lesbian people. Lily's revolution is starting early.

"Never doubt that a small group of thoughtful, committed citizens can change the world," Margaret Mead once said. "Indeed, it is the only thing that ever has." What the world is seeing in the lives of openly gay and lesbian people, and what the world will continue to see as more and more people embrace their own courage to love one another, is a spiritual revolution shaking the very foundations of what it means to be human.

 How God works is a mystery. We cannot know before we have walked the walk where God is leading or what God has in mind for us.

Two young, teenaged boys in different parts of the country were emerging into their adolescence while struggling with the shame of their homosexuality. Adolescence is a brutal task, and for gay teenagers it is positively deadly: Nearly one in ten gay children don't make it to their twenties. In two different parts of the country, two mothers' sons had planned their suicides.

In two different parts of the country, both of these young men read a news story about Barry and me and then—and this is the miracle—found a copy of a feature article in *OUT* magazine that carried a photograph of us embracing. They saw two men with ordinary courage who had worked hard to live into a reconciling faith, two men for whom God made sense even though the religious institution taught shame. In two different parts of the country, two mothers and two fathers were spared devastation when their two babies called a suicide hotline and found counselors. Two young men discovered their courage to love and chose life.

Notes

1 Bawer, Bruce. "Devotions," in *Coast to Coast: Poems by Bruce Bawer.* Brownsville, OR: Story Line Press, 1993.
2 Spong, J. S. *Living in Sin? A Bishop Rethinks Human Sexuality.* San Francisco: Harper & Row, 1988, p. 202.
3 Carter, Stephen L. *Integrity.* New York: HarperCollins, 1996, p. 19.
4 "Report of the Task Force on Changing Patterns of Sexuality and Family Life." Prepared at the request of the 111th Convention of the Diocese of Newark, New Jersey, 1985.
5 Keen, Sam. *Beginnings Without End.* New York: Harper & Row, 1975, p. 66.
6 Bonhoeffer, D. *The Cost of Discipleship.* New York: Collier Books, 1949, p. 47.
7 Bawer, Bruce. "Bedtime," in *Coast to Coast: Poems by Bruce Bawer.* Brownsville, OR: Story Line Press, 1993.
8 Dillard, Annie. *Teaching a Stone to Talk.* New York: Harper & Row, 1982, p. 20.
9 Pearson, Carol S. *The Hero Within.* San Francisco: Harper & Row, 1986, p. 1.
10 L'Engle, Madeleine. *The Glorious Impossible.* New York: Simon & Schuster, 1990.
11 Rourke, Mary. "The Heretic?" Los Angeles: *Los Angeles Times Magazine,* February 25, 1996.
12 Moore, Thomas. *Care of the Soul.* New York: HarperPerennial, 1994, p. 17.
13 Ibid., p. 11.

Permissions

Scripture quotations are from the Revised Standard Version of the Bible, copyright © 1946, 1952, and 1971 by the Division of Christian Education of the National Councils of the Church of Christ in the U.S.A. Used by permission.

"Devotions" and "Bedtime" by Bruce Bawer reprinted by permission of Story Line Press, publisher of Bruce Bawer's book *Coast to Coast.*

Living in Sin? A Bishop Rethinks Human Sexuality by John Shelby Spong, copyright © 1989 by the Rt. Rev. John Shelby Spong. Reprinted with permission of HarperCollins Publishers Inc.

Integrity by Stephan Carty, copyright © 1996 by Stephan Carty. Reprinted with permission of HarperCollins Publishers Inc.

Beginnings Without End by Sam Keen, copyright © 1975 by Sam Keen. Reprinted with permission of Sam Keen.

The Cost of Discipleship by Dietrich Bonhoeffer, translated from the German by R. H. Fuller with some revision by Irngard Booth, copyright © 1959 by SCM Press, Ltd. Reprinted with the permission of Simon & Schuster.

Teaching a Stone to Talk by Anne Dillard, copyright © 1982 by Anne Dillard. Reprinted with permission of HarperCollins Publishers Inc.